T0305496

Behavioral Political Economy and Democratic Theory

Drawing on current debates at the frontiers of economics, psychology, and political philosophy, this book explores the challenges that arise for liberal democracies from a confrontation between modern technologies and the bounds of human rationality.

With the ongoing transition of democracy's underlying information economy into the digital space, threats of disinformation and runaway political polarization have been gaining prominence. Employing the economic approach informed by behavioral sciences' findings, the book's chief concern is how these challenges can be addressed while preserving a commitment to democratic values and maximizing the epistemic benefits of democratic decision-making. The book has two key strands: it provides a systematic argument for building a behaviorally informed theory of democracy; and it examines how scientific knowledge on quirks and bounds of human rationality can inform the design of resilient democratic institutions. Drawing these together, the book explores the centrality of the rationality assumption in the methodological debates surrounding behavioral sciences as exemplified by the dispute between neoclassical and behavioral economics; the role of (ir)rationality in democratic social choice; behaviorally informed paternalism as a response to the challenge of irrationality; and non-paternalistic avenues to increase the resilience of the democratic institutions toward political irrationality.

This book is invaluable reading for anyone interested in behavioral economics and sciences, political philosophy, and the future of democracy.

Petr Špecián, Charles University and Prague University of Economics and Business, Czech Republic.

Routledge Frontiers of Political Economy

The Political Economy of Transnational Governance
China and Southeast Asia in the 21st Century
Hong Liu

Economics, Science and Capitalism
Richard Westra

Production, Value and Income Distribution
A Classical–Keynesian Approach
Enrico Bellino

The Failure of Markets
Energy, Housing and Health
Craig Allan Medlen

Marx's *Capital*, Capitalism and Limits to the State
Theoretical Considerations
Raju J Das

Behavioral Political Economy and Democratic Theory
Fortifying Democracy for the Digital Age
Petr Specián

Economics, Social Science and Pluralism
A Real-World Approach
Victor A. Beker

Corporations, Accounting, Securities Laws, and the Extinction of Capitalism
Wm. Dennis Huber

For more information about this series, please visit: www.routledge.com/
Routledge-Frontiers-of-Political-Economy/book-series/SE0345

Behavioral Political Economy and Democratic Theory

Fortifying Democracy for the Digital Age

Petr Špecián

LONDON AND NEW YORK

First published 2022
by Routledge
4 Park Square, Milton Park, Abingdon, Oxon OX14 4RN

and by Routledge
605 Third Avenue, New York, NY 10158

Routledge is an imprint of the Taylor & Francis Group, an informa business

© 2022 Petr Špecián

The right of Petr Špecián to be identified as author of this work has been asserted in accordance with sections 77 and 78 of the Copyright, Designs and Patents Act 1988.

British Library Cataloguing-in-Publication Data
A catalogue record for this book is available from the British Library

Library of Congress Cataloging-in-Publication Data
Names: Špecián, Petr, author.
Title: Behavioral political economy and democratic theory : fortifying democracy for the digital age / Petr Špecián.
Description: 1 Edition. | New York, NY : Routledge, 2022. |
Series: Routledge frontiers of political economy |
Includes bibliographical references and index.
Subjects: LCSH: Economics–Psychological aspects. |
Democracy. | Rationalism.
Classification: LCC HB74.P8 S64 2022 |
DDC 330/.01/9–dc23/eng/20211210
LC record available at https://lccn.loc.gov/2021060450

ISBN: 978-1-032-22973-7 (hbk)
ISBN: 978-1-032-22975-1 (pbk)
ISBN: 978-1-003-27498-8 (ebk)

DOI: 10.4324/9781003274988

Typeset in Bembo
by Newgen Publishing UK

In memory of dad

Contents

Illustrations

Figures

Tables

Acknowledgments

The bulk of this book was written during the spring and summer of 2021 on my research visit to Central European University (CEU) in Vienna. Nonetheless, its structure and underlying ideas have been much longer in the making. Accordingly, there are many people to whom I owe my gratitude for their indispensable role in the process that led to the finished manuscript.

Prague University of Economics and Business and Charles University have both been exceptionally supportive throughout my career. Special thanks are due on account of their generous decision to relieve me from my teaching duties in the summer semester of 2021 to spend a sabbatical abroad. I am particularly grateful to Zdeněk Chytil, Ján Pavlík, Gabriela Seidlová Málková, Hedvika Novotná, and Michal Mirvald in this regard.

My stay at CEU has been supported by a habilitation scholarship via AKTION Austria—Czech Republic. Both the financial means and the organizational support provided by AKTION proved indispensable. At the same time, the research visit would not be possible—let alone successful—without Andres Moles, who graciously agreed to supervise my stay and supported me throughout by priceless suggestions and encouragements.

I thank Pavel Potužák and Marek Hudík for their inspiring professionalism, endless enthusiasm for economics, and help with finding a proper title for this book; Jan Švarcbach for his nagging to finally get the book done; Andy Humphries for supporting my project; Viktor Ivanković for valuable comments; Ondřej Havlíček, Libor Fůs, Ondřej Špaček, Mirek Vacura, Ondřej Bečev, Tomáš Ondráček, and Filip Tvrdý for the various direct and indirect ways they helped me move forward during the years when this volume had been hatching; Petr Krauwurm, Petra Chudárková, and Matěj Dražil for help with editing some of the chapters. Above all, I am grateful to my family—especially to Jitka—for their universal support, as well as patience and endurance during all the long hours I have spent behind the closed doors of my study. To anyone whose just desert I omitted to mention, I owe my apology (and a beer).

The work on Chapters 3 and 5 was supported by the Czech Science Foundation (GACR) under Grant 20-06678S. Some of the book's other parts are derived from my earlier writings, mostly published in the Czech language. All of them have been substantively revised and updated for inclusion in this volume. I thank the original publishers for their kind permission to use the material.

- Chapter 1 is based on the article Špecián, P. (2015) 'Potřebuje ekonomie psychologii?' [Does Economics Need Psychology?], *Teorie vědy/Theory of Science*, 37(3), pp. 279–301.
- "The Problem of Rational Ignorance and the Wisdom of Crowds" section is based on the article Špecián, P. (2017) 'Ekonomická analýza referenda' [An Economic Analysis of a Referendum], *Politická ekonomie*, 65(4), pp. 460–475. doi:10.18267/j.polek.1155.
- The sections "(Ir)rationality, Sovereignty, and Welfare;" "In Our Best Interest;" and "Searching for True Preferences" are derived from the article Špecián, P. (2019) 'The Precarious Case of the True Preferences', *Society*, 56(3), pp. 267–272. doi:10.1007/s12115-019-00363-8.

Introduction

It may feel long ago, but democracy's victorious march through the world once appeared unstoppable. In the late 20th century, the third wave of democratization spread across the globe, and Francis Fukuyama's (1992) prophecy of the end of history in the embrace of liberal democracy became a global bestseller. Today, democratic optimism is waning. The word "democracy" remains at the top of popularity charts in virtually every country, but its actual implementation is faltering. As *Freedom House* has put it in its latest annual report, "democracy and pluralism are under assault" (Repucci, 2021). And indeed, even the most established liberal democratic regimes in Western Europe or the United States struggle to contain the onslaught of populism with authoritarian and nativist features. Not to mention many of the previously promising new converts to the "Western" model of governance—such as Poland or Hungary—that have apparently lost their way.

For many advocates of democracy, the year 2016 with its Brexit referendum that led to Great Britain leaving the European Union and Donald Trump's victory over Hilary Clinton in the U.S. presidential election marked a moment of deep disillusion and confusion. The ripples of this shock still reverberate through both the public debates and the scholarly discourse. And rightfully so. Should the "liberal elite" accept the democratic choices that they cannot be reconciled with—such as those regarding Brexit and Trump—as not only legitimate but also epistemically superior to their own judgment? Or is it time to admit that there truly is something disturbing in the current developments and that liberal democracies are losing their sure footing?

A growing incidence of nativist or populist backlash would perhaps be easily explicable amid a deep economic crisis, such as the Great Depression of the 1930s or even the Great Recession of 2008. Yet, the economic fundamentals seem to have lost much of their explanatory power concerning the political outcomes. With unemployment at record lows, robust economic growth, and unprecedented standards of living, the discontent with the established political has been rife even before the coronavirus emergency. Undoubtedly, a debate about the role of inequality and changes in the labor markets driven by globalization and automation is still worth having (e.g., Stiglitz, 2012; Rodrik, 2018; Frank *et al.*, 2019). Nonetheless, trying to explain the democratic crisis,

DOI: 10.4324/9781003274988-1

many have turned toward the information revolution brought about by digital technologies. The digital revolution is—in its way—deeply democratic: it is upending the traditional, elite-controlled ways of knowledge production and information dissemination (Gurri, 2018). However, the extent to which this epistemic democratization is compatible with the liberal-democratic political order remains unclear.

In the debates on the disruptive potential of the digital revolution, concerns regarding digital disinformation rose to prominence. Sadly, it appears that the steep decline in the costs of information dissemination and audience targeting may represent a greater boon to disinformation peddlers than to information providers. Disinformation and, consequently, misinformation thrive in an environment where the citizens have instant access to a vast stock of online news sources that vary significantly in quality and ideological bent, and can assist the spread of whatever content they find worthwhile with unprecedented ease. A link to the democratic crisis does not appear difficult to draw. As Bakir and McStay (2018, p. 159) put it, the proliferation of online disinformation such as the infamous *fake news* leads to the "production of wrongly informed citizens."

In concurrence with these political and technological upheavals, the early 21st century has also witnessed rapid progress within behavioral science in search for the predictable deviations from rational behavior and their use in policy design. Economics, the most theoretically coherent and arguably also the most influential of the social sciences, experiences a wholesale import of findings from psychology and other behavioral sciences (Thaler, 2016). Its neo-classical fundament has been modified and enriched by numerous behavioral insights (cf. Angner, 2019). Today, most economists are ready to recognize that human behavior cannot be predicted, much less explained, without considering the empirical findings regarding the nature and limitations of human cognition.

The shift in the scientific understanding of human behavior has also produced a voluminous discussion regarding its policy implications. In the face of systematic mistakes—that is, *predictable irrationality* (Ariely, 2009)—traditional normative foundations of applied economics deferential to preferences revealed through choices lose much of their appeal. What if people's welfare, as perhaps the prime objective of liberal democratic governance, is not best realized through the pursuit of happiness by preference satisfaction via free choice (McQuillin and Sugden, 2011)? Behaviorally informed paternalism has become the most prominent contender in the race to provide an answer. Its proponents believe that a democratic government should use the expanding empirical knowledge of human behavior and cognition to direct people toward better choices. After all, if people end up harming themselves in predictable ways once left to their own devices—even worse: if the imperfections of their rationality end up being commercially exploited (Akerlof and Shiller, 2015)—is it not the government's duty to provide relief? So, behaviorally informed paternalists have gotten busy designing interventions to empower the government to carry out such a task. This is an exercise, in which those of a "libertarian" streak have achieved the most notoriety (Thaler and Sunstein, 2003, 2008, 2021). They offer cheap, discrete, and noncoercive fixes to irrationality, that is, *nudges*, which ostensibly help people improve their choices in ways that make them "better off as judged by themselves."

The developments described so far—democratic crisis, digital revolution, and transition toward a behaviorally informed paradigm in social science and public policy—are among the most prominent developments of our era. As one would expect, the literature on each of them is voluminous. However, they are rarely addressed in one breath. For instance, Hélène Landemore's (2020) proposal at radical reform of democracy's central institutions is motivated by the democratic crisis but only tangentially touches on digital or behavioral revolutions. Martin Gurri's (2018) penetrating analysis of how the digital revolution implies trouble for democracy is largely bereft of grounding in democratic theory, behavioral or otherwise. Mario Rizzo's and Glen Whitman's (2019) painstaking polemic with behaviorally informed paternalism lacks concern for technologies or political institutions. The examples could be multiplied.

In contrast to these recent contributions, my book is based on the premise that connections between democratic crisis, digital revolution, and behavioral paradigm shift are vital. Democracy's institutions are not timeless: they need to be assessed—and refashioned, if necessary—against the background of the temporal technology and scientific knowledge. Digital revolution may prove to be a blessing or a curse to democracy, depending on the institutional setup against which it plays out. Deployment of behavioral insights in policy can not only prop up democracy against the tides of political irrationality but also help aspiring authoritarians bury it. In short, I maintain that we can neither resolve the democratic crisis unless we understand its technological and behavioral components nor take full advantage of the technological or behavioral-scientific advances unless we manage to employ them in democracy's service.

The themes to be covered are broad and complex. Indeed, while the specific features of the conundrum we face today may have become apparent only recently, they touch upon the most prominent debates that have kept social scientists busy for decades, if not centuries. Their exploration thus requires a firm methodological fundament. Accordingly, this book will be guided by the economic approach to human behavior. While initially espoused in the context of neoclassical economics (Becker, 1978), it proves versatile enough to facilitate addressing the phenomena of interest. It will help concentrate our focus in the upcoming chapters on peoples' instrumental rationality (and its limits), responsivity to incentives (or the lack of it), and the role of equilibria, especially those institutionally reinforced. In the spirit of this approach, I shall also rely on the assumption of motivational symmetry across the realm of choice, be it private or social: self-interest will be expected to exert no lesser force in politics than it does in consumption. If citizens-qua-voters behave differently from citizens-qua-consumers, it is not because they suddenly transform into their own better selves once participating in the matters of collective choice, but because they face different incentives.

Still, there is one important caveat: while I agree with Becker (1978) that utmost effort should be dedicated to explaining human behavior in rational terms, I lack any confidence that the persisting residuum of irrationality will prove unimportant for democracy's fate. This is perhaps well in line with Becker's (1993, p. 402) later admission that he may have overstated the case for rationality, albeit for a good cause. Be that as it may, the resultant method I shall apply throughout the book can perhaps best be called a behaviorally informed economic approach: while its attention is first dedicated to preferences, incentives, and equilibria, it always keeps a wary eye toward the signs that the bounds to human rationality are being encountered. As such, it represents a contribution to an emerging field of *behavioral political economy*, that is, to "psychologically informed, economic analysis of behavior and its effects in the political arena" (Schnellenbach and Schubert, 2015, p. 396).

This book is a treatise in democratic theory and revolves around the current challenges liberal democratic societies face. But on the most fundamental level, it is also a book about rationality and its limits. Indeed, rationality stands at the core of the most important recent debates among democratic theorists. The skeptics treat citizens' political irrationality as an inherent setback, if not a dealbreaker for democracy (Caplan, 2008; Somin, 2013; Achen and Bartels, 2016; Brennan, 2016). Democratic optimists tend to play down its threat, attacking the validity of the empirical claims regarding democracy's failures, invoking democracy's potential in idealized circumstances, or emphasizing the obstacles that remain in the way of people's will (Mackie, 2003; Landemore, 2012; Matsusaka, 2020). With rational citizens, democracy cannot fail; with irrational ones, it must fail—or so it may appear in the light of this controversy.

I believe a more nuanced analysis of political irrationality is required. By any historical standard, liberal democracy represents a political regime exceptionally supportive of human flourishing. At the same time, it would be foolhardy to presume it invulnerable to irrationality's onslaughts. Therefore, I eschew an early commitment to any fixed position among the feuding camps of democratic theorists. This means, for instance, that although I am generally sympathetic with Caplan's (2008) theory of rational irrationality, my argument also considers probable that human irrationality—at least in some of its shapes—will prove impervious to incentives. Similarly, my baseline notion of democracy is fairly minimalist and conceives it in the Arrowian (1963) tradition as an inclusive system of decision-making that avoids exogenous value imposition, but I also work in dialogue with the epistemic democrats (Landemore, 2012; Goodin and Spiekermann, 2018) toward its interpretation in epistemic and ultimately instrumental terms.

The central question of my book is how the challenges of our time can be addressed while preserving a commitment to democratic values and maximizing the instrumental benefits of democratic decision-making. An important inspiration for my efforts has been J. T. Kelly's book *Framing Democracy* (2012), which breaks the path in considering a broad range of democratic theories in terms of their (often implicit) behavioral assumptions and assessing the promise of various institutional solutions to the political fallout of bounded rationality. I take his contribution as an initial step in a grand project. The project is to construct a behaviorally informed democratic theory that employs scientific knowledge on quirks and bounds of human rationality to inform the design of resilient democratic institutions. My book represents an attempt to advance this project further. The recent developments have proven highly informative and enable me to proceed in heretofore largely unexplored directions. Themes like behaviorally informed paternalism and digital disinformation, while otherwise fervently debated, have attracted scant attention from democratic theorists so far. In the following chapters, I take the opportunity to highlight their importance for our understanding of how democracy can and should work.

Overview of the Book's Structure

Chapter 1 focuses on the paradigmatic shift from imperialist "neoclassical" economics to behavioral economics. Traditionally, economics has been set apart from the other social sciences by its emphasis on theory. The basic principles of behavior have been presumed intuitively known to humans due to their virtue of being agents in the world. To the extent these principles are universal (that is, not limited to any specific area of human endeavors), the economic approach offers a template for a general theory of human behavior. Such "economic imperialism" has always been controversial among economists, let alone other social scientists. But it is only in the last decades that a strong rival has arisen. This rival—*behavioral economics*—seeks to enhance the discipline's scientific and practical performance by importing findings from behavioral sciences, especially psychology. The sustained growth in behavioral economics' prominence can be interpreted as a part of the process of a broader assertion of behavioral science in the study of the social realm.

Chapter 1 revolves around the central issue of contention between behavioral and neoclassical economics: the economic agents' rationality. Rationality—axiomatically grounded—serves as the backbone of the neoclassical theory of rational choice in terms of its content and form. Behavioral economists, in their turn, highlight rationality's limits, or *bounds*, especially as a trigger of systematic deviations of human behavior from the patterns rational choice theory predicts. They seek to ground their theories in the empirical findings regarding the workings of the human mind instead of abstract a priori principles. Against this background, Chapter 1 examines the behavioral economics' potential to deliver on its promise to supersede neoclassical economics' performance. It concludes that its capacity to bring lasting improvements in the scientific understanding of the human condition is most unquestionable in areas where weak incentives toward rational behavior prevail. Prominently, mass liberal-democratic politics, as viewed from the perspective of a regular citizen, represent one such area.

Chapter 2 explores the relationship between democracy and rationality while stressing the need for a democratic theory that comes to terms with the challenge of political irrationality. Constructing such a theory is no mean feat. Even if individual preferences are assumed rational, aggregating them into social preferences presents a thorny task. Famous problems, such as Arrow's Impossibility Theorem, force serious compromises to enable the collective decision-making system to be even operational. The hope is that the inevitable flaws and trade-offs in its design will only rarely produce severe empirical repercussions and that democratic social choice is capable of remarkable performance on account of its epistemic virtues often summarized under the label of the wisdom of crowds. Encouragingly, rigorous arguments supporting the hypothesis of the wisdom of crowds—Condorcet's Jury Theorem most prominent among them—show that mere ignorance cannot undermine it. A peculiar anti-expertise, that is, the ability to be more likely wrong than right, is required for any trouble to ensue.

Unfortunately, systematic deviations from rational behavior documented by the behavioral economists produce effects analogical to such anti-expertise. Widely shared default heuristics and mental models are likely to trigger a biased assessment of the available information and inadequate intuitions. While the usual aggregation procedures—simple majority rule most prominent among them—are highly effective in weeding out random mistakes, they cannot defuse systematic bias. The problem is aggravated by the fact that the incentives a democratic citizen faces in democratic social choice because of her negligible probability of being pivotal do not favor any investment in debiasing techniques. Even where the bias is collectively detrimental and the cost of countering it is low, the baseline incentive setup favors its persistence.

Chapter 2 argues that the behavioral paradigm shift forces us, as a democratic society, to dedicate more systematic attention to comparing the alternative sets of rules of the political game in terms of their expected resilience toward the political ramifications of irrationality. The task of curtailing irrationality is not an a priori impossible one. Indeed, liberal democracies' considerable success is at least partially attributable to their ability to maintain what I call a *democratic equilibrium,* that is, to the capacity of their institutional framework to contain irrationality's excesses without sacrificing responsivity to the citizens' preferences. However, as technological changes revolutionize their underlying information economy, the "tried and true" solutions may no longer suffice.

Chapter 3 analyzes how the surge of misinformation—triggered as a side-effect of the digital revolution and epistemic democratization—may upset the democratic equilibrium. As people increasingly turn away from mass media and perceive the world through the personalized lens of online platforms, there seems to be a growing risk of irrationality's centrifugal forces overwhelming liberal democracy's defense mechanisms. In my treatment of the issue, I have drawn on the extensive debate surrounding "fake news," that is, fabricated reports disguised as news, whose growing prevalence (and, possibly, influence over the outcomes of democratic choice) has been a major concern since 2016.

Analyzing fake news, Chapter 3 shows the prominence of a perspective that puts the public into the position of victims. The dominant approach invokes rationality's bounds and emphasizes the exploitation of the vulnerable public by predatory falsehood peddlers. Such perception also informs most of the existing proposals to stem the tide of disinformation. However, I demonstrate that much depends on the exact nature of epistemic irrationality inherent in the receptivity toward fake news: is it "hardwired," susceptible to learning, or a by-product of rational optimization in service of goals unaligned with truth-seeking (such as reputation management)?

The victim-oriented policy response to fake news represents a bet on the first two possibilities. However, I show that such a gamble is risky for democracy. If fake news consumption is driven by the third trigger—that is, rational irrationality rather than bounded rationality—it poses an even more significant threat to the democratic equilibrium than the mainstream analysis suggests. It can still facilitate runaway political polarization and is resistant to policy measures that would rely on the public's voluntary cooperation. Moreover, the framing in terms of victimhood is inherently problematic from the democratic perspective since trust in regular citizens' capabilities of sound decision-making lies at the very core of the democratic faith. Victimhood rhetoric, in contrast, pictures the public as helpless sufferers awaiting the assistance of (presumably benevolent) epistemic elites. Thus, it offers a distinctly paternalist outlook projected into the policy realm in the forms of various "debunking" or "deplatforming" efforts often teetering on the edge of censorship.

Chapter 4 develops the concerns regarding the paternalist treatment of irrationality further. Overwhelmingly, the current debate revolves around irrationality in consumers' choices and considers the theme of political irrationality a separate issue. I show that no neat separation between these two realms is feasible. While already apparent on the problem of fake news, the issue represents a central problem for behaviorally informed paternalism, once duly generalized. Namely, an expansion of the scope of paternalist intervention in consumption increases the relative importance of the political channel through which the people's preferences are transmitted. To fortify the claim that both realms—collective and individual choice—need to be considered in conjunction, I introduce the *Sovereignty Principle*: a normative benchmark that unifies notions of consumers' sovereignty (that the paternalists question) and citizens' sovereignty (that they subscribe to). I defend the Sovereignty Principle as an expression of central democratic values and argue that behaviorally informed paternalism finds itself on a collision course with it.

To support these claims, Chapter 4 discusses how behaviorally informed paternalism strives to reshape the usual notions of the relationship between human choices and human welfare, appealing to "true preferences" that need to be filtered out of the confusing clutter of the actual choices. However, a closer analysis of the proposed methods of true preference identification shows that none of them avoid making problematic value judgments. I argue that the promise of politically neutral expert interventions to help people fulfill their true preferences cannot be realized. In democratic societies, providing the government with a mandate to carry out interventions to defuse bounded rationality leads to a higher degree of reliance on the political channel of preference revelation. Citizens-qua-voters are increasingly called upon to control public intervention into their lives of citizens-qua-consumers. In the absence of transparent and neutral criteria for true preference identification, such a path is rather treacherous—especially when appreciating the particularly weak incentives toward rationality that the democratic citizens face and the ongoing democratic crisis.

Once we admit the widespread limitations of the consumers' rationality in the private markets, it is unavoidable to also concede the same—if not worse—regarding a voter in the political marketplace of modern democracy. Thus, behaviorally informed paternalism provides a precarious solution to the problem of bounded rationality. Above all, paternalists fail to present an effective solution to the age-old problem of guarding the guardians, that is, of exogenous value imposition. Behavioral experts tasked with overseeing that people do not harm themselves by their own systematically mistaken choices will gain a difficult-to-control power over a wide area of their lives. At the same time, democratic control of these experts appears difficult, especially if they engage in designing inconspicuous micro-interventions, such as "nudges" that many paternalists favor. The issue is reinforced by the fact that political choices can be subject to covert influence probably more easily than consumption choices. In short, paternalism—even if behaviorally informed—does not provide a satisfactory solution to irrationality against the background of the upheavals currently threatening liberal democracies.

To bypass the shortcomings of the paternalist approach while retaining the commitment to reflect the findings of behavioral science, Chapter 5 looks for ways to limit the harmful effects of irrationality without compromising the Sovereignty Principle. It suggests that the growing knowledge regarding the quirks and limitations of human rationality can be used in the service of a reform that produces an institutional setup more resilient toward the threat of political irrationality and no less democratic than the current political setup. To address this issue, Chapter 5 emphasizes the perspective of what economists call *mechanism design*, that is, intentional shaping of incentives to produce the desired outcome. The chapter culminates in a proposal for an "Anti-Psychological State" whose constitutive features align with the Sovereignty Principle.

In this context, I draw on the existing reform proposals that escape the paternalist mold. In particular, I consider two "marginal reforms:" *boosts*, that is, competence-building techniques (Hertwig and Grüne-Yanoff, 2017), and *budges*, behavioral regulations preventing exploitation of rationality's bounds (Oliver, 2013). I also explore two "radical reforms," namely, *open democracy* (Landemore, 2020)—which is a mix of deliberative democracy and lottocratic representation—and *quadratic voting* (Weyl, 2013) that enables recording of preference intensity. Where marginal reforms aim to enhance decision-makers' performance on the background of the current political institutions, radical reforms strive to refashion them.

While of considerable interest, these proposals tend to be plagued by difficulties if considered in the political context: those that are behaviorally informed do not address citizens' political incentives, and those that see incentives as central remain mostly behaviorally uninformed. However, not all hope is lost. Beyond establishing the criteria to evaluate the promise of these proposals vis-à-vis the threat of political irrationality, I explore and document their potential for synergy. If we take advantage of their complementary features, the examined marginal and radical reforms can be treated as building blocks for *an Anti-Psychological State* that seeks to defuse political irrationality while not sacrificing democratic responsivity. Chapter 5 illustrates this on an example of an institutional configuration that augments the template of open democracy using boost, budges, and quadratic voting.

Bibliography

Achen, C.H. and Bartels, L.M. (2016) *Democracy for Realists: Why Elections Do Not Produce Responsive Government*. Princeton, NJ: Princeton University Press.

Akerlof, G.A. and Shiller, R.J. (2015) *Phishing for phools: the economics of manipulation and deception*. Princeton: Princeton University Press.

Angner, E. (2019) 'We're All Behavioral Economists Now', *Journal of Economic Methodology*, 26(3), pp. 195–207. doi:10.1080/1350178X.2019.1625210.

Ariely, D. (2009) *Predictably Irrational: The Hidden Forces that Shape Our Decisions*. New York: HarperCollins.

Arrow, K.J. (1963) *Social Choice and Individual Values*. Second edition. New Haven: Yale University Press.

Bakir, V. and McStay, A. (2018) 'Fake News and The Economy of Emotions: Problems, Causes, Solutions', *Digital Journalism*, 6(2), pp. 154–175. doi:10.1080/21670811.2017.1345645.

Becker, G.S. (1978) *The Economic Approach to Human Behavior*. Chicago: University of Chicago Press.

Becker, G.S. (1993) 'Nobel Lecture: The Economic Way of Looking at Behavior', *Journal of Political Economy*, 101(3), pp. 385–409. doi:10.2307/2138769.

Brennan, J. (2016) *Against Democracy*. Princeton: Princeton University Press.

Caplan, B. (2008) *The Myth of the Rational Voter: Why Democracies Choose Bad Policies*. New edition. Princeton: Princeton University Press.

Frank, M.R. *et al.* (2019) 'Toward Understanding the Impact of Artificial Intelligence on Labor', *Proceedings of the National Academy of Sciences*, 116(14), pp. 6531–6539. doi:10.1073/pnas.1900949116.

Fukuyama, F. (1992) *The End of History and the Last Man*. New York: Free Press.

Goodin, R.E. and Spiekermann, K. (2018) *An Epistemic Theory of Democracy*. Oxford: Oxford University Press.

Gurri, M. (2018) *The Revolt of the Public and the Crisis of Authority in the New Millennium*. San Francisco: Stripe Press.

Hertwig, R. and Grüne-Yanoff, T. (2017) 'Nudging and Boosting: Steering or Empowering Good Decisions', *Perspectives on Psychological Science*, 12(6), pp. 973–986. doi:10.1177/1745691617702496.

Kelly, J.T. (2012) *Framing Democracy: A Behavioral Approach to Democratic Theory*. Princeton: Princeton University Press.

Landemore, H. (2012) *Democratic Reason: Politics, Collective Intelligence, and the Rule of the Many*. Princeton: Princeton University Press.

Landemore, H. (2020) *Open Democracy: Reinventing Popular Rule for the Twenty-First Century*. Princeton: Princeton University Press.

Mackie, G. (2003) *Democracy Defended*. Cambridge; New York: Cambridge University Press.

Matsusaka, J.G. (2020) *Let the People Rule: How Direct Democracy Can Meet the Populist Challenge*. Princeton: Princeton University Press.

McQuillin, B. and Sugden, R. (2011) 'Reconciling Normative and Behavioural Economics: The Problems to Be Solved', *Social Choice and Welfare*, 38(4), pp. 553–567. doi:10.1007/s00355-011-0627-1.

Oliver, A. (2013) 'From Nudging to Budging: Using Behavioural Economics to Inform Public Sector Policy', *Journal of Social Policy*, 42(4), pp. 685–700. doi:10.1017/S0047279413000299.

Repucci, S. (2021) *Freedom in the World 2020. A Leaderless Struggle for Democracy*, *Freedom House*. Available at: https://freedomhouse.org/report/freedom-world/2020/leaderl ess-struggle-democracy (Accessed 19 May 2021).

Rizzo, M.J. and Whitman, G. (2019) *Escaping Paternalism: Rationality, Behavioral Economics, and Public Policy*. Cambridge; New York: Cambridge University Press.

Rodrik, D. (2018) 'Is Populism Necessarily Bad Economics?', *AEA Papers and Proceedings*, 108, pp. 196–199. doi:10.1257/pandp.20181122.

Schnellenbach, J. and Schubert, C. (2015) 'Behavioral Political Economy: A Survey', *European Journal of Political Economy*, 40, pp. 395–417. doi:10.1016/j.ejpoleco.2015.05.002.

Somin, I. (2013) *Democracy and Political Ignorance*. Redwood City: Stanford University Press.

Stiglitz, J.E. (2012) *The Price of Inequality: How Today's Divided Society Endangers Our Future*. First edition. New York: W.W. Norton & Company.

Thaler, R.H. (2016) 'Behavioral Economics: Past, Present, and Future', *American Economic Review*, 106(7), pp. 1577–1600. doi:10.1257/aer.106.7.1577.

Thaler, R.H. and Sunstein, C.R. (2003) 'Libertarian Paternalism', *The American Economic Review*, 93(2), pp. 175–179.

Thaler, R.H. and Sunstein, C.R. (2008) *Nudge: Improving Decisions About Health, Wealth, and Happiness*. New York: Yale University Press.

Thaler, R.H. and Sunstein, C.R. (2021) *Nudge: Improving Decisions About Money, Health, and the Environment*. Final edition. New York: Penguin Books.

Weyl, E.G. (2013) 'Quadratic Vote Buying', *SSRN Electronic Journal*. doi:10.2139/ssrn.2003531.

1 The Paradigmatic Struggle in the Theory of Human Behavior

In medieval times, philosophy was considered subservient to theology. A similar pretense of intellectual superiority has come to characterize many economists' attitudes toward psychology—and the other social sciences—during the 20th century. A classic manifesto of an econo-centric view of the social scientific endeavor is Gary Becker's influential text *The Economic Approach to Human Behavior* (1978). Here, Becker explains the intellectual and methodological foundation of a research program, now often labeled "economic imperialism," which raises a claim on territories traditionally considered a sovereign field of other disciplines. While not under such an intensive siege as sociology, psychology receives a merely ancillary role in the program whose ambition is nothing less than formulating a general theory of human behavior based on the template of economics. Psychology's humble purpose is to contribute to the economists' efforts by providing them with information on people's preferences. Psychologists can help figure out what people want, but once that is reasonably clear, the heavy lifting of an actual explanation accrues to economists.

Although Becker's thoughts cast a long shadow, the card seems to be turning. Despite a stubborn initial opposition of a sizeable part of the economic profession, an approach that takes psychology much more seriously is on the rise. It already exercises a strong influence on how economics is done and thought about by its practitioners. Also, it has earned much attention from both policymakers and the public. Called "behavioral economics," its ascent to prominence has been marked by Nobel Prizes awarded to Daniel Kahneman in 2002 and Richard Thaler in 2017. It sees the road to progress as leading in the opposite direction from what Becker has conceived. In the behavioral economists' view, it is time for psychology to reject its subordinate position and colonize the economic models of human behavior. As Thaler (2017) quipped in his Nobel Banquet speech: "I discovered the presence of human life in a place not far, far away, where my fellow economists thought it did not exist: the economy." Instead of an economic man, *homo economicus*—a sometimes helpful but ultimately misleading caricature rooted in unrealistic assumptions—economic thought should henceforth embrace the actual humans with all their cognitive quirks and limitations.

DOI: 10.4324/9781003274988-2

Unfortunately, the foundational features of the "imperialist" economic approach championed by Becker and the relevance of the critiques based on the demands for an improved psychological foundation of economic models are frequently misconstrued. Therefore, this chapter will examine the competing research programs while highlighting their significant differences and dispelling the illusory ones. Only then will it be possible to appreciate the proper role of rationality and its limitations in the quest for a general theory of human behavior. Thus, I shall set up a framework for examining the potential of democratic social choice in the later parts of the book.

Economic Approach to Human Behavior

The term *mainstream economics* is both clumsy and dependent on a debatable diagnosis of what represents "mainstream" at any given moment. Therefore, I shall avoid taking a stance on whether behavioral economics is more mainstream today than the approach aligned with the spirit of Becker's manifesto. I shall call the latter simply *neoclassical*. This designation is not without its risk because the term is contested (cf. Lawson, 2013). Nonetheless, it represents a label that remains in common use, especially in debates surrounding the clashes of "orthodox" economic schools with their "heterodox" adversaries. Because my use aligns with standard historical delineations of the economic paradigms (Morgan and Rutherford, 1998), I hope it will not sow too much confusion.

What is characteristic of neoclassical economics, then? To outline its basic features, I shall follow the footsteps of the Chicago economists who have provided its most prominent methodological reflection and extended its reach most broadly. To this day, their ideas frequently shape how economics is passed to a new generation of students through renowned textbooks, such as Gregory N. Mankiw's (2021) *Principles of Economics*, currently in its ninth edition.

For novice economists who encounter such an introductory text, the first thing to notice—especially if they happen to have an opportunity to compare with the other social sciences—is the emphasis on an abstract theory. Although applications are always present and play an important role in facilitating understanding, they remain mere manifestations of the underlying general principles. Mankiw (2021, p. 13) leaves little space for doubt that the economic approach contains a sizable dose of deductive reasoning: "The field of economics is based on a few big ideas that can be applied in many different situations. (…) Keep these building blocks in mind. Even the most sophisticated economic analysis is founded on these (…) principles." Thus, neoclassical economics starts from principles considered essentially self-evident to any human by virtue of his being an agent in the world—for instance, "people respond to incentives" (cf. Landsburg, 2012, p. 3)—and rigorously explores their implications to arrive at conclusions that are often remote and unexpected. This does not make neoclassical economics nonempirical: one still needs many additional working assumptions to formulate any useful (i.e., testable, among other things) theory that would attempt to solve a specific problem. Nevertheless, the core principles are considered largely immune from falsification and permit the use of the characteristic mathematical organon, as I shall yet discuss.

The preoccupation of the neoclassical approach with theory suggests the potential breadth of its scope. According to Becker's (1978) classic exposition, economics cannot be distinguished from other social sciences based on a difference in the field of study. If human behavior follows general principles, they will manifest themselves in any area of human endeavors. If one were to limit the scope of economic study to, say, activities that involve an explicit calculation of profits or monetary prices, such a delimitation would be arbitrary, or at least not implied by the economic approach itself in any way. Lionel Robbins (2007 [1932], p. 15) realized this, formulating perhaps the most famous definition of economics: "Economics is the science which studies human behaviour as a relationship between ends and scarce means which have alternative uses."

The definition includes several attention-worthy components. Nevertheless, let us not divert our attention from the issue of scope now. Once we realize that one of the "scarce means which have alternative uses" is time, it becomes clear that the subject of economic science, so defined, must be coextensive with *any* human behavior. Whatever goal people might pursue, whichever resources they might have at their disposal, they will always have a limited amount of time at their disposal, be it in the context of an anonymous market exchange or their most intimate personal relationships. Therefore, if our examination aims to distinguish economics from other social sciences, we cannot succeed by relegating individual disciplines to different areas of study.

As Becker (1978) points out emphatically, what sets economists apart from the other social scientists is their specific approach to the study of social phenomena. Becker suggests that this approach, here referred to as neoclassical, rests on three distinct cornerstones: maximizing behavior, market equilibrium, and stable preferences. Each deserves a brief exposition.

Maximizing behavior means that any agent chooses such from the available alternatives that provides him with the greatest net benefit. An agent in this context does not have to be a person; it can be anything whose behavior can be best described as rationally goal-directed (more on rationality later). Such an agent represents a basic analytical unit taken as a "black box" that the economist engaged in the given modeling exercise does not analyze further. The black box may enclose an individual mind, but it may also represent large social composites as corporations or even states. How "large" or "small" the agents postulated by the economist will be depends primarily on practical considerations, especially on purpose the corresponding model is intended to serve, and the level of analytical detail necessary to solve the research problem at hand (cf. Rodrik, 2015, chap. 1). The definition of an agent will differ in response to whether one seeks to explain the changes in the demand for potatoes, the position of ice cream vendors on a beach, or the patterns of international trade.

The most generic and most fervently debated agent of neoclassical economics is the consumer. The model consumer's goal is utility maximization, which typically causes a lot of confusion. The confusion tends to result from conflating the economic sense, in which the concept of utility is used today, with the intuitive, psychological meaning of the term. In the 19th century, the term *utility* was used following the tradition of utilitarian philosophy founded by the English philosopher Jeremy Bentham as synonymous with pleasure and referred to the psychic experience of satisfaction. Thus, Stanley Jevons (1965 [1871], p. 37), one of the fathers of modern economics, stated that "pleasure and pain are undoubtedly the ultimate objects of the Calculus of Economics."

Over time, however, the utilitarian understanding of utility has proved too much of a hindrance to economic science. It became clear that significant analytical conclusions can be achieved without utility being measured or even measurable. Moreover, employment of any other than a purely formal notion of utility would require reliance on the validity of a particular psychological theory of mental states and acceptance of utilitarian ethics as a value guide. Perhaps unsurprisingly, neoclassical economists concluded that the price is not worth paying. Therefore, "utility" is treated formalistically to refer to the consumers' assumed ability to rank alternatives according to their relative subjective desirability. Saying that the agent strictly prefers alternative x to alternative y is equivalent to saying that x provides the agent with greater utility than y. This approach is called *ordinal* as only the order of the alternatives in the individual's preference ranking matters: all considerations of utility's magnitude are purged from the analysis. Thus, the utility itself is an empty drawer that can be filled with anything: for the sake of acquiring testable predictions, one often needs to approximate formal utility with something measurable, such as wealth or income.

Market equilibrium refers to the vantage point neoclassical economics takes to address the issues of social coordination. A society consists of individuals variously equipped with resources, needs, and desires. When individuals' property rights are enforceable, markets represent a prominent medium of coordination that allows the individuals to engage in mutually beneficial transactions and thus achieve otherwise unattainable levels of satisfaction.[1] The context of exchange motivates the individuals to reveal subjective valuations: those who value the respective goods relatively little will be motivated to sell, and those who value them relatively lot will be motivated to buy. While prospective buyers and sellers, guided by self-interest, haggle over the terms of trade, they unintentionally convey vital information about the scarcity of the good relative to other goods in the economy—the relative prices are established as a side product of the decentralized interactions. Equilibrium denotes a stable situation toward which the market gravitates. Competition among the buyers and sellers eliminates surpluses and shortages through price adjustment and converges on a price that "clears" the market. At this price, the quantity supplied equals the quantity demanded. As a result, the equilibrium price remains stable until an exogenous shock alters the balance of supply and demand and forces the market to seek a new equilibrium reflective of the novel situation.

The concepts of the market and the equilibrium can be interpreted broadly. The price does not need to be quoted in monetary terms, for instance. It points to the value of any sacrifice of time, effort, or resources—that is, to any opportunity cost—the buyer must incur to acquire the given good. According to neoclassical economics, the market logic is quite universal. It applies even when an explicit calculation of monetary prices would be considered offensive and morally reprehensible by many cultures. Becker (1978, p. 10) himself speaks of the marriage market, for example: "According to the economic approach, a person decides to marry when the utility expected from marriage exceeds that expected from remaining single or from additional search for a more suitable mate."

Equilibrium can be more broadly understood as any situation where none of the participants are motivated to a unilateral change in their behavior. As such, it subsumes a Nash equilibrium used by a branch of economics called game theory to explain strategic interactions. This concept is crucial in the famous prisoner's dilemma game, for example, where it shows how the pursuit of self-interest does not have to imply socially beneficial outcomes. Equilibrium, you see, is not inherently a measure of success, just of stability. For two prisoners motivated to betray each other more than to cooperate, following self-interest leads to stability behind bars.

Stable preferences represent the most controversial of the cornerstones highlighted by Becker. An agent's preferences denote a set of binary evaluative relations between alternatives in terms of "better," "worse," and "equally desirable." Correspondingly, behavior that the economists observe and attempt to predict is understood as a result of interaction between the preferences that characterize what the agent wants (or more precisely: wants more or less than something else) and the constraints that limit the availability of alternatives in the given situation. The trouble is that preferences are never directly observable. All one can do is infer them from indirect evidence. As such, they can be encountered at various levels of immediacy. For instance, an observer may conclude that the consumer weakly prefers green apples to red apples—that is, considers the green at least as desirable as the red—if they choose a green apple over a red one when both are available (assuming equal price, quality, etc.). A preference thus manifested is relatively immediate.

On the other hand, there are also compelling reasons to believe that people prefer health over disease. In this case, however, a reconstruction of the preference from the observed behavior becomes a more perilous task: there is no first-order choice between health and disease to speak of. A preference for health over disease, conceived by an observer, is consistent with many possible behaviors. The prime advantage of the reconstructed background preferences, or "meta-preferences," is that their generality makes them significantly more likely to remain stable, especially in contrast to the often-ephemeral immediate preferences. While anyone's appetite for red and green apples may change from day to day, a meta-preference for, say, a tasty and nutritious diet is persistent.

When Becker (1978) incorporates stability of preferences among the cornerstones of the economic approach, he highlights all the trouble that follows from permitting the preferences to change in the course of an analysis. Of course, one might be tempted to narrow down the understanding of preferences to their immediate, first-order cases for the sake of making the process of their reconstruction more transparent, even more scientific. However, the narrow perspective would inevitably create the need to admit the fleeting nature of the first-order preferences and ultimately prove counterproductive. *Any* change in behavior can be easily "explained" by a presumed change in preferences: one can easily claim success in explaining even the most sudden and unexpected changes in individuals' or groups' behavior if one is free to announce that these agents no longer possess their original values and tastes. According to Becker (1978, pp. 12–13), insistence on the preferences' stability provides the best remedy against this facile, pseudoscientific "explanation," which empties our theories of empirical content, making historical behavioral data no longer useful for predicting behavior. If the preferences are stable, then the observed changes in behavior must result from observable changes in the constraints faced by the agents. The use of *deus ex machina* in the form of an explanation by reference to presumed preference changes is rendered beyond the pale.

However, the fragility of the first-order preferences (red versus green apple) is frequently too palpable to presume them stable. Meta-preferences hidden behind many different types of behavior represent a significantly better candidate for persistence. This does not eliminate their major weakness: recovering them by exact or even tractable methods is difficult. Suppose, for instance, that people in Scandinavia crave designer clothes while people in the Amazon lust for rare bird feathers. Are these different behaviors all projections of "the same" meta-preference for social status? If we are overly cavalier in hypothesizing about the meta-preferences, we risk slipping into "just so stories" devoid of predictive power. In other words, the methodological benefits of using meta-preferences in the place of first-order preferences are not clear-cut. As we shall see in Chapter 4, the problem remains unresolved with significant ramifications for democratic theory. Be that as it may, it is in determining the content and shape of the stable preferences where Becker (1978, p. 14) sees an opportunity for psychology—especially "sociobiology" (in the following, I shall occasionally refer to evolutionary psychology instead)—to contribute to the endeavor of the general science of human behavior.

Despite Becker's (1978, p. 14) assurances that "the value of other social sciences is not diminished even by an enthusiastic and complete acceptance of the economic approach," the acceptance of his manifesto had been less than enthusiastic outside economics. Ongoing controversies surrounding the preferences' stability played an important part. Perhaps this is why Edward Lazear (2000)—writing more than 20 years after Becker's original exposition of the economic approach—discarded stable preferences from the shortlist of the cornerstones. His retrospective celebration of neoclassical economics' imperial achievements replaces stable preferences by the efficiency criterion. This move brings economics closer to applied policy by emphasizing the normative layer of the economic analysis. As we are yet to discuss, efficiency offers a degree of guidance in evaluating alternatives in terms of their desirability and makes it easier for it to formulate practical recommendations. Inefficiency means waste: resources that could have been used to satisfy human wishes and desires do not find their best possible use. Eliminating such a wasteful treatment offers an option to increase someone's utility without sacrificing anybody else's, a so-called *Pareto improvement*.

Whether or not do we accept Becker's or Lazear's list of the cornerstones as the better representation of what the neoclassical approach "really is about," they serve as a demarcation criterion for distinguishing economics from the other social sciences. They represent the methodological background for a general theory of human behavior that speaks the mathematical language of equilibria and constrained optimization. Its primary explanatory tool is the rational choice theory (Zafirovski, 2000; cf. Gilboa, 2010). Its baseline model of a human being is the (in)famous *homo economicus*.

An Empire of Rational Choice

Perhaps the most salient trait of "the economic man" is his ahistorical nature. *Homo economicus* represents the baseline model of a rational decision-maker who is not bound to any particular—historical, sociological, or psychological—circumstances. It is an "ideal type" of an agent that remains after individual character, biographical context, or cultural setting are purged from consideration (cf. Špecián, 2019). The baseline model aspires to represent a Babylonian official, a medieval monk, or a contemporary American businessperson equally well. Clearly, this does not mean that specific context is irrelevant for solving a specific economic problem—an economist interested in the grain prices in the second millennium BC would better be ready to read up on ancient Babylonia. Nonetheless, the fundamental methodological framework is not expected to vary with the historical scenery.

The already-examined notion of constrained optimization represents the backbone of this framework: an agent maximizes his or her utility subject to a given constraint. No doubt, it will be necessary to consider how stable meta-preferences project themselves into the first-order preferences that shape observable behavior in a particular setting. Here, economists may indeed be compelled to ask historians, sociologists, and psychologists for advice. However, once a utility function is estimated, the preferences are treated as given. Likewise, the specific case-relevant constraint is not truly ahistorical and needs to be based on data often gathered by other disciplines. However, no context alters the nature of constrained optimization as a general exercise.

Apart from the fact that *homo economicus* does not inhabit any specific country or epoch, it has other essential traits. Rationality is the most important by far. For the constrained optimization framework to be useful, one must assume that the maximizing agents proceed rationally in the instrumental sense, that is, they use the best available means to achieve their goals. At the same time, it does not matter if the instrumentally rational behavior results from conscious reasoning; its exact psychological underpinning is irrelevant.

A great controversy stems from the fact that *homo economicus* is considered selfish, which means that it only cares about its own consumption with complete disregard of the other agents' outcomes. However, the selfishness assumption is a matter of analytical convenience more than anything else. It can be discarded, if need be, without sacrificing the methodological fundament of neoclassical economics as such. Hudík (2015, p. 167), for instance, makes a persuasive case that its alleged dependence on selfishness misrepresents the economic approach: "even in applied economics, selfishness is not a typical assumption and certainly not an unavoidable one." Instead, *motivational symmetry* is presumed in the economic approach. However selfish or altruistic people may be in their consumption behavior, we expect them to be guided by the same motivations also in other walks of life, including politics.

Thus, the rationality assumption is not coextensive with the selfishness assumption since an economic agent's "self-interest" can be defined as broadly as you like. Also, it does not contradict a commonsense understanding of human behavior. That might be surprising, given how eagerly many people embrace irrationality as an explanatory device to shed light on peculiar behaviors.[2] However, even those most vocally skeptical about human rationality would be lost in the regular walks of life if they could not rely on a fundamental explanatory principle of what can be called "folk psychology" or "theory of mind." Folk psychology represents an intuitive way by which we connect the people's observed behavior—arguably including our own behavior (Carruthers, 2011)—with their mental states: beliefs, desires, or intentions. Alexander Rosenberg (2012a, p. 39) summarizes this explanatory principle as follows: "If any person, agent, individual [x], wants some outcome, d, and believes that an action, a, is a means to attain d under the circumstances, then x does a." What else does the principle delimit if not the intuitive notion of instrumental (goal-directed) rationality?

Thus, despite the complex mathematical apparatus that it often relies upon, neoclassical economics takes the commonsense notion of how human behavior works seriously. Perhaps except for the fact that it puts less credit into verbally declared intentions, brushing them off as "cheap talk," and espouses consistency as rationality's guiding principle. The hard-necked reliance on rationality assumption creates perhaps the most salient friction point between neoclassical economics and the other social sciences. Nonrational factors such as habit, tradition, or power relations are effectively purged from neoclassical economics. This explanatory asymmetry has long raised concerns regarding the compatibility of economics and other social scientific endeavors (e.g., Etzioni, 1983). Even the dispute with behavioral economists is, at its core, a dispute over rationality. The mainstay of the behavioral economists' attack on the neoclassical approach is the evidence of systematic—and therefore predictable—occurrence of behavior incompatible with the precepts of instrumental rationality.

What exactly does rationality, as postulated by neoclassical economists, entail then? A frequent target of criticism is what we can call "hyperrationality" (Elster, 2008) or "unlimited rationality" (Gigerenzer, 2010). For instance,

Richard Thaler and Cass Sunstein (2021, p. 9) maintain that: "If you look at economics textbooks, you will learn that Homo economicus can think like Albert Einstein, store as much memory as Google does in the cloud, and exercise the willpower of Mahatma Gandhi." Such an agent is clearly superhuman, a sophisticated robot rather than an actual flesh-and-bone human being. Jon Elster (2008, p. 64), who strives to provide a more precise—albeit less colorful—description, defines hyperrationality as "the search for the action that would have been optimal if one ignored the costs of the search itself." Therefore, in his view, hyperrationality assumes that the agent's decision-making process disregards the difficulties with obtaining information and the constrained processing capacity of the human brain. Under the assumption of hyperrationality, thinking is neither laborious nor time-consuming, and cognitive abilities are unlimited—so, each agent can flawlessly and immediately perform the complex optimization tasks addressed by the technical appendices of economic papers.

That hyperrationality does not represent a psychologically accurate picture of human reasoning is beyond dispute. However, what remains controversial is if this critique strikes the heart of the neoclassical approach. Does it indeed expose its principal limitations or even overall inadequacy? One ought to tread carefully here. Admission of necessity to consider the cost of information acquisition and information processing means no revolution in economic thinking. In fact, it aligns neatly with its basic precepts as no consistent champion of the neoclassical approach would doubt the need to take *all* the costs of the existing alternatives into consideration.

The cognitive and information costs are occasionally ignored to keep a particular model tractable—that much is true. It is also the case that their inclusion may lead to complications in empirical research due to the paucity of data. However, these problems are pragmatic and do not invalidate the neoclassical approach in general. After all, the economics of information had belonged among the accepted components of the neoclassical discourse before behavioral criticism. In his Nobel lecture, George Stigler (1983, p. 539) even delights in the absence of opposition to spreading his information economics gospel through the profession. In short, if the expected benefits of information processing do not exceed the expected costs of obtaining it, it is rational not to seek such information. The fact that one lacks omniscience, forgets, or does not always adhere to his resolutions may conflict with the textbook models of *homo economicus*. Its conflict with the notion of rational optimization as such is less clear, though. One can be rationally ignorant of things not worth knowing, rationally forget what is not worth remembering, or rationally reconsider former resolutions as their actual requirements become visible. In other words, rejection of hyperrationality, be it understood in a sense established by Elster (2008) or in the context of Thaler's and Sunstein's (2021) critique of textbook models, is not equivalent to rejection of rationality.

Nonetheless, the rationality assumption as utilized by neoclassical economics is not invulnerable to behavioral criticism. Its weak spot is its axiomatic underpinning that emphasizes consistency above all else. The axioms pertain to the form preferences are supposed to take that guarantees consistent valuation of alternatives. Their chief implication is that even in an environment characterized by imperfect information and nonzero processing costs, instrumentally rational behavior must be devoid of systematic mistakes. Mistakes are permissible—the agent can make many of them, and sizable ones too—but they need to be random (cf. Caplan, 2008, chap. 1). Suppose Josephine wants to arrive at work at 9 am straight. This is not an easy task, given she needs to commute over the city. Some days, the traffic will be unexpectedly thicker than usual; other days, the streets may be wondrously empty. As a result, Josephine will sometimes arrive too late or too early. However, this is fine only if she arrives at 9 am *on average*, that is, if her mistakes are randomly distributed around the intended outcome (I take the liberty here to presume that late arrival is as bad as early arrival). If her mistakes are *systematically* skewed in one direction, there are only two possible explanations: either we are wrong about Josephine's goal of arriving at 9 am straight or she is irrational. Behavioral economists are trying to identify the various contexts in which the latter seems a preferable explanation, as we shall see.

But first, let me address four axiomatic principles in the very core of the disagreement over the validity of neoclassical rationality assumption: completeness, transitivity, independence from irrelevant alternatives, and invariance (Tversky and Kahneman, 1986; Gintis, 2016, chap. 5).

Completeness means the agent's ability to compare alternatives—that is, alternative bundles of goods or, more broadly, alternative states of the world—in terms of their relative desirability. A binary relation of preference is supposed to exist for any two alternatives. The relation can be defined using a notion of weak preference, that is, "at least as good as." Would you like a red apple better than a green apple? Would you prefer Godzilla to beat King Kong or vice versa? A neoclassically rational agent is supposed to have a response to these questions. It is fine to be indifferent, but an inability to compare is impermissible from the perspective of the completeness axiom. Incomplete preferences make the economic agent susceptible to the fate of the proverbial Buridan's ass that starved to death between two stacks of hay whose relative desirability it could not judge.

Transitivity axiom, in its turn, precludes vicious cycles from appearing in the preference ordering. It states that an agent that weakly prefers x to y and y to z must also weakly prefer x to z. Non-transitive preferences may either render the agent unable to choose or make them vulnerable to riskless exploitation, neither of which is consistent with being "neoclassically rational" (Rizzo and Whitman, 2019). The latter problem is typically illustrated using a "money pump" thought experiment (Hausman and McPherson, 2006, pp. 46–47). Suppose Alex prefers an apple to an orange (x to y), an orange to a banana (y to z), but—in violation of transitivity—a banana to an apple (z to x). An unscrupulous schemer can exploit their irrational preferences to pump out their resources, suggesting a series of deals: Alex is willing to buy an orange for a banana and a penny, an apple for an orange and a penny, a banana for an apple and a penny; you get the idea. A sufficient number of repetition rounds would allow the schemer to get Alex's last penny without any risk.

The third axiom, *independence of irrelevant alternatives*, only becomes important if the set of alternatives under consideration is constrained (cf. Gintis, 2016, chap. 5.1). Do note that this is not the same issue as affordability, since even in a constrained set some alternatives may be unaffordable. For instance, one needs to choose from the available menu in a diner, but one's budget makes the steak an unviable alternative. In such situations, neoclassical rationality requires the preference ranking of two alternatives to be independent of whether any third option, which has no substantive relation to any of the other two, is available on the menu or not. In other words, the preference for an apple over an orange (or vice versa) must be independent of whether a banana is also available. If the independence axiom is violated, the agent is, again, vulnerable to exploitation: this time, it may take the form of a "decoy." Let me use Hansen's (2016, pp. 166–167) example of an *asymmetric dominance effect* for illustration. Suppose Clara is shopping for a laptop. Initially, there are two alternatives on the menu, exhibit A with 300 GB storage and a €400 price tag and exhibit B with a 200 GB hard drive costing €300. Whatever preference she might have, the preference needs to be independent of any third option added to the menu to qualify as rational. Can the presence of exhibit C with a meager 250 GB of storage and a hefty €450 price persuade Clara to choose A over B? Can an exhibit D with 150 GB worth €350 sway her toward preferring B over A? If yes, Clara's preferences are not independent of irrelevant alternatives, and a cunning seller can take advantage of that using a suitable decoy to manipulate her choice toward the item with a higher margin.

The last axiom from the canonical list is *invariance*. It requires that the preference ordering remains the same, no matter how the alternatives are described— or "framed"—as long as all the descriptions provide equivalent information. In other words, the relative desirability of any alternative is supposed to persist even if the alternative is described in different terms. Invariance allows circumventing the thorny issue of how an agent interprets and understands the situation at hand. Instead of asking about the agent's understanding, which is a matter of an uncomfortable degree of subjectivity, we simply ask if the information is available. As Herbert Simon (1986, p. S210), a forefather of today's behavioral economics, has put it, neoclassical economics postulates "one world" identical for the agent and the observer. Perhaps the most famous experiment demonstrating a violation of the invariance axiom remains the "Asian disease," which I shall discuss later.

The axiomatic fundament of neoclassical rationality cannot be as casually sacrificed as the assumption of hyperrationality. It is cemented into the very foundation of the rational choice theory. The behavioral economists' experimental demonstrations of systematic and predictable violations of these axioms by real-world economic agents—that is, by the people whose behavior economic models are supposed to predict and explain—are therefore worrisome from the neoclassical perspective. Substantive reformation or even abandonment of the axiomatic underpinning of the rationality assumption would indeed represent a major paradigmatic shift. The least the behavioral economists take their experimental findings to suggest is a split between the descriptive and the normative theory of human behavior. The former, relying on a heavy infusion of psychological findings into its considerations, explains how humans do behave; the latter suggests how they should behave optimally. In Tversky's and Kahneman's (1986, p. 272) words: "the dream of constructing a theory that is acceptable both descriptively and normatively appears unrealizable."

It is readily apparent that the suggested theoretical split threatens to undermine the ambitions of the neoclassical approach much more seriously than any specific setback in applying economic theory to nonstandard themes. As already stated, the habitat of *homo economicus* is supposedly not limited to "economic behavior" in a narrow sense of exchange with explicitly calculated prices. Following the steps of Becker's manifesto, neoclassical economics aspires to imperial status and claims territories previously occupied by other social sciences: clearly without much regard for the natives' objections. From the imperialist perspective, the difference between a market for vegetables and a market for children is merely the (un)availability of readily available monetary prices. True, there is a long-standing controversy over how bothersome the explicit prices' absence truly is (Coase, 1978). Nonetheless, practical obstacles can be waved off as partial or temporary and are of minor importance from the overall perspective of the gargantuan undertaking of unification of the social sciences under the banner of neoclassical economics.

The neoclassical economists' skeptical attitude toward the possible contribution of psychology is grounded in the claim that scientific economics does not strive to describe mental states but to predict behavior. That, at least, is a classic position defended by Milton Friedman in the single most influential text in the history of economic methodology, *The Methodology of Positive Economics*. Friedman (1953, p. 7) suggests that the goal of economics—and any other value-free science—lies in delivering testable predictions of yet unobserved phenomena. If there is any realism at play in neoclassical economics, it is the *behavioral* realism of its predictions, not the *psychological* realism of its assumptions. So, according to Lehtinen and Kuorikoski (2007, p. 116): "… if a result is demonstrably robust with respect to the unrealistic psychological or behavioral assumptions, the falsity does not matter."

The approach delineated by Friedman is also frequently called "as if" methodology (cf. Boland, 1979) because its central claim is that the agents may behave as if the model assumptions are fulfilled even if they are not. Friedman (1953) illustrates that using an example of an expert billiard player. The player's behavior can be predicted using a complex mathematical model built around an assumption that the player behaves

> as if he knew the complicated mathematical formulas that would give the optimum directions of travel, could estimate accurately by eye the angles, etc., describing the location of the balls, could make lightning calculations

from the formulas, and could then make the balls travel in the direction indicated by the formulas.

(Friedman, 1953, p. 21)

Such a model may provide a high degree of predictive precision—which is the ultimate measure of its scientific merit—disregarding the fact that the billiard player performs no such calculations and, psychologically speaking, applies expert intuitions and "just figures out" from what angle with what force a particular ball needs to be hit. While the billiard player's actual cognitive process may be of great interest to psychologists, economists do not care about it until its consideration would facilitate a more precise prediction of the player's behavior. Because the point of the social scientific enterprise is not formulating realistic assumptions but deriving accurate predictions, psychology's role is purely instrumental. If it cannot offer enlightening answers to questions such as: "What does the agent maximize?" it is irrelevant for imperial economics.

To commemorate its successes on the eve of the new millennium in one of the profession's leading journals, Edward Lazear (2000) has presented a long list of the presumably conquered territories: economics of discrimination, crime, family, demography, social interactions, religion, human capital, personnel economics, politics, health, or law. His rhetoric is elated, if not triumphant:

> The power of economics lies in its rigor. Economics is scientific; it follows the scientific method of stating a formal refutable theory, testing the theory, and revising the theory based on the evidence. Economics succeeds where other social sciences fail because economists are willing to abstract.
>
> (Lazear, 2000, p. 102)

It is perhaps one of history's remarkable ironies that these confident remarks have been uttered at the very moment when economic imperialism in Gary Becker's footsteps was to face unprecedented, possibly even shattering challenges. Two years after Lazear's text has been published, the psychologist Daniel Kahneman has received a Nobel Prize in economics "for having integrated insights from psychological research into economic science, especially concerning human judgment and decision-making under uncertainty" (The Nobel Prize, 2002). Not so long after that, the Great Recession of 2008 caught the economists unaware and espoused their predictive failures in all their nakedness: the prestige of neoclassical economics in the public's eyes has been shaken, perhaps beyond mending. Do these events initiate a novel stage of development in economic thought? Did psychology become ready to turn the tide and colonize economics?

Behavioral Paradigm Shift

Behavioral economics has gained momentum as a prominent research program that rivals the neoclassical approach in a context of a so-called cognitive revolution in the study of human behavior (Sent, 2004). The label "behavioral" is somewhat unfortunate because the revolution repudiates behaviorism as an attempt to explain behavior without a reference to mental phenomena and strives to open the "black box" of the human mind. Its oldest polemics with neoclassical economics addressed the realism of economic assumptions and were swiftly rejected as irrelevant in the tradition of Friedman's instrumentalism. Behavioral economics became a serious rival to the neoclassical mainstream only when the psychologists gave up on external criticism and decided to beat the economists in their own game. The central line of their attack rests on the claim that a psychologically realistic model of an economic agent's mind represents a necessary condition for the behavioral realism of the economic predictions. Accordingly, the theories built upon a better understanding of how a human mind works—especially considering its various limitations—promise to improve the scientific performance of economics. It is not the intrinsic value of the assumptions' realism that is being advertised here, but a pledge that "increasing the realism of the psychological underpinnings of economic analysis will improve economics on its own terms—generating theoretical insights, making better predictions of field phenomena, and suggesting better policy" (Camerer and Loewenstein, 2004, p. 3). The outlined strategy is clear: it is simple for the neoclassical economists to ignore anyone who applies a different set of evaluative criteria to appraise theories on account of their incompatibility with the economic way of looking at things. However, they cannot turn a blind eye toward rivals who outperform them on equal terms.

As the title of one of the popular books by a prominent behavioral economist and social psychologist Dan Ariely (2009) concisely announces, the trump card of the psychologistic approach against neoclassical economics is "predictable irrationality." This slogan points to a belief—grounded today in extensive empirical evidence—that deviations from rational behavioral presumed by the neoclassical models are neither random nor fleeting. Seen from the perspective of behavioral economics, the human being will not always make the right choices (not even "on average") and converge toward the optimal solution due to learning. People can be expected to make systematic and predictable mistakes. Moreover, these mistakes are significant and robust enough to exert tangible influence in the real world beyond a laboratory's doors.

In their famous "heuristics and biases" research program, behavioral economists managed to experimentally demonstrate that the human mind does not work "as if" it was hiding a flawless computation mechanism. Instead, it relies on relatively simple rules of thumb—heuristics—that enable it to economize on its cognitive capacity while providing very satisfactory outcomes, at least in some circumstances. The circumstances matter, though. Heuristics can also systematically misfire when the right mental levers are pushed, leading to systematic mistakes—biases. Arguably, the most omnipresent heuristics stem from cognitive adaptations to an ancestral environment: think hunters and gatherers on an African savanna (cf. Petersen, 2015). Thus, biases are easily exacerbated when the heuristics are used in the very different environment of modern society. One way or another, heuristics—and the biases they bring along—are necessary for orientation in the complex system of the world that surrounds us while relying on the limited cognitive capacity we possess.

From the point of view of neoclassical rationality, cognitive shortcuts become problematic once they systematically trigger types of behavior that clash with the expected behavior of a rational agent. As a result, predictions based on the neoclassical rationality assumption may be less precise than predictions based on a more psychologically realistic model of a human mind. If sufficiently robust and significant, such an improvement in predictive power may force neoclassical economists to capitulate and admit the importance of psychological realism. With their surrender, economics, once an imperial science, may effectively become a province of psychology. As Thaler (2015, p. 340) puts it:

> When all economists are equally open-minded and are willing to incorporate important variables in their work, even if the rational model says those variables are supposedly irrelevant, the field of behavioral economics will disappear. All economics will be as behavioral as it needs to be.

It would be superfluous to catalog all the heuristics and biases discovered by behavioral economists. An excellent primer to the topic is Daniel Kahneman's *Thinking, Fast and Slow* (2011), for instance. Moreover, Rizzo and Whitman (2019, chaps 4–5) have recently offered an exceptionally detailed critical reflection of the state of the field. I shall limit myself to demonstrating their significance on a prominent example of the invariance axiom violation. It comes from an experimental study that tests if differences in framing influence the preference ranking of alternatives. The scenario is one with a fictitious "Asian Disease." The disease's outbreak is expected to kill 600 people; there are two possible programs to combat it, each with known consequences (Tversky and Kahneman, 1986, p. S260):

- If Program A is adopted, 200 people will be saved.
- If Program B is adopted, there is 1/3 probability that 600 people will be saved, and 2/3 probability that no people will be saved.

An alternative scenario with an identical setting was presented to a different group of test subjects (Tversky and Kahneman, 1986, p. S260):

- If Program C is adopted, 400 people will die.
- If Program D is adopted, there is 1/3 probability that nobody will die, and 2/3 probability that 600 people will die.

To an attentive reader, it is evident that Program A is identical to Program C, and Program B is the same as Program D. No information is withheld; each setup is transparent. From a perspective of a neoclassically rational agent, there is no relevant difference within each pair. Although the economic theory does not predict if a rational agent should prefer A to B or vice versa, once you commit to a preference in one direction, the invariance axiom requires that you must preserve the same direction in your choice between C and D. The Asian Disease experiment is taken as a falsification of this prediction. When alternatives are framed from the perspective of gains, most experimental subjects state a preference for A over B; if the problem is framed through the lens of losses, the preference reverts, with the majority choosing D over C.

Of course, methodological objections come quickly to one's mind: the experimental design is interindividual, the exercise is merely hypothetical with no "skin in the game," and so on. However, framing effects have been examined and demonstrated many times since (cf. Kelly, 2012). The existing evidence that framing matters for the preferential ordering thus appears strong. The preferences' frame-dependence is a significant hurdle for the neoclassical approach. If people differ in their perception of what is in the strictest sense identical, how is one to construct a general theory of their behavior without delving into psychological intricacies? The presence of framing undermines not only the invariance axiom but possibly also the independence axiom. It has also been illustrated that the framing of choices from the perspective of human decision-makers tends to be narrow. People tend to consider not all the relevant features of a problem but only the particularly salient ones—such as those where an alternative's dominance is easily recognized—which opens the way for the decoy effect described above. Arguably, the issue of framing offers a particularly convenient starting point for an attack against the neoclassical approach used as testified by Ariely's (2009) battle cry "everything is relative."

Indeed, it would seem from some of the behavioral economists' more radical statements that the neoclassical approach with its rational choice perspective on human behavior is destined to fail, if not already at the brink of extinction. Despite such impressions, a lively controversy persists. The implications of experimental findings, such as the Asian disease, for the economic theory are not so easily drawn. Upon a closer look, three distinct points of view retain a strong voice in the debate. The first perspective views behavioral economics as an alternative to the rational choice theory, which replaces the older approach with a new one that relies on psychological realism and represents a radical step toward making the aprioristic and navel-gazing economics more scientific (Simon, 1986; Gigerenzer, 2010). The second one—espoused by Colin Camerer and George Loewenstein (2004) or Richard Thaler (2015, 2016), for instance—is less non-compromising. It perceives the rationality-based models as a sometimes useful but ultimately too narrow subset of behavioral models. Here, the behavioral research program aims to integrate economics into a broader context of the behavioral sciences and broaden the scope of its models' useful application. The third perspective, one most skeptical of the behavioral economists' achievements, largely dismisses the threat to the neoclassical orthodoxy. In its view, the anomalies uncovered by the behavioral economists are not entirely uninteresting and may occasionally deserve a footnote or two. Still, they cannot aspire to be more than a commentary highlighting some partial challenges of the rationality-based approach (Levine, 2012). According to these skeptics, behavioral economists promise a revolution in economic thinking since the 1970s. However, it forever remains a few years in the future: the imminent end of the neoclassical rule is continuously being announced but always postponed at the last minute to a more opportune moment.[3]

To the extent there is a development of the three views' relative strength, the proponents of behavioral economics seem to have been shifting from the first one to the second (cf. Sent, 2004; Thaler, 2015). Their critics keep to the third one, but their numbers may be dwindling if the Nobel Prizes and the composition of publications in the top journals offer any guidance.

One issue has proven especially contentious: does behavioral economics provide sufficiently generalizable contributions to help update the theory of human behavior? The behavioral economists' insights are scattered across the landscape, and their subordination to a coherent theoretical framework appears problematic (Posner, 1998). Moreover, while the general case for the influence of rationality's bounds on human behavior is potent, not all findings to support it have withstood scrutiny equally well. During the recent "replication crisis" that hit some disciplines, such as social psychology, very hard, many canonical experiments that became part of conventional wisdom failed in replication efforts (cf. Schimmack, 2020). Although psychology as a discipline proved remarkably open to self-correction and swiftly proceeded against the use of "questionable research practices," there is a lingering shadow of doubt over the robustness of numerous findings. For instance, the sizable research in priming, that is, the possibility to influence human behavior by subliminal cues, fared particularly poorly. Little wonder that scholars skeptical toward overzealous policy applications conclude that "when incentives, learning, group debiasing, and self-regulation have not been adequately assessed, it is not clear which results we can confidently export to the world of public policy" (Rizzo and Whitman, 2019, p. 234).

The replication crisis only accentuates a principal worry the theoretically minded economists share: while *homo economicus*—whatever its flaws and limitations—possesses a precisely delimited substance, it is not particularly clear what its replacement is supposed to be. True, the efforts to find a single, universally valid model are probably futile, and economists must always engage in risky model selection (Rodrik, 2015). However, flexibility in model selection is not the same as an absence of a unifying outlook on what the proper economic approach is supposed to be. While individual findings of behavioral economists are often remarkable, a degree of systematization necessary to transplant them into a novel context is conditional on theoretical advances. In short, while the theoretical underpinnings of the neoclassical approach are clear, the theoretical foundations of the behavioral approach remain largely obscure: *homo economicus* cannot be supplanted by a list of 150 psychological biases. Behavioral economists propose integrating rational choice into a broader framework, but such a framework is currently not at hand. If history is to be our guide, one can scarcely hope for an actual scientific revolution to take place without it (Kuhn, 1996).

Table 1.1 Methodological comparison of neoclassical and behavioral economics

Neoclassical economics	Behavioral economics
Deduction	Induction
Model	Experiment
Prescriptive	Descriptive
One world	Interpretation, framing
Optimization	Satisficing

On the road toward considering the long-term potential of behavioral economics to advance the general theory of human behavior, it is perhaps best to start by comparing it to the neoclassical approach on a methodological level. Whatever controversies may reign concerning theoretical prospects of the behavioral revolution, the methodological modifications it suggests have some distinct contours. The most salient methodological differences between neoclassical and behavioral economics are summarized in Table 1.1. Above all, such a comparison elucidates how accepting the behavioral approach would minimize the difference between economics and the other social sciences.

Many differences between the two approaches have already been hinted upon during the preceding discussion. Nevertheless, a concise summary may prove helpful.

Perhaps the most striking characteristic of neoclassical economics is the extent of its reliance on deduction from basic principles, whose application to various contexts is sought and tested. The approach is conditional on a certain kind of intransigence: any explanations relying on ad hoc changes in preferences or presumption of agents' irrationality are treated skeptically, if not briskly rejected as paradigmatically incompatible. It would be a mistake to presume that neoclassical hypotheses cannot be falsified, though. Neoclassical economists fully agree that the shards of evidence produced by empirical research are vital to further their scientific aspirations: economics is ultimately an empirical science (e.g., Stigler, 1983). At the same time, they also firmly believe that a coherent picture of the social world cannot be built without reliance on overarching principles of behavior. Surrendering a coherent theoretical framework once thorny anomalies come at sight would be foolhardy unless its replacement is already available. Empirical research in the social sciences faces many challenges, and a mere list of empirical conclusions, however striking they might be, cannot substitute for a theory.

Given the complexity of the social world that is composed of an immense number of human relationships that flexibly respond to changing circumstances, it remains impossible to perform a "decisive experiment" that would serve as a definitive falsification of any general hypothesis, let alone a whole approach, such as the neoclassical one. To mention a particularly vexing problem for the social scientists, the predictions derived from a theory represent a valid test of the theory if and only if the conditions under which the prediction has been made remain constant. That means that the prediction is binding only *ceteris paribus*, that is, in otherwise equal circumstances. The problem of omnipresent confounding variables cements the role of an abstract theory. Its perhaps paradoxical advantage is that it does not strive to become a faithful image of reality. It only presents hypotheses about the critical relationships among the variables while the potentially disturbing influences whose elimination can never be guaranteed in realistic situations are bracketed out using the ceteris paribus condition.

Consider the demand for apples as a simple example. The neoclassical workhorse model of a competitive market predicts that an increase in the price of apples will lead to a reduction in the quantity of apples that people will buy. Under what conditions is the prediction binding? When can we add its failure to the burden of the economic theory from which it follows? The forecast is only binding if the price of apples changes while any other relevant variable either remains constant or is controlled for. Prices of other products, changes in weather, advertising, as well as innumerable other influences represent potential confounding variables. In short, the set of the potential confounding variables is open, and a definite list of factors that could frustrate the forecast despite its theoretical underpinning being correct cannot be established (cf. Rosenberg, 1996). Thus, the ceteris paribus condition is necessary to reduce the complexity of the social world to manageable levels, but its employment makes empirical falsification of hypotheses arduous.

One way or another, in behavioral economics, there is a much more pronounced tendency to build the theory from the bottom up using the experimental results. It thus follows in the footsteps of Herbert Simon's (1986, pp. 223–224) call for the empirical foundations to economics. The prospect theory represents a prominent example (Kahneman, 2003; Thaler, 2015, chap. 4). Built upon a foundation of experimental results, it postulates a point of reference as a baseline for people's evaluation of alternatives when making decisions under uncertainty. Experimental results also establish its emphasis on "loss aversion," that is, on the fact that losses and gains relative to the reference point are evaluated asymmetrically. Risk aversion is typical in the domain of gains. In the domain of losses, people become risk-seeking and willing to risk larger losses to avoid certain smaller ones.

The prescriptive/descriptive distinction is somewhat contentious as neoclassical economists do not perceive their theory as normatively oriented. Remember, neoclassical economists use the assumption of axiomatic rationality to generate predictions of what people *will* do, not recommendations of what they *should* do. Nonetheless, it remains the behavioral economists' frequent charge that the neoclassical theory remains descriptive only as far as people comply with its standards of rationality but becomes prescriptive once it addresses someone who "misbehaves" (cf. Thaler, 2015, chap. 4). Prima facie, the charge certainly does not seem unfounded. After all, Friedman himself emphasized that he models an *expert* billiard player using his "as if" approach. Thus, it may indeed be the case that the rational choice theory only offers reliable predictions of an expert solution to a problem. Since people who make significant choices often lack expertise in making them—how often do you buy a car or take a mortgage?—"as if" rationality-based predictions may deviate a lot from what they will actually do (cf. Thaler, 2015, chap. 6). That does not mean that the prediction is entirely useless, though. True, it is useless *as a prediction*. But it might be quite important as a *recommendation*. In short, a prediction of expert behavior turns normative when it provides less experienced agents with advice on how they should act to be more successful.

In other words, the normatively correct solution to a problem predicted based on the assumption of neoclassical rationality and the empirically frequented solution exposed by the behavioral economists' inductive methods are not always the same. Consider a simple mathematical problem "$x = 3 + 3 \times 3$." The normatively correct answer is $x = 12$, but an empirically frequented one will also be $x = 18$ (run a Twitter poll!). That does not mean that behavioral economists say that the answer 18 is as good as 12 because many people choose it. They emphasize that if we make the rationality assumption a cornerstone of our prediction, these predictions will be less precise than if we consider human propensity to make systematic mistakes. This possibility is particularly worrisome to neoclassical economists since it is the criterion of predictive success upon which their scientific legitimacy rests.

The postulate of "one world" is equivalent to assuming that the decision problem is perceived identically by the agent and the observer, that is, the economist who decides to model the situation (Simon, 1986). Thus,

> if a theorist knows the ends of some decision-maker, he can predict what actions will be taken to achieve them as follows: (1) he calculates the most reasonable way for the decision-maker to reach his goals, and (2) he assumes this way will actually be chosen because the decision-maker is rational.
>
> (Downs, 1957, p. 4)

The one world assumption is a controversial step because it eliminates the whole issue of interpretation that has been a prominent topic in the social sciences since Max Weber (2019 [1922]), at least. However, to open the door to the problems of interpretation would undermine the invariance axiom and force a significant transformation of the neoclassical approach. This, of course, presents an opportunity for behavioral economists who emphasize the issues of interpretation connected to the framing effects. As we have already seen in the case of the Asian Disease, subtle changes in wording may lead to significant changes in preference ordering, although the information provided remains the same. The implications are potentially far-reaching. Ariely (2009), for instance, suggests that human behavior will differ substantially depending on whether an interaction is framed as market exchange or as social exchange. He posits that once we detect clues that the situation instantiates the former scenario, we start calculating costs and benefits through the lens of narrow self-interest. If an otherwise equivalent situation is categorized as the latter case, though, we will take a much broader perspective, which might be labeled as ethical (cf. Sandel, 2012). If you ask a lawyer friend to help you move to a new apartment, they might gladly agree, although no financial compensation is on the table. However, your daring inquiry about legal services at a discount rate may enrage the same friend. Because the neoclassical approach remains blind to social framing, situations like these elude its explanatory powers.

The final point of the comparison is optimization versus satisficing. While a rational economic agent strives to find the best available solution to the problem at hand, a boundedly rational agent is satisfied with the first solution that seems "good enough." Doing that, they do not rely on an exhaustive cost-benefit analysis, be it conscious or not, but on simple heuristics. These heuristics do not guarantee the choice of the best available alternative because they may fail systematically in certain circumstances. But they economize significantly on cognitive effort. It appears that the resulting ratio of the quality of choice relative to the cost of making it is often attractive (cf. Gigerenzer, 2010). If one can identify the agents' heuristics, one can also recognize situations where they will lead to systematic mistakes and, in turn, achieve more precise predictions.

Toward a New Theory of Human Behavior

As already apparent from the preceding examinations, a prominent epistemic criterion for evaluating the scientific value of hypotheses, models, and theories is their predictive success. Why should predictive success and not, say, originality or elegance be decisive? Sociologically speaking, the last two criteria undoubtedly exercise some influence. A brief examination will clarify the normative precedence of predictive success. The world we live in is complex, and the pragmatically important causal links among different variables are far from obvious. Because we cannot see how things are related, we build hypotheses and theories about it. How can we tell which hypotheses and theories are better than others, however? According to Friedman's (1953) classic argument, this is possible only when examining their internal logical consistency and their correspondence with the experience of the world. When testing theories against the world, it is necessary to see that indefinitely many mutually incompatible theories can be created that fit the existing data equally well. In short, the available data can be subsumed into many different internally coherent narratives. The data used to construct a particular narrative cannot test its validity, of course. The only way the relative performance of distinct theories can be assessed is by evaluating them against new data (Friedman, 1953). The prediction criterion is not of merely philosophical interest: the practical value of science rests upon its predictive success. Only if we can predict the consequences of our actions can we also direct them to the consequences deemed most desirable.

I employ the benchmark of predictive success based on normative considerations, not descriptive ones. No matter how sociological factors influence theory selection, predictive success provides a guiding light toward which sciences aspire (cf. Collins and Evans, 2017). At least to the extent they want to be treated as relevant to decision-makers. Since economists, compared to other social scientists, seem particularly eager to be perceived as worthy partners for the practical men and women in the world of business and politics (Fourcade, Ollion and Algan, 2015), I presume the prediction requirement will keep exercising its gravity toward them, independent whether they are of the neoclassical or behavioral bent. Based on these considerations, it appears that three preliminary questions need to be assessed before we can conclude anything about the promise implementation of psychology bears for the economists' quest after the general theory of human behavior.

1   Is predictive success conditional on a model's or theory's "realism"?
2   Is the neoclassical framework successful in generating reliable and precise predictions?
3   Can broader employment of behavioral sciences' findings increase economists' predictive success, even in the long run?

Predictive Success and "Realism"

So how about the relationship between predictive success and realism? Well, the answer depends on what precisely is meant by "realism." As suggested above, in the context of the billiard player example, there seems to be no necessary connection between a theory's descriptive realism of our assumptions and its predictive success. However, the problem of the "reality" under consideration is significant in its own right. It appears one can use different languages to speak about the economic phenomena that tend to operate in their own specific realities, or at least emphasize distinct layers of reality, among which it is not easy to traverse. That is testified by the infeasibility of translation between the languages. When addressing the economic phenomena in the most "realistic" way, should one use the language of basic sciences, such as physics, or stick to the traditional language reliant on folk psychology?

While the idea that physicalist language might be appropriate to describe economic phenomena can seem strange, it is not so long ago when it was popular enough for Ludwig von Mises (2010 [1949]) to dedicate significant efforts to its defeat (cf. Špecián, 2012). Even today, economists are sometimes charged with "physics envy" (Mirowski, 1992), apparently not without reason (Lazear, 2000). And indeed, there are solid reasons for finding the physicalist language appealing. What is ultimately "real" about our world, if not the elementary particles and their interactions (cf. Rosenberg, 2012b)? Moreover, physics has achieved tremendous success in recovering laws—or highly reliable regularities, if you will—of their behavior and utilized them to generate accurate predictions. Despite its appeals, the language of physics has not found much use in economics so far, except for rare applications in macroeconomic modeling. How is that?

It appears translatability is the prime culprit. If we were to benefit from grounding our economic theories in the "tried and true" foundation of physics, we would first need to express the economic problems in the physics' language. However, the language of the basic sciences like physics is fundamentally different from the language used by the "human sciences" that include economics as well as all the other social and behavioral sciences (Rosenberg, 2005). It is different because it repudiates any notion of purpose or function from its dictionary. The language of basic sciences is structuralist and defines its concepts via reference toward a particular physical structure. In contrast, the language of human sciences defines its concepts via reference to the functions and purposes that physicalist language principally cannot understand. As a result, a definition of an "atom" has little in common, structurally speaking, with a definition of a "consumer." Although any existing consumer is, in the end, a particular configuration of atoms, a *concept* of a consumer is untranslatable into the language of atomic structures. Its meaning is not constituted by a reference to the physical characteristics of consumers (cf. Fodor, 1974). It points to a class of agents' intentions and functions in the economy. The very notion of agency finds itself firmly beyond the expressive capabilities of the physicalist language. An identical purpose may be realized with indefinitely many different configurations of atoms, which may not share common features from the physical point of view. Thus, physical realism does not seem attainable for the current economic science unless it resigns on functional understanding, which hardly seems possible.

The current economics, be it neoclassical or behavioral, overwhelmingly speaks the language of folk psychology. It is based on an intuitive theory of mind. It models behavior as an outcome of an interaction between what people want and what they can achieve, utilizing concepts like tastes and beliefs. The reliance on folk psychology in neoclassical and behavioral approaches only differs in grade as the latter strives to peek into the black box of the human mind. The language of folk psychology is naïve, that is, not based on any expertise that would not be ubiquitous, but also superbly effective as a prediction tool. Any regular person's everyday "folk understanding" of other people's behavior suffices to predict their actions with a degree of success sufficient to build massive, well-coordinated societies. The bad news for economists—and other social scientists—is that it seems remarkably difficult to increase the predictive success beyond what folk psychology allows in its naïve form (Rosenberg, 2005).

One way or another, if we expect the scientific progress resulting from the behavioral revolution to stem from increased realism, we may be disappointed. In its mainstream applications, behavioral economics offered a relatively minor shift within the language of folk psychology and did not move all that far beyond the neoclassical "as if" methodology (Berg and Gigerenzer, 2010). Consider the famous distinction between the two systems of the human mind—the fast, intuitive *System 1* and the laborious, reflective *System 2* (Kahneman, 2003, 2011)—usually called the dual process theory. The systems do not label any specific apparatus of neural machinery that "really" trigger the distinctive cognitive processes. The distinction between them is made for modeling purposes more than anything else; interaction between two systems within a single agent helps resolve some problems that are hard to tackle using a single utility function. Its realism seems to be restricted to getting closer to the intuitive understanding of human behavior as a struggle between "sense and sensibility" (Sperber and Mercier, 2017). We are yet to see whether neuroeconomics can bring the desired revolution in the degree of realism employed (Marchionni and Vromen, 2010).

Considering how problematic the very idea of realism appears at a closer examination, perhaps it is good news, after all, that realism—whatever its precise meaning—is not necessary as far as a theory or model "works," that is, keeps providing precise and reliable predictions. If such is the case, it may be an unnecessary luxury to ponder its degree of realism. That seems to be the case of quantum physics, where the proverbial rebuttal to redundant philosophizing on the true nature of things is "shut up and calculate." Unfortunately for the social scientists, it seems such a nonchalant attitude may backfire in the face of predictive failure. As Daniel Hausman (1994) argues—using a metaphor of a car engine—if we want to fix something broken, we will do much better if we know how it works. A theory that strives for realism, be it defined as it may, is trying to create a map of a particular territory. If the map fails in guiding us in the right direction, the mapmakers do not try to correct it at random but strive to increase its resemblance to the territory. From this perspective, "realism" is not an intrinsic good. But it allows intuitive ideas about what the territory looks like to offer clues to improve the predictive power of a theory. Thus, it can guide us to include some previously neglected aspects of our understanding of the social world, and we can hope it helps. Not because the intuitive understanding is necessarily "realistic" in any strict sense, but because it works rather well in its tasks.

Given how convoluted the problems surrounding realism as a normative criterion appear, our task would be much simpler if neoclassical economics just worked and achieved an astounding degree of predictive success. Alas, that is not the case.

Neoclassical Predictive Success

Deirdre McCloskey (1983, p. 488) provokes economists with what she calls *an American question*: "If you're so smart, why aren't you rich?" The question points toward the market test of the quality of economic predictions. Knowledge of the future—especially knowledge of the *economic* future—is valuable. In short, good predictions earn money. The very fact that economists are not growing fabulously wealthy proves how meager their predictive success is. As far as some economists do become rich, it is more likely by selling their advice than acting upon it themselves. McCloskey (1983, p. 487) goes too far when she claims that prediction in economics is impossible, but she sure is up to something. There is little doubt that economic models and theories have trouble surpassing folk psychology's predictive success, especially in the long run. Clearly, the predictive failure results neither from the lack of talent nor from the lack of effort: economics steadily attracts many of the brightest, most educated, and most-hardworking people on the planet (Fourcade, Ollion and Algan, 2015). Therefore, it is worth examining where the actual stumbling blocks lie.

Following Rosenberg (2005), three roadblocks on the path toward predictive success in the social sciences appear exceptionally sturdy. One of them is the already mentioned untranslatability between the functionalist language of the predictively unsuccessful human sciences and the structural language of the predictively successful basic sciences. It precludes the possibility to build the laws of economics upon the laws of physics. Social sciences are thus forced to limit their ambitions to less reliable generalizations. The other two issues are "reflexivity" of the social-scientific predictions and the propensity of competing goal-oriented agents—like humans—to engage in arms races. As I shall illustrate, they limit the scope of any generalizations to a particular historical period in the development of life on our planet. Even worse, the possible generalizations may be fleeting and imprecise.

Predictions are reflexive if the agents whose behavior they predict become aware of them, incorporate them into their expectations, and adapt their behavior in their light. In short, people's behavior is changed by the existence of a known prediction of their behavior. The resulting problem for a social scientist is that her prediction may become self-refuting or self-fulfilling. In either case, they neither represent a valid test of their underlying theory nor offer guidance to its improvement. Imagine a scenario where a prediction is made regarding the future development of the price of gold. Assuming it is credible, people will consider the prediction when making their investment decisions, and such consideration will alter the path along which the price develops. Simply put, a credible prediction of a *future increase* in the price of gold will trigger a *current increase* in the price of gold, rendering itself invalid. Thus, it represents a self-refuting prophecy. In contrast, predicting a bank's impending insolvency may motivate its clients to withdraw their savings in the volume that indeed triggers the insolvency rendering the prophecy self-fulfilling.

Arms races are perhaps even more worrisome for scientists eager to achieve predictive success, especially in the long run. They are not limited to people but appear in any evolutionary landscape in the form of the Red Queen phenomenon (Ridley, 2003): a competition among goal-oriented agents turns into a runaway process in which innovative strategies evolve and obsolete ones disappear with no equilibrium stable in the long run. A zebra develops camouflage patterns making it difficult for the lions to see it, which creates selective pressure on the lions to adapt their perception, which creates selective pressure on zebras to improve their camouflage patterns, and so on. A firm develops a new product that captures market share from other firms, who are thus also pushed toward innovation, resulting in a similar continuous process of change. The main difference between people and zebras in this context is that people are much more inventive and flexible than zebras making their arms races much faster and less predictable. While a biologist may safely presume that zebras' camouflage patterns will not change significantly in a decade or even a century, an economist can rarely afford a luxury of a similar expectation. The problem can perhaps be best described as one of indefinitely many equilibria.

Cultures provide people with sets of rules that enable them to solve coordination problems. They allow individuals to form mutually coherent expectations to facilitate cooperation; they indicate "focal points" that enable us to converge toward a particular cooperative equilibrium among the indefinitely many possible ones (Schelling, 1980). The trouble is that the currently focal equilibrium may not remain so. In general, people's incentives are mixed: we are not pure cooperators; we compete too. There are always incentives for some agents to disrupt the current focal points. For instance, a reader of Jane Austen's novels may notice that cooperation works in her world of landed gentry, but the distribution of the equilibrium payoffs is distinctly skewed toward men to the disadvantage of women and toward landlords to the disadvantage of everybody else. The open horizon of multiple equilibria stimulates the agents to consider how the current balance could be disrupted for the sake of achieving another one that they deem more desirable. As a result, the stability is fleeting. Any social formation may crumble as the world of the gentry has crumbled. Sometimes, a strong external shock is necessary, but sometimes, even a barely perceptible random trigger may initiate a chain reaction that destabilizes the whole system and forces it to search for a new equilibrium (consider the sudden disintegration of the Soviet Bloc or the startling phenomenon of the Arab spring). The resulting fluidity of interaction impedes predictive success.

Where does that leave us? Our previous considerations are not limited in their relevance just to neoclassical economics but seem rather general in their skepticism. Nevertheless, let me examine if there is at least some hope that behavioral economics improves economic science's predictive success despite all the pressing limitations.

Behavioral Economics' Promise

Above, I have expressed a degree of skepticism regarding the amount of progress toward "realism" that behavioral economics offers. Nevertheless, the methodological comparison still suggests that behavioral economics represents a significant change in a perspective on social phenomena relative to the neoclassical approach as it is more uncompromisingly empirical. If we retain predictive success as the key benchmark in theory evaluation—despite all the reasons to temper our optimism regarding the ultimate prospects of its improvement—does behavioral economics have the potential to break the predictive stalemate even in the long run? Or are its achievements short-lived?

Behavioral economics does not appear much better capable of achieving reduction to the basic sciences than neoclassical economics. At least currently, as its language remains grounded in folk psychology. If neuroeconomics can make a substantive difference in this regard remains to be seen. Accordingly, much depends on behavioral economists' ability to identify limits to reflexivity and overcome or diminish the arms race problem. Depending on the degree of their success, their strive to capture parameters neglected by the neoclassical approach may bear fruits in terms of an increased long-run predictive success. There are two areas, in particular, that deserve close attention: the first is where the human capacity of behavioral adaptation reaches its limits; the second is where incentives toward rational behavior are weak or nonexistent.

Humans are an animal species with certain biologically hardwired constraints. Not even the most ardent cultural determinist believes that people can grow four meters tall or run with the speed of sound. However marvelous our adaptive capacities may be, there will be limits we cannot overcome unless our nature is altered. While such a "change of nature" is possible—no, inevitable— on an evolutionary timescale, it is too slow to matter over any pragmatically relevant period. To the extent the hard constraint of our nature matters for our cognitive makeup, we may learn that our systematic mistakes are triggered in a way we cannot control. In short, any debiasing efforts may be futile with respect to some of the biases that burden us. Such biases will mislead us as reliably and inevitably as optical illusions do. Accordingly, their identification would give behavioral economics an edge in predictive success, even in the long run. In this vein, Oliver (2015, p. 703, emphasis mine) asserts that: "behavioural economic phenomena are classifications of *innate* human decision-making behaviour. That is, *we do not choose to be*, for example, loss averse; *we just are*."

So, how stable are the biases discovered so far? The jury is still out, I am afraid. On the one hand, many key findings of behavioral economics have withstood the replication efforts exceptionally well (e.g., Ruggeri *et al.*, 2020), dispelling any reasonable concern that they might represent mere experimental artifacts or even a product of questionable research practices. Moreover, "misbehaving" has been reported not only in hypothetical scenarios like the Asian Disease but in high-stakes situations with behavioral finance as one of the particularly dynamic subfields of behavioral economics. This gives credence to Richard Thaler's (2016, p. 1585) triumphalism when he proclaims that he does "not know of any findings of 'cognitive errors' that were discovered and replicated with hypothetical questions but then vanished as soon as significant stakes were introduced."

But do we have evidence that the immovable limits of human adaptability have been identified? There are ample reasons for caution here. Human adaptability can be easily underestimated; while our mind is not a blank slate (Pinker, 2003), it certainly comes as close to one as anything evolution has ever produced. Heyes (2018), for instance, argues that the observed cognitive variance is much more extensively culturally conditioned than the mainstream claims suggest. And while there is no denying that significant progress has been made since the times when psychological studies restricted their pool of subjects—although not the proclaimed generalizability of their results—to the undergraduates at a few elite universities, it remains the case that most of the available evidence comes from examining those who are native or at least culturally affiliated to what has been called the WEIRD societies: Western, Educated, Industrialized, Rich, and Democratic (Henrich, 2020). Moreover, the evidence on cultural conditioning implies that even WEIRDness itself is not a constant. Can we be in any way certain that a snapshot of the current psychological biases will retain relevance through many rounds of an arms race between the bias exploiters and the exploited, for instance? Chapter 3 will demonstrate that this is an imminently pressing question for democratic societies in the context of the digital revolution.

On a less abstract level, it is especially worrisome that the number of high-quality empirical studies that account for the possible debiasing effects of incentives and learning remains too limited to draw definite conclusions (Rizzo and Whitman, 2019, pp. 196–197). Given the current state of knowledge, we have only the murkiest idea of how various biases may interact—and counteract—in realistic settings and of their case-by-case elasticity vis-à-vis incentives and learning.

Consider a recent high-profile study by Enke *et al.* (2021) that is sometimes advertised as a definite demonstration that incentives do not matter when it comes to irrationality. The authors use an experimental setup on a large sample of Kenyan university students to demonstrate that introducing high stakes (worth about a month's median income) does not appreciably debias the subjects relative to a low-stakes scenario. Yet, there are important caveats to underscore.

Enke *et al.* (2021) show that incentives do not influence performance in most experimental tasks, but they work in the usual direction with respect to the expended effort. The subjects in the high-stakes scenario spent about 40% more time attempting to find the correct solution. So, it is not that the incentives do not influence the subject's behavior but that the elicited behavioral change does not improve performance. While this is a significant finding—the more notable that it deviates from predictions the authors have elicited from a group of experimental economics' experts prior to their study—it is not quite clear how relevant it is for the question of "debiasing in the wild."

For instance, one of the experimental questions asks the subjects about the size of the population of Uzbekistan in 2018 (Enke *et al.*, 2021, p. 14). Certainly, it is interesting that the provided answers correlate significantly with an arbitrary number derived from the participants' birthdate, demonstrating an anchoring bias. But on the face of it, it is hardly surprising that incentives do not influence performance. It appears a safe bet that most people are just completely unaware of the correct answer, independent of whether €1 or €1,000 are at stake. The extra effort can make no difference if there is nothing to draw on. Tellingly, the participants themselves report no greater confidence in their answers when the stakes are high.

Moreover, in the one task—the cognitive reflection task[4]—where one can actually improve one's odds just by thinking harder (i.e., without prior possession of specific information or cognitive skills), effort does bear fruit, and performance in the high-stake scenario improves. Thus, as the authors themselves suggest, it appears that perhaps: "the difficulty in overcoming cognitive biases is often conceptual in nature, and that higher effort does not easily induce 'the right way of looking at the problem'" (Enke *et al.*, 2021, p. 33).

So it seems fair to summarize the evidence by Enke *et al.* (2021) the following way: incentives do stimulate effort but do not improve performance in cases where the effort is futile. Note, however, that in realistic scenarios where irrationality is a concern—that is, in the wild—we tend to be much less threatened by this possibility. "No man is an island," and any society engages in an extensive division of cognitive labor. In short, the experimental subjects would just google the population of Uzbekistan had they been allowed the possibility. And if they were regularly rewarded for knowing such trivia, many would learn them by heart. Therefore, the study merely implies that people try harder to solve problems if the stakes are high but cannot increase their success rate unless equipped with proper tools. Regarding the question of the limits of human adaptive capacity, they offer nothing to dispel the concern that behavioral economics' predictive improvements will prove short-lived in high-stakes environments.

How about the low-stakes environments, though? They present a much safer bet in the search for persistent predictive improvement attributable to the behavioral economists' exploits. Where there is no cost associated with irrationality, there is no reason to avoid it. Intuitions based on fast, mostly nonconscious heuristics offer swift and effortless—albeit biased—solutions. A critical examination of these intuitions, on the other hand, requires an investment, which is not worth making unless there is an appreciable cost associated with being wrong. In short, the space in which the knowledge of behavioral economics can most easily be expected to be permanently valid is the same as the area where incentives for individuals to behave rationally are lacking. Low stakes for an individual are not the same as low stakes in the aggregate, however. Indeed, it is crucial from the perspective of this book that regular democratic citizens find themselves in just such a low-stake situation when making their political choices. As Schnellenbach and Schubert (2015, p. 396) state laconically, "we can expect cognitive biases to be at least as, and probably more important in politics than in the marketplace." This is far from inconsequential, as we are about to see.

Conclusion

Under the imperial banner raised by Gary Becker, the neoclassical approach has provided a beachhead for an attempt to conquer the neighboring social sciences. However, the success of the grand venture of economic imperialism is questionable. Whatever its appeals, it did not lead to many undisputed accomplishments if we consider the prediction criterion the guiding light in theory evaluation. Quite to the contrary, there has been a growing concern that its foundational rationality assumption represents an inadequate tool to tackle human behavior within the traditional domain of economics or outside of it.

The research program of behavioral economics, which rivals the neoclassical approach and pushes for reevaluation of its methodology, has uncovered numerous instances of "misbehaving." Understandably, the evidence that the deviations from rational behavior are not random but systematic is worrying for the sympathizers of the neoclassical perspective. If people indeed are "predict-ably irrational," economics may ultimately find itself a province of psychology. However, as I have argued, it is perhaps still too early for confident conclusions. There remains a significant possibility that irrationality responds to incentives and learning. Many predictive improvements may yet be undermined as they trigger adaptation. Perhaps somewhat paradoxically, the efforts to exploit people's mistakes may thus lead to a greater degree of convergence of their behavior to the rationality ideal.

Nonetheless, some areas remain where the convergence is especially unlikely: namely, those where the incentives for instrumentally rational behavior are lacking. If the systematic mistakes themselves are not costly while avoiding them requires exertion of resources or effort, we need to expect their persist-ence: even where they become exploited by third parties. Perhaps the most consequential of such areas is democratic social choice, where a single voter exercises almost no influence over its outcome. The next chapter ponders this finding's relevance for the democratic theory.

Notes

1 Because the main emphasis has been traditionally put on noncoercive interactions, Abba Lerner (1972, p. 259) once stated that "economics has gained the title of queen of the social sciences by choosing solved political problems as its domain." However, non-coercion is just one of the assumptions that may be relaxed for the sake of addressing the problem at hand. In neoclassical view, war and strife are ultimately no less amenable to an economic approach than trade is (cf. Mesquita, 1985). I keep to the traditional domain to ease the explication.
2 Remarkably, this eagerness is somewhat asymmetric: we tend to see others as more irrational than ourselves (Pronin, Lin and Ross, 2002).
3 Intriguingly, Hudík (2019) argues that behavioral and neoclassical approaches are more complementary than the mainstream controversy would suggest. However, the extent to which complementarism gets embraced by the members of the economic profession remains to be seen.
4 The task includes a series of "trick questions" where there is a salient, but wrong, intuitive answer, and finding a correct answer requires one to override the initial intuition. One of the paradigmatic setups—also used by Enke *et al.* (2021)—is the "bat and ball" problem (Frederick, 2005, p. 26): "A bat and a ball cost \$1.10. The bat costs \$1.00 more than the ball. How much does the ball cost? __ cents." (In case you wonder, the intuitive answer is 10 cents, and the correct one is 5 cents.)

Bibliography

Ariely, D. (2009) *Predictably Irrational: The Hidden Forces that Shape Our Decisions.* New York: HarperCollins.
Becker, G.S. (1978) *The Economic Approach to Human Behavior.* Chicago: University of Chicago Press.
Berg, N. and Gigerenzer, G. (2010) 'As-if Behavioral Economics: Neoclassical Economics in Disguise?', *History of Economic Ideas*, 18(1), pp. 133–165.

Boland, L.A. (1979) 'A Critique of Friedman's Critics', *Journal of Economic Literature*, 17(2), pp. 503–522. doi:10.2307/2723302.

Camerer, C. and Loewenstein, G. (2004) 'Behavioral Economics: Past, Present, Future', in Camerer, C., Loewenstein, G., and Rabin, M. (eds) *Advances in Behavioral Economics*. Princeton: Princeton University Press, pp. 3–51.

Caplan, B. (2008) *The Myth of the Rational Voter: Why Democracies Choose Bad Policies*. New edition. Princeton: Princeton University Press.

Carruthers, P. (2011) *The Opacity of Mind: An Integrative Theory of Self-Knowledge*. Oxford; New York: Oxford University Press.

Coase, R.H. (1978) 'Economics and Contiguous Disciplines', *The Journal of Legal Studies*, 7(2), pp. 201–211. doi:10.2307/724212.

Collins, H. and Evans, R. (2017) *Why Democracies Need Science*. Cambridge; Malden: Polity Press.

Downs, A. (1957) *An Economic Theory of Democracy*. First edition. Boston: Harper and Row.

Elster, J. (2008) *Reason and Rationality*. Translated by S. Rendall. Princeton: Princeton University Press.

Enke, B. *et al.* (2021) *Cognitive Biases: Mistakes or Missing Stakes?* SSRN Scholarly Paper ID 3824526. Rochester: Social Science Research Network. doi:10.3386/w28650.

Etzioni, A. (1983) 'Toward a Political Psychology of Economics', *Political Psychology*, 4(1), pp. 77–86. doi:10.2307/3791174.

Fodor, J.A. (1974) 'Special Sciences (or: The Disunity of Science as a Working Hypothesis)', *Synthese*, 28(2), pp. 97–115. doi:10.1007/BF00485230.

Fourcade, M., Ollion, E. and Algan, Y. (2015) 'The Superiority of Economists', *Journal of Economic Perspectives*, 29(1), pp. 89–114. doi:10.1257/jep.29.1.89.

Frederick, S. (2005) 'Cognitive Reflection and Decision Making', *Journal of Economic Perspectives*, 19(4), pp. 25–42. doi:10.1257/089533005775196732.

Friedman, M. (1953) 'The Methodology of Positive Economics', in Friedman, M. (ed) *Essays in Positive Economics*. Chicago: University of Chicago Press, pp. 3–43.

Gigerenzer, G. (2010) *Rationality for Mortals: How People Cope with Uncertainty*. New York; Oxford: Oxford University Press.

Gilboa, I. (2010) *Rational Choice*. First edition. Cambridge, MA: MIT Press.

Gintis, H. (2016) *Individuality and Entanglement: The Moral and Material Bases of Social Life*. Princeton: Princeton University Press.

Hansen, P.G. (2016) 'The Definition of Nudge and Libertarian Paternalism: Does the Hand Fit the Glove?', *European Journal of Risk Regulation*, 7(1), pp. 155–174. doi:10.1017/S1867299X00005468.

Hausman, D.M. (1994) 'Why Look Under the Hood?', in Hausman, D.M. (ed.) *The Philosophy of Economics: An Anthology*. Cambridge: Cambridge University Press, pp. 183–187.

Hausman, D.M. and McPherson, M.S. (2006) *Economic Analysis, Moral Philosophy and Public Policy*. Second edition. Cambridge: Cambridge University Press.

Henrich, J.P. (2020) *The WEIRDest People in the World: How the West Became Psychologically Peculiar and Particularly Prosperous*. New York: Farrar, Straus and Giroux.

Heyes, C.M. (2018) *Cognitive Gadgets: The Cultural Evolution of Thinking*. Cambridge, MA: The Belknap Press of Harvard University Press.

Hudík, M. (2015) 'Homo Economicus and Homo Stramineus', *Prague Economic Papers*, 24(2), pp. 154–172. doi:10.18267/j.pep.506.

Hudík, M. (2019) 'Two Interpretations of the Rational Choice Theory and the Relevance of Behavioral Critique', *Rationality and Society*, 31(4), pp. 464–489. doi:10.1177/1043463119869007.

Jevons, H.S. (1965 [1871]) *The Theory of Political Economy*. Fifth edition. New York: A. M. Kelley.

Kahneman, D. (2003) 'Maps of Bounded Rationality: Psychology for Behavioral Economics', *The American Economic Review*, 93(5), pp. 1449–1475. doi:10.2307/3132137.

Kahneman, D. (2011) *Thinking, Fast and Slow*. London: Allen Lane.

Kelly, J.T. (2012) *Framing Democracy: A Behavioral Approach to Democratic Theory*. Princeton: Princeton University Press.

Kuhn, T.S. (1996) *The Structure of Scientific Revolutions*. Chicago: University of Chicago Press.

Landsburg, S.E. (2012) *The Armchair Economist: Economics and Everyday Life*. New York: Free Press.

Lawson, T. (2013) 'What is This "School" Called Neoclassical Economics?', *Cambridge Journal of Economics*, 37(5), pp. 947–983. doi:10.1093/cje/bet027.

Lazear, E.P. (2000) 'Economic Imperialism', *The Quarterly Journal of Economics*, 115(1), pp. 99–146. doi:10.2307/2586936.

Lehtinen, A. and Kuorikoski, J. (2007) 'Unrealistic Assumptions in Rational Choice Theory', *Philosophy of the Social Sciences*, 37(2), pp. 115–138. doi:10.1177/0048393107299684.

Lerner, A.P. (1972) 'The Economics and Politics of Consumer Sovereignty', *The American Economic Review*, 62(1/2), pp. 258–266. doi:10.2307/1821551.

Levine, D.K. (2012) *Is Behavioral Economics Doomed? The Ordinary versus the Extraordinary*. Cambridge: Open Book Publishers.

Mankiw, N.G. (2021) *Principles of Economics*. Ninth edition. Boston: Cengage Learning.

Marchionni, C. and Vromen, J. (2010) '"Neuroeconomics: Hype or Hope?"', *Journal of Economic Methodology*, 17(2), pp. 103–106. doi:10.1080/13501781003756667.

McCloskey, D. (1983) 'The Rhetoric of Economics', *Journal of Economic Literature*, 21(2), pp. 481–517.

Mesquita, B.B. de (1985) 'The War Trap Revisited: A Revised Expected Utility Model', *American Political Science Review*, 79(1), pp. 156–177. doi:10.2307/1956125.

Mirowski, P. (1992) 'Do Economists Suffer from Physics Envy?', *Finnish Economic Papers*, 5(1), pp. 61–68.

Mises, L. von (2010 [1949]) *Human Action: The Scholar's Edition*. Auburn: Ludwig von Mises Institute.

Morgan, M.S. and Rutherford, M. (1998) 'American Economics: The Character of the Transformation', *History of Political Economy*, 30(5), pp. 1–26.

Oliver, A. (2015) 'Nudging, Shoving, and Budging: Behavioural Economic-Informed Policy', *Public Administration*, 93(3), pp. 700–714. doi:10.1111/padm.12165.

Petersen, M.B. (2015) 'Evolutionary Political Psychology: On the Origin and Structure of Heuristics and Biases in Politics: Evolutionary Political Psychology', *Political Psychology*, 36, pp. 45–78. doi:10.1111/pops.12237.

Pinker, S. (2003) *The Blank Slate: The Modern Denial of Human Nature*. Reprint. London: Penguin Books.

Posner, R.A. (1998) 'Rational Choice, Behavioral Economics, and the Law', *Stanford Law Review*, 50(5), pp. 1551–1575. doi:10.2307/1229305.

Pronin, E., Lin, D.Y. and Ross, L. (2002) 'The Bias Blind Spot: Perceptions of Bias in Self Versus Others', *Personality and Social Psychology Bulletin*, 28(3), pp. 369–381. doi:10.1177/0146167202286008.

Ridley, M. (2003) *The Red Queen: Sex and the Evolution of Human Nature*. Second edition. New York: Harper Perennial.

Rizzo, M.J. and Whitman, G. (2019) *Escaping Paternalism: Rationality, Behavioral Economics, and Public Policy*. Cambridge; New York: Cambridge University Press.

Robbins, L. (2007) *An Essay on the Nature and Significance of Economic Science*. Auburn: Ludwig von Mises Institute.

Rodrik, D. (2015) *Economics Rules: The Rights and Wrongs of the Dismal Science*. New York: W.W. Norton.

Rosenberg, A. (1996) 'Laws, Damn Laws, and Ceteris Paribus Clauses', *The Southern Journal of Philosophy*, 34(S1), pp. 183–204. doi:10.1111/j.2041-6962.1996.tb00820.x.

Rosenberg, A. (2005) 'Lessons from Biology for Philosophy of the Human Sciences', *Philosophy of the Social Sciences*, 35(1), pp. 3–19. doi:10.1177/0048393104271921.

Rosenberg, A. (2012a) *Philosophy of Social Science*. Fourth edition. Boulder: Westview Press.

Rosenberg, A. (2012b) *The Atheist's Guide to Reality: Enjoying Life without Illusions*. New York: W.W. Norton.

Ruggeri, K. *et al.* (2020) 'Replicating Patterns of Prospect Theory for Decision Under Risk', *Nature Human Behaviour*, 4(6), pp. 622–633. doi:10.1038/s41562-020-0886-x.

Sandel, M.J. (2012) *What Money Can't Buy: The Moral Limits of Markets*. First edition. New York: Farrar, Straus and Giroux.

Schelling, T.C. (1980) *The Strategy of Conflict*. Cambridge, MA: Harvard University Press.

Schimmack, U. (2020) 'A Meta-Psychological Perspective on the Decade of Replication Failures in Social Psychology', *Canadian Psychology/Psychologie canadienne*, 61(4), pp. 364–376. doi:10.1037/cap0000246.

Schnellenbach, J. and Schubert, C. (2015) 'Behavioral Political Economy: A Survey', *European Journal of Political Economy*, 40, pp. 395–417. doi:10.1016/j.ejpoleco.2015.05.002.

Sent, E.-M. (2004) 'Behavioral Economics: How Psychology Made Its (Limited) Way Back into Economics', *History of Political Economy*, 36(4), pp. 735–760.

Simon, H.A. (1986) 'Rationality in Psychology and Economics', *The Journal of Business*, 59(4), pp. 209–224.

Specián, P. (2012) 'Svět a věda u Ludwiga von Misese. Esej o misesovské metafyzice [World and Science by Ludwig von Mises: An Essay on Misesian Metaphysics]', *Filozofia*, 67(4), pp. 335–346.

Specián, P. (2019) 'The Precarious Case of the True Preferences', *Society*, 56(3), pp. 267–272. doi:10.1007/s12115-019-00363-8.

Sperber, D. and Mercier, H. (2017) *The Enigma of Reason: A New Theory of Human Understanding*. London: Allen Lane.

Stigler, G.J. (1983) 'Nobel Lecture: The Process and Progress of Economics', *Journal of Political Economy*, 91(4), pp. 529–545. doi:10.2307/1831067.

Thaler, R.H. (2015) *Misbehaving: The Making of Behavioral Economics*. Kindle edition. New York: W.W. Norton.

Thaler, R.H. (2016) 'Behavioral Economics: Past, Present, and Future', *American Economic Review*, 106(7), pp. 1577–1600. doi:10.1257/aer.106.7.1577.

Thaler, R.H. (2017) 'Banquet Speech', *NobelPrize.org.* Available at: www.nobelprize.org/prizes/economic-sciences/2017/thaler/speech/ (Accessed 15 September 2021).

Thaler, R.H. and Sunstein, C.R. (2021) *Nudge: Improving Decisions about Money, Health, and the Environment.* Final edition. New York: Penguin Books.

The Nobel Prize (2002) *The Sveriges Riksbank Prize in Economic Sciences in Memory of Alfred Nobel 2002, NobelPrize.org.* Available at: www.nobelprize.org/prizes/economic-sciences/2002/press-release/ (Accessed 21 June 2021).

Tversky, A. and Kahneman, D. (1986) 'Rational Choice and the Framing of Decisions', *The Journal of Business*, 59(4), pp. S251–S278. doi:10.2307/2352759.

Weber, M. (2019 [1922]) *Economy and Society: A New Translation.* Translation edition. Translated by K. Tribe. Cambridge, MA: Harvard University Press.

Zafirovski, M. (2000) 'The Rational Choice Generalization of Neoclassical Economics Reconsidered: Any Theoretical Legitimation for Economic Imperialism?', *Sociological Theory*, 18(3), pp. 448–471. doi:10.1111/0735-2751.00111.

2 Democracy and Rationality

Modern mass democracy in its familiar form represents an exceptionally fertile ground for behavioral economists. That, at least, seems to be implied by the conclusion of the previous chapter that predictable irrationalities are most likely to flourish in low-stakes environments, including those where an individual's choice is not decisive for the outcome. I shall now proceed in the assessment of the validity and ramifications of this claim. However, before such exercise can even begin, there is one exceptionally thorny question to address: what is democracy?

The plentitude of mutually incompatible definitions political theory offers can testify how ambiguous and confusing is the term's use (Dufek, 2018). In particular, there is a cleavage between the normatively inclined theorists whose demands are often so ambitious that no actual political regime can hope to qualify and descriptively oriented ones whose lenient requirements offend the sensibilities of many a democratic idealist (Dufek and Holzer, 2013). Since there is no hope that these disagreements will be settled anytime soon, let me just brazenly put forward a definition I shall rely upon in the following parts of the book: democracy is a mechanism of collective choice among alternatives that is *inclusive* and *avoids exogenous value imposition*. That is, all the society's members are allowed to participate in the collective choice, and any resulting social valuation of alternatives must result from aggregation of these individuals' preferences.[1] This preliminary definition is fairly minimalist, and draws upon the foundational writings of the neoclassical theory of democracy (Downs, 1957; Arrow, 1963). If it appears too vague, do not protest just yet: it will undergo various clarifications as we proceed.

It will quickly become apparent that even this minimalist concept of democracy can turn out impossibly demanding if we also share the neoclassical desire to derive a social preference ordering that would conform with the requirements of axiomatic rationality. Moreover, the lesser the degree of idealization we are willing to tolerate, the more numerous the challenges we encounter. For instance, citizens' ignorance of the relevant political facts—which tends to be quite extensive—needs to be considered. Worse yet, we must face the inadequacies of the neoclassical rationality assumption and appreciate the implications of human reason's quirks and imperfections. We'd better get started.

DOI: 10.4324/9781003274988-3

Choice: Individual and Collective

As already observed, neoclassical economists take market exchange as a paradigmatic case of social coordination. In its context, markets serve both an instrumental and an epistemic function. Their instrumental role is primary: they allow scarce resources to find their most desired uses relying on the individual participants' self-interest as their motive force. In other words, a market is a means toward satisfaction of the people's wants, whatever they might be. To succeed instrumentally, however, markets must also resolve a paramount epistemic challenge along the way. Their instrumental performance depends on their ability to gather the fragments of relevant knowledge scattered among numerous individuals and transform them into easily perceptible relative prices of the various commodities, as famously highlighted by F. A. Hayek (1945).

Suppose you would want to understand the process that brings your morning cup of coffee to your kitchen table or even thank all the people who make this possible (Jacobs, 2018): this would be an unusually complex and onerous task even if you cut many corners doing so. Fortunately, an ordinary coffee drinker will never find its accomplishment necessary. They just need to be aware of the location of the nearest vendor and willing to pay the market price. The massive epistemic network in the background remains conveniently hidden because the market functions in a *decentralized* fashion. In other words, the aggregation necessary to shift from the level of individual preference satisfaction to the level of social resource allocation proceeds in a piecemeal way. Each person can choose to enter a transactional relationship with any other willing person or abstain from it. Thus, the market possesses a built-in tendency toward welfare improvements because transactions only happen if all their participants consider them beneficial (more on welfare in Chapter 4).

However, this does not make the markets' appeal universal. Few economists—let alone regular citizens—would nowadays subscribe to a "market fundamentalist" view that all of the world's ills are best addressed by the decentralized mechanism of free competitive exchange. And for good reasons too. One key issue is that her purchasing power will determine the strength of an individual's voice in the marketplace. While not always problematic, this fact clashes with our moral intuitions that such weighting may not be universally appropriate. It may be preferable for everybody's voice to carry equal weight, for instance: a core of the democratic maxim of "one person, one vote." Even where we are comfortable with differentiation, it is not necessarily the case that it should be based on economic factors, such as income and wealth because they represent a questionable proxy for a person's worth (cf. Sandel, 2020, chap. 5).

Also, the markets frequently falter on their own terms due to the imperfection of the conditions under which they operate. Many well-known market failures may deteriorate their instrumental and epistemic function and undermine their ability to solve the task of efficient resource use satisfactorily. One prominent issue is that not all the relevant costs and benefits associated with a particular transaction are always considered due to spillover effects, that is, *externalities*.

These situations lead to inadequate market pricing because the transactions' side-effects influencing the well-being of third parties remain neglected. So, the associated costs and benefits are not fully considered. The neglect is rational from the perspective of the market participants, and it often cannot be resolved in a decentralized fashion because of prohibitive transaction costs and other hurdles. The most notorious example is climate change: tiny spillover effects of billions of individual choices add up to trigger a rather palpable spillover of the world's oceans due to the melting icecaps (cf. Nordhaus, 2013).

The limits of the individualistic solutions that can be achieved via markets call for the introduction of collective choice, which I shall identify with *politics*.[2] In neoclassical economics, the collective choice is approached from the same direction as individual choice, that is, presupposing that all individuals in society possess preferences that conform to axiomatic rationality. Their preferences are presumed internally consistent (complete, transitive, and invariant), context-independent, and stable. As Anthony Downs (1957, p. 47) puts it in his classic *An Economic Theory of Democracy*: "fixed political tastes seem far more plausible to us than fixed consumption tastes." A resulting set of assumptions constitutes what Robert Sugden (2018, p. 7) has called *integrated preferences*. How can we analyze democracy from this angle?

The relationship between individual and collective choice is clearly complex. Both politics and markets are deeply socially embedded and cannot be neatly disentangled, except for modeling purposes. Nevertheless, it seems that one can emphasize either the parallel or the sequential dimension of their relationship. The sequential perspective focuses on whether politics precede markets—and thus represent a more fundamental social structure—or the other way around (e.g., Graeber, 2011). The parallel perspective is concerned with the division of labor among them: which social functions are better performed via collective choice, and which are best left to private choice? Let us consider education, for instance. Its provision can be both private and public; given neither the alignment of market outcomes with human values nor their flawless performance in preference satisfaction can be guaranteed, how successfully can markets be substituted with political coordination mechanisms in education provision? Mind that on the market, each agent is free to search for a solution that fits her individual situation best. In contrast, the centralized solutions achieved by the political process are collectively binding. Once the collective decision of the public provision of education has been made, one will be coerced to pay taxes necessary to finance the program. In short, there are numerous pros and cons of each solution to consider.

It is this parallel perspective from which neoclassical economics views the mechanisms of individual and collective choice. Despite frequent allegations of the opposite, the neoclassical approach in its imperial guise is not wedded to a "neoliberal" adoration of free markets. Its spirit lies more in analyzing alternative institutional frameworks from the perspective of their relative performance, that is, in terms of efficiency (cf. Lazear, 2000, pp. 101–102). Moreover, such comparisons are not necessarily of the "markets-or-politics" kind. What unites them instead is an instrumental outlook: how well does a particular institution serve its purpose? In this vein, I shall strive to analyze the relative performance of different political regimes, especially those that fit under my minimalist definition of democracy. Not all political regimes are born equal, and neither are all regimes described as democratic.

Therefore, my central question is: "How well does democracy—in a particular institutional setup—function to the people's benefit?" From this point of view, democracy's value does not stem merely from its virtue of being a democracy. The outcomes it delivers as a mechanism of collective choice matter.[3] This is well in line with the neoclassical understanding. Downs (1957), for instance, views democracy as a regime in which (1) the government seeks to maximize the political support it receives from the citizens, and (2) collective choices are made by the majority rule. Thus, he cautiously embraces the claim that democracy is a decision-making mechanism "in which the decider makes each choice on the basis of the preferences of those affected by it and weights the preferences of each in proportion to the degree to which he is affected" (Downs, 1957, p. 257).

While any definition of democracy can be extensively debated, it seems that the one utilized by Downs—or me—would hardly raise many eyebrows among the regular democratic citizens who do not consider political theory their favorite pastime. After all, the idea that the government should be responsive to the people and its policies must reflect their preferences is not an exotic invention of neoclassical economics. It corresponds with what Achen and Bartels (2016) somewhat disparagingly call the *folk theory of democracy*. As the "folk" label suggests, this theory represents the most widespread popular understanding of what democracy stands for, namely that:

> Ordinary people have preferences about what their government should do. They choose leaders who will do those things, or they enact their preferences directly in referendums. In either case, what the majority wants becomes government policy (…).
>
> (Achen and Bartels, 2016, p. 1)

One way or another, an instrumental view of democracy is necessary to assess the promise of behavioral economics' contribution to democratic theory. As already pointed out in Chapter 1, behavioral economists consider neoclassical theory inadequate—if not inferior—as a predictive device due to its overreliance on the rationality assumption. At the same time, they make little effort to divorce from the neoclassical perspective normatively: rational choices may be scarcer than we once thought, but they still represent the trusted standard of how one should choose (cf. Rizzo and Whitman, 2019). That pertains to collective choice too.

Like the market, democracy must achieve epistemic success if it is to perform well instrumentally. The ability to satisfy people's wishes and desires is conditional on efficient information gathering and processing. Unless the democratic mechanism enables identifying what the people truly want, it is impossible to deliver it. Markets discover to satisfy people's wishes and desires individually; democracy must find ways to achieve the same goal collectively. However, along the way toward collectively satisfying individual desires, there is a sizable pitfall that Downs (1957, p. 160) calls *the central problem of political theory*, namely, "how can social goals be developed from differing individual values?"

To explore the intricacies of "the central problem," it is best to start from a Downsian baseline model of a democratic voter—a *homo politicus*—which is broadly analogical to *homo economicus*. As already suggested, *homo politicus* is a neoclassically rational agent with integrated preferences. In the role of a democratic citizen, such an agent is expected to "select a government" (Downs, 1957, p. 7), that is, vote for the party—or, more broadly, the alternative—they most prefer *on political grounds*. Note that the rationality of *homo politicus* is not only delimited by the familiar axioms but also of a relatively narrow kind. If one votes a certain way on other than political grounds—say, to get along with the members of one's family—such behavior is counted as irrational because "it employs a political device [that is, a vote] for a non-political purpose [namely to appease one's significant others]" (Downs, 1957, p. 7). Only as far as this narrow political rationality approximates voters' actual behavior, can democracy aspire to fulfill its epistemic and instrumental function.

Hopefully, the features of "the central problem" have become more discernible by now. Three issues will guide the remainder of my debate of democracy's predicament in this chapter:

1   Even if political information is assumed free, the citizens' *individual* political rationality may not suffice to produce rational *collective* outcomes. Let me call this the *problem of social choice*.
2   If obtaining political information is costly, rational citizens will not seek it because a single vote carries too little weight to justify the requisite investment. As a result, uninformed citizens may fail to identify the parties and policies best aligned with their values and tastes. This is the *problem of rational ignorance*.
3   The citizens may not be politically rational. Here, we need to distinguish two possibilities:
    a   The citizens are politically irrational (as Downs defines the concept) but rational when viewed from a broader perspective that allows for nonpolitical goals. Since they are irrational for rational reasons, this can be labeled the *problem of rational irrationality*.
    b   The citizens are irrational no matter how broad a perspective one takes. They make systematic mistakes and engage in self-defeating behavior. Using the parlance of behavioral economics, I shall address the issue as the *problem of bounded rationality*.

Downs' legacy lies mainly in espousing the problem of rational ignorance. The social choice problem has been most famously explored by Kenneth Arrow

(1963), who established the corresponding field of study. The twin issues of rational irrationality and bounded rationality fall under the purview of the behavioral political economy of democracy. Let me dedicate the rest of the chapter to exploring these individual facets of "the central problem."

The Problem of Social Choice

The problem of social choice represents a formidable challenge even in the most idealized circumstances. A few conceptual clarifications are necessary before it can be scrutinized. From the neoclassical perspective, the voters' preferences are supposed to be integrated (i.e., internally consistent, context-independent, and stable), as we already know. Still, one might be tempted to imagine them too narrowly, as "a preference for higher taxation," for instance. If taken at face value, such a narrow framing is impermissible because, for the preference theory to be applicable, the alternatives must be mutually exclusive. There are many possible worlds with taxation levels exceeding the status quo, and one must rate their relative desirability. Therefore, the preferences are understood in a broad sense of the preferences among alternative *social states*:

> The most precise definition of a social state would be a complete description of the amount of each type of commodity in the hands of each individual, the amount of labor to be supplied by each individual, the amount of each productive resource invested in each type of productive activity, and the amounts of various types of collective activity, such as municipal services, diplomacy and its continuation by other means, and the erection of statues to famous men.
>
> (Arrow, 1963, p. 17)

As Arrow (1963, p. 17) makes clear, there is no presumption of narrow selfishness implied in this definition: not only consumption *tastes* but also ethical *values* influence people's appraisal of the social states. In line with the ordinal view of utility that precludes the imposition of exogenous evaluative standards, the agents are completely free to apply any valuation criteria in their assessment of the relative desirability of various social states. Both utilitarian and deontological ethics are permissible, for instance, as well as any other ethical framework or a lack of it. Various individuals in a society may—and perhaps often do—possess quite different preferential orderings of the social states. After all, with uniform preferences, there would be no meaningful difference between individual and collective choice.

It is immediately apparent that the expectation that individuals can readily make up their mind regarding their preference between any two imaginable social states is a rather demanding one. Do note that the preferences are defined relative to outcomes—that is, social states that result from a particular social choice. Thus, the problem of scarce information on the voters' side is discreetly removed: the neoclassical assumption of "one world" identical for the decision-maker and the observer appears in its most potent form. The voters are tacitly presumed to know what policies are feasible as well as their causal impact. Otherwise, the voting procedure could not be pictured as a process of aggregation of their outcome preferences. Accordingly, the voters in the neo-classical social choice context are not merely rational but hyperrational in the strict sense that they search for the best alternative ignoring the costs of the search itself (Elster, 2008, p. 67). The more remarkable it is that attempts at pref-erence aggregation via social choice still lead into impossibilities.

To illustrate these impossibilities, it suffices to consider a situation with merely three alternative social states (x, y, z) and three voters (A, B, C) because any more complex setting leads to analogical outcomes. Therefore, suppose x is the continuation of the status quo, y represents a state where a certain amount of money from a collective budget has been spent to build a public swimming pool, and z is a state where the same amount has been used to finance a public school. Anna, Bert, and Cecilia represent the collective of (hyper)rational voters whose individual preferences supply the information necessary for social evalu-ation of the alternative social states.

Collective choice requires an aggregation rule that will translate any set of individual preference orderings into a social preference ordering (Figure 2.1; cf. Mas-Colell, Whinston and Green, 1995, p. 790).[4]

Suppose we already know Anna's, Bert's, and Cecilia's *individual* preferences regarding the social states (operator P denotes a strict preference):

Anna	$xPyPz$
Bert	$yPzPx$
Cecilia	$zPxPy$

Still, how does a *society* consisting of Anna, Bert, and Cecilia evaluate the alter-native social states? Anna and Bert prefer the school (y) over the swimming pool (z); does that imply that y is *socially preferred* to z? Only if you have a particular aggregation rule already at hand. If the aggregation rule appoints Cecilia dic-tator whose preferences override everybody else's, then the pool (z) will be

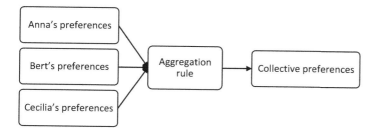

Figure 2.1 Preference aggregation.

socially preferred. If the rule requires unanimity, then the status quo (x) will prevail over both the school (y) and the pool (z), not precisely because it is collectively chosen but because the unanimity rule makes it exceptionally difficult to override (cf. Arrow, 1963, p. 45). And we do not need to stop with these standard options: there is an infinite variety of possible rules. Arrow (1963, p. 24) uses an example of a "Platonic case" where the same social preference ordering is generated for any set of individual preferences.

If you feel that the Platonic case—which represents what we might today call "perfectionism" (Conly, 2012), that is, an idea that values are objective, not subjective, and people should be coerced to pursue them even if they do not come to appreciate them—finds itself on a collision course with the fundamental democratic values, you are right, of course. This implies a more general lesson: not all possible aggregation rules are equally attractive. Unfortunately, it is not only exotic rules, such as the Platonic case, that exhibit troublesome flaws. The (simple) majority rule, which is often treated as essentially synonymous with democracy (cf. Downs, 1957; Goodin and Spiekermann, 2018), also has its fair share of shortcomings.

Simple majority rule means that in a collective of N decision-makers, an alternative must obtain the support of $N/2 + 1$ decision-makers to be strictly collectively preferred. In our stylized case, two out of the three voters must strictly prefer one alternative over another for it to win in the respective duel. Given Anna's, Bert's, and Cecilia's preference profiles, a startling problem will emerge. Clearly, no alternative can receive majority support if all three compete simultaneously: in such a case, the status quo (x) would persist, but it would not be *chosen*. Only Anna would vote for it. Bert would choose a pool (y), and Cecilia would push for a school (z). However, the attempt to resolve the stalemate by introducing pairwise competition leads to a worrying outcome: x prevails over y due to Anna's and Cecilia's support; y wins over z because Anna and Bert prefer it; z defeats x through Bert's and Cecilia's vote. By now, the problem is obvious: the collective preference ordering becomes a vicious circle. If simple majority voting is used to aggregate Anna's, Bert's, and Cecilia's preferences, there is no way to tell which alternative is the most preferred by their collective or "society." Although their individual preferences are rational—even hyperrational—simple majority rule cannot derive rational social preferences on their basis.

If one alternative is chosen anyway, its selection is not implied by the voter's preferences but by the arbitrary circumstances of the voting process. One particularly worrisome implication is that an agenda-setter may orchestrate the election so that *their* preferred alternative wins, even if they have no voting rights on their own. How could such a scheme succeed? Suppose the agenda setter most prefers the status quo (x). It will become the ultimate winner if the first round of voting sees y prevail over z only to be defeated by x in the second round. However, the agenda setter could have also arranged for y or z to win. For that to happen, it would suffice to assign the alternatives into the sub-contests differently. For instance, if x competes with z in round number one, it loses, and after round two, y becomes the ultimate winner.

The problem was first noticed by Nicolas de Condorcet in the 18th century and later popularized by Duncan Black (1958). In honor of the great Enlightenment thinker, it has been called Condorcet's Paradox. Accordingly, when no alternative can prevail over all the remaining ones in a pairwise competition, we say there is no Condorcet winner. As we have seen, no alternative is the best from the social perspective in such a case. A troublesome result indeed.

Unfortunately, it gets much worse. If we broaden the search for a normatively appealing aggregation rule, we will discover that the problem of cycles and other similarly disturbing failures to produce a social ordering based on individual preferences are not limited to the majority rule. Sadly, they are unavoidable, as Kenneth Arrow (1963) demonstrated.

In the good neoclassical tradition, Arrow's discussion of aggregation rules is deductive. He strives to provide a general, principle-based conclusion. His efforts have produced what became famous as Arrow's Impossibility Theorem. It states that an aggregation rule that produces a social preference ordering consistent with the twin ideals of rationality and citizens' sovereignty (Arrow, 1963, p. 31) represents a logical impossibility. The significance of Arrow's Theorem follows from the fact that the normative requirements whose mutual consistency he examined are not peculiar at all. Quite to the contrary! They shape the core of the neoclassical credo and underlie the folk theory of democracy. Let me consider them in more detail following Sen (2017, chap. 3*), who stays faithful to Arrow's (1963) original version of the proof but makes some important clarifications.

What features would make a social preference ordering compliant with the ideal of rationality? The requisite social rationality is the good old neoclassical rationality elevated to a collective level. As such, it involves (1) *completeness*, (2) *transitivity*, and (3) *independence* of irrelevant alternatives.[5] To qualify as rational, the social preference ordering must be complete (1), that is, able to rate any two social states in terms of "better," "worse," or "equally desirable." Also, it must be transitive (2): that makes it immune to the problem of vicious circles demonstrated by Condorcet's Paradox. Finally, it must comply with the independence of irrelevant alternatives (3), which means adding alternatives to the menu or subtracting them will not influence the social preference relations between the remaining alternatives. This implies that the use of any information on preferences' intensity—let alone interpersonal comparisons of utility—is ruled out.

Independence assumption precludes aggregators that incentivize voters to misrepresent their preferences, that is, to vote strategically (Mueller, 2003, p. 591).[6] Why would anybody do that? Consider the following case. Suppose you are a strategically minded voter with a preference ordering $zPyPx$ (i.e., you strictly prefer the pool over the school and the school over the status quo). In a majority vote, you are confident that the pool can beat the status quo but skeptical about its ability to prevail over the school. If the school competes with the status quo in a binary contest, your preferences imply you should vote for it. However, such sincerity could jeopardize the chance of your most preferred alternative, the pool, to ultimately prevail. If the school wins the first round of the election, it is likely to beat the pool in the second round. That gives you an incentive for preference misrepresentation: if voting for the status quo over the school despite your binary preference that says otherwise can push your most preferred alternative—that is, the pool—closer to the ultimate victory, you are better off if you behave strategically. In short, whether z is present on the menu or not may exert influence over your revealed preference in the contest between x and y, which is a violation of independence.

The remaining criteria call for a democratic solution to the social choice problem, albeit relatively weakly: they require that the peoples' preferences be neither prohibited nor ignored. Broadly speaking, citizens' sovereignty is incorporated in three conditions: (4) unrestricted domain; (5) strong Pareto principle; and (6) non-dictatorship.[7] Again, the conditions appear prima facie unproblematic. Unrestricted domain (4) means that the voters must not be prevented from expressing any preference they might have. Whatever Anna's, Bert's, and Cecilia's preference orderings of the status quo (x), the school (y), and the pool (z) are, the aggregator cannot exclude any of them from consideration. Strong Pareto principle (5) requires that if each voter strictly prefers, say, x over y, x is strictly socially preferred to y. More plainly, if everyone favors a continuation of the status quo over the school, the status quo must be collectively chosen. In any other cases, the Pareto criterion remains silent. Non-dictatorship (6) is what it sounds like: it prohibits the existence of a voter whose preferences would always be decisive for the social preference ordering.

The problem is—as Arrow has demonstrated—that if there are more than two alternatives to choose from, the six conditions cannot be simultaneously fulfilled.[8] An aggregation rule that complies with conditions (1)–(5) would necessarily be a dictatorship. A non-dictatorial system is only possible if some of the conditions (1)–(5) are weakened (') or abandoned entirely (¬). Note that the problem does not only apply to some specific subset of preference aggregation mechanisms but also apply to *any logically possible aggregation rule*. Want dictatorship (¬6)? No, you don't. Want consensus? It will violate completeness (¬1) because it cannot evaluate the relative desirability of multiple alternatives that all enjoy unanimous support. Also, it will not comply with independence (¬5) as it creates incentives for strategic voting (could there be any more convenient opportunity of strategizing than possession of veto power?). Want majority rule? It violates transitivity (¬3) and enables cycles, as illustrated by Condorcet's Paradox. Due to incentives for strategic voting being present, it also violates independence (¬5). The list of various voting rules' flaws could go on forever. Thanks to Arrow, one thing is certain: there will always be a flaw.

Can Arrow's result be easily escaped or sidestepped? Despite vast effort invested in doing just that, the answer is no. As Sen (2017, p. 273) summarizes the discussion: "weakenings tended to produce new problems, which could all be converted into Impossibility Theorems by axiomatically demanding the removal of those infelicities." Let us consider a few examples (cf. Mueller, 2003, chap. 24.2; Feldman and Serrano, 2005, pp. 288–291). Weakening the transitivity (2') condition escapes the implication of dictatorship but does not produce inclusive democracy either because it leads to the emergence of oligarchy or at least a veto-power-wielding elite. Weakening of unrestricted domain (4') requires the permissible preferences to be single-peaked, which is hardly applicable in a real-world democratic context. And abandoning independence (¬3) is conditional on solving the inscrutable problem of how the preferences' intensity is to be measured—otherwise, it opens the door for strategic voting.

What is the meaning of Arrow's Impossibility Theorem for the democratic theory? It undermines the view of the ideal democratic process as a pure transformation of scattered individual preferences into a consistent ideal of a *common good* or a *general will*. As it demonstrates, there is no such thing as a neutral voting system: inevitably, "random elements enter" the social choice, as Arrow (1963, p. 10) has put it. Whatever the outcome of the collective decision-making, it would be different if some other aggregation rule was used, even if all the voters' individual preferences remained the same. Thus, democratic social choice is impossible without an arbitrary component. This matters from the instrumental perspective, of course, because the Impossibility Theorem shows there is no straightforward way to determine the welfare function a society is supposed to maximize. The aim of social choice remains uncomfortably vague: if a society is not quite certain where it is headed, it becomes difficult to evaluate if it is on the right track.

Still, one should not despair prematurely. While it can be deductively proven that no aggregation rule offers a guarantee that bothersome issues, such as voting cycles, will not arise, it remains an empirical question if they occur with significant frequency and how much damage they wreak. Perhaps it should not come as a surprise that evaluating the instrumental success of alternative social choice mechanisms cannot be concluded a priori. After all, it is not like the markets, besides their other problems, escape the logic of the Impossibility Theorem: the problem of incomplete social ordering plagues them too. Therefore, we cannot avoid the painstaking task of addressing the trade-offs between the different systems.

In other words, even if all possible voting systems are imperfect, some are more imperfect than others. Take the majority rule: it does not live up to all the neoclassical ideals, but there remains much to speak for it (Dasgupta and Maskin, 2008). True, its resistance to voting cycles and strategic voting cannot be vouched for, but how frequently do they occur? The evidence on the cycles' occurrence is scarce (Mueller, 2003, chap. 5.13; Goodin and Spiekermann, 2018, p. 33). In a similar vein, strategic voting may be an inconsequential threat where there is a large number of voters, that is, on most occasions when one participates in a democratic collective choice: exertion of effort on strategizing if one's probability of being decisive is negligible is perhaps not a reasonable investment (Landemore, 2012, p. 156; Goodin and Spiekermann, 2018, p. 49).

So, to assess democracy's potential more productively, we must descend from the Olympian heights of hyperrationality and examine it in less idealized conditions, namely, with ignorant or even irrational citizens.

The Problem of Rational Ignorance and the Wisdom of Crowds

With "merely" rational voters, the problem of ignorance emerges. Hyperrationality assumption sidesteps the epistemic dimension of social choice. Once we abandon this assumption—as we should—we must deal with the fact that both valuations *and beliefs* will be aggregated in a democratic social choice.[9] If the citizens are to achieve states of the world they prefer, their degree of awareness of the feasible policies and their probable consequences will matter. However, information gathering tends to be costly. It takes time and effort to read the parties' programs and learn the candidates' track records. It would seem much depends on the voters' willingness to shoulder these costs.

Downs (1957, pp. 222–223) examines the issue of rational voters' willingness to pay for political information deductively. His conclusion is not encouraging. Due to an individual voter's negligible impact on the outcome of a social choice in the modern mass democracy (see below), voters have no incentive to invest in information gathering and processing. They can be expected to possess political information as far as it is free. Thus, they may receive it as a side-effect of other activities: chatting with friends, listening to radio, or reading news. Some of them might even find political information intrinsically entertaining. However, no investment can be expected for the sake of increasing the quality of one's vote per se. The citizens who do not have politically savvy friends, do not enjoy reading political news, and change the radio station every time music gets interrupted by the commentator's voice will remain ignorant. And rationally so—the instrumental benefits of political information do not justify the costs of its gathering. Thus, the concept of "rational ignorance" has been conceived.

Perhaps one might be tempted to dismiss Down's prediction of rational ignorance as mere aprioristic speculation. Certainly, *homo politicus* would rationally choose ignorance, but that does not imply "real" people do that. However, the prediction is upheld by empirical research. Pervasive voter ignorance is an undisputed fact (e.g., Somin, 2013; Achen and Bartels, 2016). Suffice to say that perhaps a third of the electorate seems to deserve an unflattering label of "know-nothings" (Somin, 2013, p. 35). In their case, knowing nothing needs to be taken literally because these citizens are completely uninformed even about the most basic political trivia. They do not know the key officeholders, have no idea what powers entail to the prominent public offices, cannot connect historical political choices with their originators, and lack any stable political worldview or ideology. Even those citizens who are not precisely "know-nothings" can frequently be characterized as "know-very-littles." In short, Jason Brennan (2016), in his critique of democracy, can muster an embarrassingly

large amount of empirical evidence when he derides a majority of the democratic citizens as "hobbits":

> Hobbits are mostly apathetic and ignorant about politics. They lack strong,
> fixed opinions about most political issues. Often they have no opinions at
> all. They have little, if any, social scientific knowledge; they are ignorant
> not just of current events but also of the social scientific theories and data
> needed to evaluate as well as understand these events. Hobbits have only a
> cursory knowledge of relevant world or national history. They prefer to go
> on with their daily lives without giving politics much thought.
>
> (Brennan, 2016, p. 4)

On the face of it, the problem of rational ignorance appears serious. But how
much does it truly matter for democracy's epistemic performance? Surprising
as it might be, its effect can be benign under the right conditions. That, at
least, has been suggested by many scholars who highlight democracy's epistemic
virtues: in their view, a large numbers of nonideal decision-makers—such as the
ignorant voters described above—can be trusted to deliver accurate collective
judgment on complex issues like the ones any modern polity must face.

In this venue, let me turn attention to the concept of *the wisdom of crowds*,
which has been popularized by James Surowiecki (2004). It denotes a phenomenon where an aggregate judgment of a group is more accurate than an
individual judgment of any of its members. This can happen even if some of
the group's members possess substantial expertise while the group is not very
sophisticated on average. In short, if the wisdom of crowds appears, numbers
beat competence. Surowiecki's paradigmatic example points to a situation when
Francis Galton—an English scientist and Charles Darwin's cousin—discovered
that in a weight-judging competition to guess the weight of an ox, the average
guess of the crowd was more accurate than any of the expert estimates.

Galton's case study represents a proof of possibility: it demonstrates that the
wisdom of crowds does emerge with a non-zero probability. However, there
remains a world of difference between admitting its occasional occurrence and
an across-the-board reliance on it characteristic for a democracy responsive
to popular opinion. What needs to be carefully examined are the conditions
that trigger its appearance. Surowiecki (2004, p. 10) suggests four such
conditions: diversity, independence, decentralization, and aggregation. *Diversity*
means that different individuals must have different information at their disposal or different perspectives of looking at the problem at hand. *Independence*
requires that the individuals' views are not determined by the views of others.
Decentralization enables the agents to concentrate on a partial aspect of the
problem at hand, that is, to specialize and to use local knowledge. *Aggregation*
points to a need for an appropriate aggregation mechanism, such as the market
or a voting system that transforms individual judgments into a collective decision. If these conditions are not fulfilled, the benefits of having an extensive
collection of decision-makers fail to materialize.

However intriguing, Surowiecki's book provides an exploratory and popularizing account of the wisdom of crowds. A more robust treatment is required if we are to take democracy's epistemic promise seriously. Most prominently, there are three rigorous proofs of democracy's epistemic superiority relative to any less inclusive mechanism of social choice: Condorcet's Jury Theorem, the Miracle of Aggregation, and Diversity Trumps Ability Theorem (cf. Landemore, 2012, chap. 6). Each of the three offers its own response to the problem of rational ignorance.

Condorcet's Jury Theorem

Condorcet's Jury Theorem, another accomplishment of the prolific Enlightenment thinker we have encountered earlier, is the most prominent of the three. Its baseline setting even manages to sidestep the complications emerging from Arrow's Impossibility Theorem because it only concentrates on problems with two alternative solutions. While this workaround is not applicable for most practical uses where the political game includes a much broader sets of options, the theorem is still intriguing: its answer to the problem of rational ignorance is that large numbers of voters can deliver an astonishing epistemic performance even if their individual competence is low. Even a know-nothing can positively contribute to the democratic social choice—or at least does no harm—unless he possesses a peculiar anti-expertise that makes him proficient in choosing the wrong alternative with higher probability than the correct one.

In the classic setup (Landemore, 2012, pp. 149–156; Goodin and Spiekermann, 2018, pp. 17–20), a group of n voters chooses between two alternatives via a majority rule. Out of the two alternatives, exactly one is correct. Condorcet's Jury Theorem demonstrates the following:
If

1   each voter recognizes the correct alternative with a probability $p > 0.5$, that is, they are better than random at their task (*competence assumption*);
2   the votes are statistically independent of each other (*independence assumption*); and
3   each voter chooses the alternative they consider correct (*sincerity assumption*);
then the probability that the group will choose the correct alternative approaches certainty as n approaches infinity.

In case you wonder, the convergence toward certainty is relatively fast. Ten thousand voters with a meager competence of just $p = 0.505$ have an almost 85% probability of choosing the correct alternative (Goodin and Spiekermann, 2018, p. 22). Demonstrating the wisdom of crowds, large numbers of voters with low individual competence can outperform small numbers of voters with high individual competence.

The assumptions of the classic setup are rather demanding, though. What if *some* of the voters are so incompetent that they tend to choose the incorrect answer? What if the voters are not *completely* independent? Fortunately, the conclusion holds even if the assumptions are weakened (Grofman, Owen and Feld, 1983; Goodin and Spiekermann, 2018, chap. 3). It is enough when the voters are better than random *on average*, that is, each incompetent voter can be outweighed by a super-competent one. Also, some degree of dependence does not undermine the conclusion completely; it just reduces the benefits that stem from the large numbers. If the voters tend to follow an opinion leader, for instance, the crowd's probability of choosing the correct alternative converges to the leader's probability as the strength of the crowd's epistemic dependence increases.

Still, how is the voters' competence to be evaluated? Can we be reasonably certain that the average voter is indeed better than random at her task? This is, of course, a thorny issue. Let me consider the perspectives of *ex ante* assessment when the voters are evaluated based on some minimum entry requirements to participate in the collective choice and *ex post* assessment when the quality of choice by the crowds (or its elected representatives) is compared to the quality of the expert choice.

From the *ex-ante* perspective, there is no consensus regarding the minimum requirements of "sufficient competence." The voters' probability of recognizing the correct alternative cannot be observed directly. The scholars who debate the issue have wildly differing views on the proxy measures of the baseline competence. The moderates claim that the current standards of eligibility to exercise the voting rights suffice, while the radicals suggest that education in civics and the social sciences, especially in economics, is needed (Landemore, 2014; Brennan, 2016). As democracy's critics like to point out, without knowing the basic rules of the democratic game and the basic realia, it is rather hard to imagine that the voters are competent to decide upon anything (Brennan, 2016). The research into "enlightened preferences" suggests that more informed voters have systematically different preferences than their less informed counterparts. Althaus (2003) or Caplan (2008) take this to mean that certain preferences (e.g., for protectionist policies) are systematically caused by ignorance. However, it is not clear that the demonstrated differences are meaningful enough to matter for the actual political outcomes (Goodin and Spiekermann, 2018, chap. 6.1.1). Also, the claim that the enlightened preferences can be easily constructed by controlling for a couple of basic parameters, such as income, strains credulity: a more knowledgeable person is not "just like me but with more information"; their whole life experience and context is probably quite different from mine (cf. Lepoutre, 2020). There is also very little agreement on whether the citizens are supposed to possess competence regarding the issues themselves—taxation, immigration, technology, and the like—or whether they can orient themselves relying on simple clues, such as the policy proposer's political allegiance or even ethnicity (Somin, 2013, chap. 4; Goodin and Spiekermann, 2018, chap. 12).

To make things worse, it does not seem probable that all political problems require the same amount of competence. Landemore (2014, p. 219), for instance, concedes that uninformed agents can hardly contribute to research in chemistry due to their lack of competence but keeps faith that the citizens' competence in the political choices can suffice. And indeed, in some questions—say, assessment of a candidate's character—the probability that a regular person "knows what he is doing" certainly appears significantly higher than in those requiring specific expertise like decisions about international agreements or technologies. In other words, sometimes we can expect common sense to perform well, sometimes we cannot. Adult human beings tend to be expert judges of human character. Not everywhere, however, do our everyday cognitive tools perform so well. Why should a layperson's opinion be worthless when it comes to chemistry but not when it comes to genetically modified organisms or nuclear energy?

An *ex post* evaluation is also riddled with difficulties. Prominent political issues tend to lack solutions whose objective validity could be easily evaluated. Does it even make sense to talk about the *correct* alternative as Condorcet's Jury Theorem presupposes?

What is meant by the correctness of a decision can be transparent in the context of a jury verdict regarding a defendant's guilt or in simple one-dimensional cognitive tasks with objectively verifiable answers, such as the value of coins in a glass or the weight of a competition ox. However, we rarely deal with such simple problems in politics (cf. Landemore, 2012). Instead, we need to presume multidimensionality and paucity of objective benchmarks of success. In short, perhaps Condorcet's Jury Theorem is applicable only when it comes to the questions of facts. What if different people have different values?

Goodin and Spiekermann (2018, chap. 4.1) address the issue and develop the following answers that gradually temper the demands on alternative's "correctness." Most strongly, one may claim that *moral realism* is true. If that were the case, whatever values prevail in a democratic contest are almost certainly the true ones. What if morality is a social construct, however? Then we can at least rely on democratic choice to reveal the respective society's current values. A third, yet milder, option is *moral separability* between the factual and evaluative layer of the political issues. Even if correct values cannot be identified via a majority rule, the relevant facts can. So, the majority choice can be expected to entail at least the correct assessment of the available alternatives' factual basis. Finally, the weakest view of correctness is moral majoritarianism: "The larger the number of voters, the more certain it is that the majority (or plurality) among them will track what is true *from the point of view of the largest segment*" (Goodin and Spiekermann, 2018, p. 42).

Unfortunately, moral majoritarianism resembles Vermeule's (2012, p. 345) suggestion to generalize Condorcet's Jury Theorem in such a way that if a voter has $p > 0.5$ probability of selecting an alternative that best corresponds to her interests, with a growing number of voters the probability grows that the alternative will be chosen that best corresponds to the individual interests of the majority of the voters. If these "interests" are not considered "correct" in any way, such reinterpretation is tautological and renders the theorem vacuous: for whatever reason, more voters choose one alternative than another; and majority choice (by definition!) leads to the victory of the alternative more people choose. Hardly a remarkable epistemic success.

Since understanding voters' competence through the lens of their ability to choose a correct alternative seems tricky in the light of the preceding debate, let me turn to the other proofs of the wisdom of crowds to see if we can sidestep the issue or at least derive similar conclusions as Condorcet's Jury Theorem with milder assumptions.

Miracle of Aggregation and Diversity Trumps Ability Theorem

Miracle of aggregation attacks the problem of ignorance from a slightly different angle. It concedes that the voters may be ignorant and that ignorance breeds mistakes. However, the mistakes are presumed random, and thus they will cancel out if many voters participate in the political decision (cf. Caplan, 2009). Suppose there is a subset of utterly ignorant voters—the know-nothings. Never mind, their votes will just evenly distribute themselves among the available alternatives rendering them unable to tip the election in one direction or the other. As far as any voters are informed, however, it is a different story. While the noise is random, the signal is not: therefore, the informed voters will *systematically* converge on some alternatives rather than others. So, even if they were in a significant minority, the informed voters will be the ones to exert the decisive influence. No candidate or policy can prevail without winning their support. In short, if all voters were utterly ignorant and had no clue what they are doing, there would be no signal. However, if some voters are somewhat competent, the signal will prevail with the standard democratic aggregation mechanisms. Since some political information is free, rational ignorance does not mean *utter* ignorance of *every voter*. The empirical evidence does not demonstrate it either. Thus, the miracle of aggregation promises to save the day.[10]

The miracle of aggregation may possess some advantage over Condorcet's Jury Theorem. While the theorem is wedded to a two-alternative case that can only be extended to a broader spectrum of alternatives by changing the voting procedure to plurality voting (Goodin and Spiekermann, 2018, chap. 3.2), the miracle of aggregation does not make any special requirements on the number of alternatives and the nature of the voting procedure. Of course, the voting procedure cannot be inclusive enough for the ignorant to veto the decision of the knowledgeable; otherwise, anything goes. Moreover, the miracle is perhaps less dependent on the notion of correctness. It only requires that the nonrandom elements that influence the voters' choice are not unrelated to the substance of the issue at hand. Democracy's instrumental performance depends on that. Despite these possible advantages, assumptions of independence and sincerity are still implicitly embraced: if the mistakes are nonrandom, there will be no miracle; if the voters strategize, their behavior also contributes to the noise that obscures or crowds out the signal.

How about the Diversity Trumps Ability Theorem (Hong and Page, 2004; Page, 2008)? What is its take on the ignorance issue? In contrast to the previous approaches, it targets the difference between information and knowledge. One thing is to possess certain information; another is how it is utilized to update the agent's beliefs and transformed into a judgment. The theorem strives to demonstrate that for the epistemic performance of the collective, the amount of information at an individual decision-maker's disposal may matter less than the diversity of the cognitive models being used to "make sense" of the information. If the knowledgeable voters utilize the same cognitive models—perhaps due to their standardized education—while the ignorant voters approach the issue using a wide variety of very different models, the latter can achieve better results than the former. In Page's (2008, p. 133) words: "collections of diverse individuals outperform collections of more individually capable individuals."

If the applied cognitive models are diverse—that is, they look at the same problem from different perspectives or use different interpretations and heuristics (Page, 2008, p. 7)—the prediction errors can be presumed not just independent but negatively correlated. Increasing the electorate's diversity thus works to clean up the noise on account of the signal systematically. At the same time, as already suggested, informed individuals, especially the trained experts, tend to share the same outlook due to their shared background and therefore lack diversity. Although an individual expert outperforms an individual layperson, of course, the greater cognitive diversity of laypeople leads to the opposite outcome at an aggregate level.

Let me consider the assumptions that imply the theorem's intriguing conclusion. Page (2008, pp. 158–165) describes these assumptions in a highly stylized context. Even so, they approximately follow the familiar tropes of Condorcet's Jury Theorem: there needs to be a sufficient number of voters (or "problem solvers"), and the issue at hand is defined as having a correct answer, albeit one that is not immediately apparent ("the problem is difficult"). Also, voters' competence and independence are of the essence. The decision-makers must possess a certain minimum competence: what Page (2008, p. 160) calls *the Calculus Condition* requires the decision-makers to be "smart" and concedes that one who has never heard of statistics cannot meaningfully contribute to solving a statistical problem. Additionally, *the Diversity Condition* requires that sufficient diversity must exist among the voters' cognitive models. Otherwise, their mistakes cannot be negatively correlated, and they can get stuck with some suboptimal solution to the problem at hand. Thus, the Diversity Condition represents a more demanding alternative to the Condorcetian independence assumption.

Although Diversity Trumps Ability Theorem has been impactful in democratic theory (Landemore, 2012; Landemore and Page, 2015), it presents the most controversial answer to the ignorance problem on technical grounds. Its mathematical underpinnings and the interpretation of its implications in the social context have come under serious critical scrutiny. Thompson (2014) argues that the list of assumptions is incomplete, and if one rectifies this shortcoming, the theorem turns into a trivial identity that lacks practical implications. She also asserts that labeling the phenomena observed in the framework of Hong's and Page's computation experiment as "diversity" is arbitrary and misleading. Although this criticism is not universally accepted (Singer, 2019), it remains an open question how significant the theoretical breakthrough represented by Diversity Trumps Ability Theorem is for the considerations of democracy's epistemic benefits (Goodin and Spiekermann, 2018, p. 98).

Be that as it may, to the extent their politically relevant predictions are not accessible to a direct empirical test, all the deductive demonstrations of democracy's epistemic superiority are only as good as the assumptions upon which they are based. We have already seen that the issue of voters' threshold competence is thorny. But it hardly presents an obvious deal-breaker as the possible solutions suggested by Goodin and Spikermann (2018) testify. Much depends on whether the other assumptions that appear in various guises in all the arguments supporting the wisdom of crowds—namely, independence and sincerity—hold water.

Behavioral Political Economy of Democracy

Let us suppose that the logically necessary flaws of the majority rule only rarely lead to significant practical complications. As we have seen, rational ignorance also presents a lesser hindrance than meets the eye. Can we rest assured that democracy will deliver on its epistemic promise? Well, not really. Chapter 1 has concluded that the realm of political choice is where the behavioral economics' findings meet perhaps the weakest opposition since there are no incentives for rationality present, at least not for an individual voter in a mass democratic social choice. Let me now examine this hypothesis in more detail as it is vital concerning the assumptions of independence and sincerity.

First, I shall consider a regular voter's incentives yet more systematically. So far, we have followed the neoclassical logic to conclude that rational ignorance is expected to prevail among democratic citizens since their individual choices are seldom decisive, that is, *pivotal*. However, if one is not pivotal, why bother voting at all?

Indeed, a rational voter can be expected to participate in the election if and only if the expected benefits of participation are greater than its expected costs (Downs, 1957, chaps 3, 14; see also Mueller, 2003, pp. 304–306). Otherwise, they will abstain. Therefore, the condition for rational participation is:

$$p \times B - C > 0$$

Here, C is the cost of participation, B is the expected net benefit from the victory of the preferred alternative, and p is the probability of one's vote being pivotal.

The participation costs can be explicit: the voter may need to pay for the transportation to the polling station, and the participation might be even subject to some monetary fee (a poll tax), although that is a remote possibility in most democratic countries today. One way or another, there will always be an implicit cost, though. A citizen who decides to participate needs to spend some time, which could have been dedicated to other activities. These costs are not exceedingly high, perhaps on the order of 25 minutes, to quote one estimate (Blais, 2000, p. 85). Nonetheless, they are inevitably positive.

The expected net benefit of the victory of the preferred alternative can be most easily illustrated on a two-alternative case (a more complex setup would produce an analogical conclusion, however). Here, it represents the difference between the voter's expected utility in the case of the preferred alternative's victory and expected utility in the case of the dispreferred alternative's victory. If there is no difference between the expected utilities, the voter is indifferent between the candidates or parties.

However, notice that the expected net benefit is not received conditional on one's participation. The preferred candidate may well win or lose independent of whether the citizen participates. Thus, an alternative's electoral victory represents a *public good* for its supporters: no one can be excluded from enjoying its benefits on account of not contributing their fair share toward its provision. Frequently, such incentive setups lead to inefficient collective outcomes with rampant free riding (cf. Olson, 1971). If one free rides, one receives the benefits of the group effort without paying the cost. Is this a credible concern? Given neoclassically rational voters, it would seem so. Downs (1957, pp. 261–262) clearly worries that voters' rationality may let democracy die of neglect.

Accordingly, all depends on the probability of being pivotal. Only if pivotal, the voter's choice will matter instrumentally, that is, it will be necessary to bring about the desired outcome. However, a mass democratic election is unlikely to be tipped by a single vote: the margins of victory tend to be in tens of thousands, even millions of votes. Using a majority rule, only if one's preferred alternative would lose by a single vote or if the election would result in a tie, one voter is decisive for the outcome. Otherwise, their marginal contribution to the outcome is zero.

So how large is the p? We need to be somewhat cautious here because its precise magnitude depends on a particular election's circumstances and difficult to estimate empirically. However, the existing findings support the obvious conclusion: the probability of being pivotal is negligible. Moreover, if "bigger" elections matter more in terms of stakes, the expected net benefits of participation (B) are inversely related to p because more citizens will participate in them. Brennan's and Lomasky's (1997, chap. 4) a priori estimate for a US presidential election with a perfectly tied electorate is 1:12,500. Not great, not terrible, you might think. However, do mind that the probability drops precipitously with even a tiny deviation from a perfect tie. For the 2008 US presidential election, Gelman *et al.* (2012) estimate it at about 1:60,000,000 on average (ranging from 1 in 10 million to less than 1 in a 100 billion for different states). Regarding more local democratic affairs, Mulligan's and Hunter's (2003) empirical estimate for US congressional elections is 1:89,000 and 1:15,000 in state legislator elections.[11]

We can therefore provide the relevant variables with the following approximate magnitudes:

$$C > 0$$

$$B \geq 0$$

$$p \approx 0$$

Therefore, a rational voter is predicted to abstain unless the expected participation of the other voters drops so much that her p rises appreciably above zero: a possibility likely equal to democracy's death of neglect. A precise calculation of the optimal participation rate is tricky and depends on numerous assumptions. However, despite the chronic complaints about the democratic citizens' low political engagement, the abstention is much rarer than the Downsian model would suggest. Millions or tens of millions of voters show up for major elections inconsistent with its prediction. What is amiss?

The apparent faux pas for the neoclassical approach has been dubbed the *paradox of voting* (not to be confused with Condorcet's Paradox, which occasionally goes under the same name). It seems the rational choice theory—proudly asserted as the leading candidate on the general theory of human behavior unifying all the social sciences under the economics' imperial banner—suffers a humiliating defeat in the clash with a mundane fact that people do vote (Green and Shapiro, 1994, chap. 4). So what does the paradox imply for our understanding of the voters' behavior?

There are multiple ways to extricate ourselves from the conundrum (cf. Mueller, 2003, chap. 14; Dowding, 2005). We can attempt to extend the size of B by assuming a significant degree of altruism among the democratic citizens, or we can add a noninstrumental benefit (D) into the equation, or we can simply divorce from the neoclassical paradigm and admit that the voters' decision to participate is not rational. However, each stratagem ultimately opens the door to political irrationality, which represents a dire threat to the wisdom of crowds, as I am going to show. The main problem is—as you may expect—that irrationality introduces non-random, systematic mistakes. But let us not get ahead of ourselves: it is instructive to inspect the stratagems first.

The *Extend B* strategy appeals to a broad definition of the voter's utility, which may well include concern about the well-being of the other members of her society (Somin, 2013, chap. 3). As discussed in Chapter 1, the individual utility does not have to be understood in a narrow sense of material well-being or wealth: it may contain both tastes and values, as Arrow (1963) has put it. As such, it may include as much altruism or other ethical goods as one sees fit. The voter can look at the election outcomes from a broad perspective—perhaps one considers a particular alternative not just "bad for me" but "bad for our society, for the world even." In short, if the voter is altruistic enough, the expected net benefits may indeed be sizable enough to overweigh the low participation costs even after being discounted by the negligible probability of being decisive. After all, political science's conventional wisdom is that the voters are not narrowly self-interested but vote "sociotropically," that is, look at the alternatives from the perspective of the whole society (Kinder and Kiewiet, 1981, p. 132). Empirically, people's material interests seem to exercise remarkably little influence over their political views, which leads some authors to hypothesize that their political choices are directed at the common good instead (cf. Landemore, 2012, pp. 196–197). Still, in the light of the negligible probabilities of pivotality, the necessary amount of altruism would have to be heroic (cf. Dowding, 2005, p. 448).

The *Add D* strategy appears less demanding as it introduces noninstrumental benefits of participation. If voters do not have an instrumental interest in voting and yet they vote, their participation can be triggered by motives that do not relate to the outcomes of collective choice. For instance, they may be driven to participation by a sense of civic duty (Riker and Ordeshook, 1968). In that case, participation would be intrinsically beneficial for them to the extent that they rationally participate independent of their votes will be pivotal. However, that the benefit is *politically* noninstrumental does not mean that it is *generally* noninstrumental. It may just be derived from achieving nonpolitical goals (Caplan, 2008). For instance, the theory of expressive voting claims that the voters' behavior can be driven by an intrinsic utility of the voting act, perhaps as an expression of one's identity (Brennan and Lomasky, 1997; Hillman, 2010). Granted that this is the case, such identity expression can still provide broadly conceived instrumental benefits, such as those stemming from declaring allegiance to a particular social group. Accordingly, one's voting behavior may represent a form of reputation management. To get along with one's associates, sharing their political outlooks may be highly desirable even if the outlook is inconsequential in the narrow political sense (I shall elaborate on this in Chapter 3).

Finally, the *Give Up R* strategy where "R" stands for rationality. One may simply admit that the neoclassical paradigm cannot disentangle the paradox of voting because people do not vote for rational reasons. Maybe they systematically overestimate p and keep voting in the delusional faith that one vote makes a difference despite experience's continuous efforts to teach them otherwise. Or they neglect to consider the costs. They might be slaves of a habit, too. The irrationality-based hypotheses could be multiplied.

In a way, these strategies leave us with as many diverse explanations for the paradox of voting as one might wish for: a true embarrassment of riches.[12] The *Expand B* and *Add D* strategies can also save the face of the neoclassical analysis of voting behavior if they are wielded carefully enough to avoid entangling the rational choice theory into tautological just-so stories ("People vote because of their civic duty and we know they feel civic duty because they vote."). Is it so inevitable that political irrationality will rear its head no matter which direction we go?

Opting for the *Give Up R* route around the paradox of voting entails admitting the voters' irrationality right from the start. As far as democratic citizens systematically misperceive even the glaring fact of the negligible probability of being pivotal, we can hardly expect them to rationally assess the complex political issues upon which they are supposed to decide. If one considers the *Extend B* or *Add D* options that promise to save the rational choice theory's face more persuasive, the comfort they offer is still quite limited. Given that the surplus benefits of participation are scant, the voters still have little to no incentive to rationally evaluate the political alternatives on the menu. At the same time, all that is needed to undermine the wisdom of crowds is systematic mistakes in judgment that cannot be overridden without an outlay of resources or effort. In other words, behavioral economics' findings are of utmost importance in the political context, whatever the relative explanatory potential of the competing hypotheses. The independence assumption will not hold whether the electorate is destined to make systematic mistakes once the right cognitive levers are pushed or merely lacks incentives to invest effort in overriding them. Let me elaborate.

The arguments supporting the wisdom of crowds show that the democratic aggregation mechanism will eliminate any random influence over individual choices (the noise) and highlight any systematic patterns (the signal). However, if there is an *undesirable* systematic influence over choices present—that is, if the voters make predictable mistakes—it will be indistinguishable from the signal. Note that such a systematic mistake is even more likely to matter at the aggregate level in the context of individual behavior: in an individual's case, noise may obscure the bias, but not so in the collective case.

Suppose Elinor suffers from both bias and low competence. In her projects, she is overoptimistic regarding the amount of time and effort necessary to accomplish them, which introduces a bias in her planning, but she is also quite incompetent when it comes to time management, introducing noise. True, both the bias and the noise can work in a sinister synergy and make Elinor miss her deadline by months. However, there is no necessary reason for them to be correlated. In the end, Elinor may be lucky and finish the project in a timely fashion because she mistakenly scheduled more time than she would have wanted. In short, the noise may counteract the bias. Not so in collective choice, though: if Elinor were a part of a team of overoptimistic individuals who make their planning decisions by a majority vote, there would be a much slimmer chance that the deadline can be met because the procedure of aggregation would tend to eliminate the noise introduced by individual incompetence and clear the path for the bias to skew the collective decision.

Unfortunately, as Chapter 1 has illustrated on the paradigmatic struggle between neoclassical and behavioral economics, the evidence on psychological biases and heuristics suggests they are very much predisposed to undermine the wisdom of crowds. Behavioral economists do not claim that some individuals are sometimes prone to some biases but that widespread biases influence numerous choices of most people. There is little reason to expect sufficient independence, mistakes canceling out, or cognitive diversity among the public whose minds follow the same shortcuts. If the crowd is exposed to a decision-making problem where the widespread heuristics are triggered outside of their proper domain, its aggregate judgment will be skewed in a way that undermines its instrumental function.

As it has become apparent in the light of the paradox of voting, independent of the exact nature of reasons that people have for participation in the democratic process, they lack incentives to invest in debiasing techniques. Thus, even if the biases would represent merely a weak default that can be overridden with a modest expense, a behaviorally informed model of voters' behavior still predicts that intuitive reasoning with all its risky shortcuts will reign freely in democratic social choice. No standard objection to the ecological validity of the anomalies uncovered by the behavioral economists holds sway here (cf. Thaler, 2015, chap. 6).

For instance, let us suppose that learning represents an effective defense from biases. However, learning requires repetition and a swift, tangible feedback. None of that can be expected to prevail in the political context: voters express their views through the ballot box infrequently, the situations they are called to assess are variable and complex, and the feedback they receive tends to be delayed and ambiguous (Achen and Bartels, 2016). Consider the best-case scenario: democratic citizens participate in elections due to their altruistic care for the common good (i.e., *Expand B* explanation is valid). It will still be the case that the idea of the general welfare that guides their actions is based just on their intuitive understanding thereof (cf. Lucas and Tasić, 2015).

To illustrate the resulting problem, I shall examine the *affect heuristic*. As Slovic *et al.* (2007, p. 1335) characterize it, affect heuristic means that:

> (…) representations of objects and events in people's minds are tagged to varying degrees with affect. In the process of making a judgment or decision, people consult or refer to an 'affect pool' containing all the positive and negative tags consciously or unconsciously associated with the representations.

The purpose of the heuristic is to save up on cognitive resources, especially when facing a complex choice. Where cost-benefit analysis is difficult, feelings still arise fast and effortlessly and supply readily available evaluative information concerning the alternatives at hand. Some alternatives elicit intuitive aversion, while others elicit intuitive proclivity. All this without the need for the evidential source of such evaluation to be consciously reflected. No matter how complex is the choice ahead, the affect heuristic swiftly provides a gut feeling to guide it. As with other heuristics, the affect heuristic often works reliably in contexts to which it is adapted: especially often-repeated situations where positive or negative conditioning can shape a stable affective association. However, elsewhere, it misfires systematically.

The collective choice rests on an evaluation of the expected costs and benefits of the alternatives under consideration. The affect heuristic is a cognitive phenomenon that may derail the wisdom of crowds if we were to rely upon it in such a task. Slovic *et al.* (2007, pp. 1342–1345) point to biases in subjective risk estimates as an example. They argue that these estimates are determined more by the feeling of dread elicited by the given risk than the probability of its actual occurrence. Accordingly, the more dreadful risks of death (such as murder) will elicit a more robust behavioral response and more urgent calls for political intervention than less dreadful risks (such as suicide), *independent of their prevalence*. Also, the perceived degree of risk is negatively correlated with the perceived benefits of a risky alternative. For example, risks of nuclear energy are judged to be inversely related to the benefits of its use: if one is provided with information suggesting high potential benefits of nuclear energy, one is also prone to consider risks of an accident minor, for example. Slovic *et al.* (2007) suggest that the information on high benefits triggers a positive affective reaction leading to a lower risk estimate; information on high risks triggers a negative affect leading to a lower estimate of benefits. Thus, independent of whether the democratic citizens cannot help themselves but view risks in a biased fashion or just "go with the flow" because they have no incentive to invest the necessary effort into reconsidering their first impressions, systematic mistakes will occur.

At the same time, the affect heuristic is just one of many quirks of rationality that exercise influence over the democratic collective choice. Boyer and Petersen (2018) have recently examined the prevalence of what they call *folk economic beliefs* that "constitute a largely unexplored background against which most information about the policy is acquired, processed, and communicated among nonprofessionals" (Boyer and Petersen, 2018, p. 3). These beliefs concern markets, immigration, social welfare, or theory of value, among other things (Boyer and Petersen, 2018, pp. 3–4). They are characterized by the propensity to view economic phenomena through the lens adapted for use in small groups at technological stasis concerned primarily with distributional issues: namely, in human ancestral environment (cf. Rubin, 2003; Petersen, 2015). However, in the modern global economy, their obsession with other people's possibly selfish intentions or their presumption of the zero-sum game nature of trade and competition are misleading and counterproductive. Consistent with our present discussion, Boyer and Petersen (2018) subscribe to the view that folk economic beliefs are highly salient in the political context, making some policy proposals more intuitively appealing than others. Sadly, that appears more than enough to thwart the emergence of the wisdom of crowds.

What does the preceding analysis imply concerning the democratic choices, then? We may expect that specific arguments and themes will have an advantage in the political discourse. For instance, intrinsically interesting information such as personalized narratives or appeals to fundamental, identity-defining values (solidarity, justice, liberty) can be expected to possess a competitive edge (cf. Feddersen, Gailmard and Sandroni, 2009). In contrast, information that is difficult to vividly imagine and generally nonintuitive will be disadvantaged. As with other failures of rationality discussed in Chapter 1, this asymmetry can be used by agenda setters like political entrepreneurs and interest groups—as well as the media—to exercise influence over the public's political judgment.

A Democratic Equilibrium

The danger posed by biases and heuristics did not escape the attention of the democratic theorists, of course (Estlund, 2008, p. 16; Landemore, 2012, pp. 165, 197). What answer can the defenders of the epistemic virtues of democracy offer? Recently, Goodin and Spiekermann (2018, chap. 4.5) have composed three responses to the concern of lacking independence in the context of Condorcet's Jury Theorem: perhaps the electorate's biases are not strong enough to undermine the wisdom of crowds (as we have seen, some degree of dependence is acceptable); or the different biases of different groups may work in the opposite directions and cancel each other out; or the group's decision will still converge at least to "what the *best responder* [that is, someone who does the best epistemically given what the situation allows] would be able to establish given all the common causes" (Goodin and Spiekermann, 2018, p. 77). Unfortunately, while these answers may work for some epistemic dependencies—such as reliance on an opinion leader—they appear feeble in the face of widespread psychological biases.

Behavioral economists' typical view is that the biases are numerous and of significant magnitudes. Therefore, hoping that their influence in an environment with no counteracting incentives is not too extensive seems baseless. Also, there are reasons to believe that the biases are a consequence of the evolutionary design of the human mind, not random disturbances to its "proper" functioning (Boyer and Petersen, 2018). Accordingly, there is little reason to expect they will cancel out in the aggregate. The best responder stratagem does not escape the problem either: it only reframes a situation that triggers a bias as inherently "misleading" but otherwise appeases with the bias's presence.

At the same time, the impact of widespread biases on democracy's performance remains an empirical problem (cf. Landemore, 2012, p. 2). It is one thing to demonstrate that they exist and can subvert the epistemic virtues of democratic social choice, but quite another to estimate how extensive the actual damage is. In this context, numerous empirical successes of democracies vis-à-vis alternative political regimes should not be overlooked (Christiano, 2011; Landemore, 2012, pp. 238–239). Any comparison requires a measure of success, which may be controversial given our commitment not to impose what the correct values are supposed to be. However, at least three stylized facts about democracies shine brightly from a broad range of normative perspectives one might want to take: (1) they do not wage war with one another (e.g., Dafoe, Oneal and Russett, 2013), (2) they are successful in preventing famines (Sen, 2000), and (3) they are more conductive of economic development than other regimes (Acemoglu *et al.*, 2019).

So, what are we to take from all this? It appears that two overlapping discussions are proceeding simultaneously. On the one hand, there is a discussion regarding the distribution of roles between the market and democratic politics. Here, libertarian authors push for broadening the purview of individual choice at the expense of collective choice. Their argument is not necessarily that an alternative system should replace liberal democracy but that fewer issues should be addressed collectively. Save for an extreme, "anarcho-capitalist" stance that all government should be abolished, these authors do not picture any substantive reshaping of the existing democratic system. What they want is "10% less democracy" (Jones, 2020), or maybe an even bigger cut to its scope, but certainly not its complete demise. On the other hand, there is also a discussion about replacing liberal democracy with a different regime of collective decision-making. Some alternatives, such as epistocracy (Brennan, 2016) or open democracy (Landemore, 2020), are defended by scholars; others are put directly into practice by aspiring autocrats (Levitsky and Ziblatt, 2018).

These two debates need to be disentangled from each other (see Chapter 5). While the optimal balance between politics and the markets represents a valid concern, I consider it of secondary importance in a situation of a demo-cratic crisis. If liberal democracy, despite all its previous successes, shakes in its foundations—as it would seem today—the more important question is if and how the political institutions can be better fortified against the threat of polit-ical irrationality.

The preceding analysis of the wisdom of crowds shows that political irration-ality might lead to poor, even self-destructive, collective choices. Yet, democracy, as we know it, has been remarkably successful in delivering human flourishing so far. What gives? Let me propose a *hypothesis of a democratic equilibrium* to resolve the apparent tension: democracy must always find a stable balance between responsivity to people's preferences and resilience toward the centrifugal forces of political irrationality. Too much responsivity and catastrophic mistakes will be made pandering to the whims of the crowd; too little of it and the régime will be captured by self-interested elites engaging in exogenous value imposition.

In a liberal democracy, the democratic equilibrium is maintained through reliance on checks and balances and the constitutional protection of citizens' fundamental rights. This solution is not without trade-offs since it introduces numerous counter-majoritarian elements and may result in a gridlock where the status quo persists without representing anyone's preferred option (cf. Posner and Weyl, 2018, pp. 86–88). Nonetheless, it has served the citizens of democratic countries well enough, as evidenced by the above-quoted empirical research and democracy's spectacular global popularity. The problem is that the democratic equilibrium achieved on the blueprint of liberal democracy may not be robust in all circumstances. The strength of political irrationality prob-ably varies depending on the citizen's political incentives and the technological infrastructure that facilitates the political discourse. Therefore, the "tried and true" containment mechanisms may prove insufficient if political irrationality surges due to changed underlying conditions. After all, the most robust conclu-sion of our examination of democracy's predicament in the current chapter is that no system of collective choice is ever perfect. There are always cracks and flaws. If political irrationality becomes strong enough, it can bring the whole construction down.

Perhaps the most significant current shock democracy needs to absorb is the digital revolution, which is well on its way. It translates the democratic discourse into the environment of social media and digital platforms that is in many ways different from the habitual infosphere dominated by mass media that proved so conductive to liberal democracy's ascent. One prominent problem is misinformation and disinformation that may exploit the bounds of human rationality. The next chapter will examine their threat more closely.

Conclusion

As we have seen, there is no feasible way of aggregating individual preferences that projects the neoclassical rationality to the social level while paying deference to the citizens' sovereignty. In short, "general will" can either be rational or be democratic, but it cannot be both. Fortunately, the principal flaws of democratic collective choice—such as the possibility of cycles and strategic voting—are not necessarily of overwhelming practical significance. Still, democracy's performance depends on whether the wisdom of crowds can be expected to emerge from the mess of individual political choices. In this context, it is worrisome that all the arguments for the wisdom of crowds share the independence assumption, in one form or another, which makes them vulnerable to widespread cognitive biases. A biased populace can be expected to make suboptimal, sometimes even self-destructive, collective choices. Political irrationality, that is, a systematic propensity to make mistakes in one's political choices, needs to be heeded as a potentially grave danger to democracy's performance and to its very survival. The study of behavioral political economy is thus of prime importance.

Where do these findings leave us? What they emphatically do *not* imply is that democracy is generally unsustainable or even impossible. After all, the last couple of centuries offer plentiful evidence that suggests otherwise. Modern democracy's founders strived to make the democratic order resilient. Still, the equilibrium maintained by the institutional devices of liberal democracy may be surprisingly fragile. There is no unequivocal *a priori* reason why this habitual configuration of democratic political institutions must deliver performance superior to other regimes. Everything depends on the specific circumstances—primarily institutional and technological ones. Thus, the historical success of liberal democracy provides no guarantee that they will continue to serve us equally well. The challenges associated with the ascent of the digital age may prove overwhelming. The unprecedented surge of mis- and disinformation on digital platforms is one of the warning signs.

Notes

1 Mild and well-substantiated requirements, such as a minimum voting age, need not be counted as violations of inclusivity.
2 Perhaps unsurprisingly, the proper delimitation of the political sphere is contested (Dufek, 2018).

3 Even among the scholars who champion democracy, few subscribe to a purely proceduralist view that democracy is desirable independent of its performance. The real controversy in the democratic theory is whether democracy's value is *merely* instrumental or *also* instrumental (cf. Brennan, 2016, chap. 1).

4 Arrow (1963, p. 23) uses the concept of *social welfare function*, which already subsumes the assumptions that the social preference ordering must be complete and transitive. I shall avoid the term and elaborate on these assumptions explicitly.

5 In case you wonder whether this makes the resulting social preferences integrated, *stability* is implied by the assumption that the individual preferences used as input are stable, and *invariance* follows from the implicit "one world" assumption discussed above.

6 Gibbard-Satterthwaite theorem, which demonstrates impossibility of voting procedures immune to strategic behavior—unless it is dictatorial or limited to collective decisions with only two possible outcomes—is closely related to Arrow's Impossibility Theorem (Blin and Satterthwaite, 1978).

7 In his original treatment, Arrow (1963, p. 28) connects citizen's sovereignty explicitly with his condition that the social welfare function must not be imposed—that is, no individual preference ordering can be considered taboo—here covered as (4) unrestricted domain.

8 If there are only two alternatives, majority rule represents the system with all the desirable features. However, this is a weak comfort given the complexities of the actual politics as the process of narrowing down the alternatives until just two are left on the table is fraught with difficulties: as we have seen on the case of Condorcet's Paradox, the issue of agenda setting is particularly salient among them. Once the last two candidates are left standing, for instance, much of the damage may already have been done.

9 Note that this endows the collective choice with a predictive dimension. In the epistemic context, majority choice can be understood as a tool of prediction with respect to the instrumentally correct solutions to society's problems (cf. Landemore, 2012, pp. 146–147).

10 It is worth noting that the number of knowledgeable voters cannot be too small relative to the whole electorate as Landemore (2012, pp. 159–160) points out. In such a case, the knowers' chance of being pivotal in the election would be meagre.

11 What if the voters do not see the instrumental benefit in being pivotal in the election but in strengthening their preferred candidate's or party's mandate (Mackie, 2012)? As Caplan (2012, p. 332) observes: "The pivotalist model focuses on a very small probability of making a substantial difference; the contributory model focuses on a substantial probability of making a very small difference." In short, the inverse relationship between p and B holds also in this context with the highly probable impact of a single vote on "boosting the mandate" bringing a negligible benefit.

12 Note that the stratagems do not pose as "either-or" explanations: some voters may be irrational while others are driven by civic duty and yet others by altruism, or all the motives may contribute to a single voter's decision to participate.

Bibliography

Acemoglu, D. *et al.* (2019) 'Democracy Does Cause Growth', *Journal of Political Economy*, 127(1), pp. 47–100. doi:10.1086/700936.

Achen, C.H. and Bartels, L.M. (2016) *Democracy for Realists: Why Elections Do Not Produce Responsive Government*. Princeton: Princeton University Press.

Althaus, S.L. (2003) *Collective Preferences in Democratic Politics: Opinion Surveys and the Will of the People*. Cambridge: Cambridge University Press.

Arrow, K.J. (1963) *Social Choice and Individual Values*. Second edition. New Haven: Yale University Press.

Black, D. (1958) *The Theory of Committees and Elections*. Dordrecht: Kluwer Academic Publishers.

Blais, A. (2000) *To Vote Or Not to Vote? The Merits and Limits of Rational Choice Theory*. Pittsburgh: University of Pittsburgh Press.

Blin, J.-M. and Satterthwaite, M.A. (1978) 'Individual Decisions and Group Decisions', *Journal of Public Economics*, 10(2), pp. 247–267. doi:10.1016/0047-2727(78)90037-3.

Boyer, P. and Petersen, M.B. (2018) 'Folk-economic Beliefs: An Evolutionary Cognitive Model', *Behavioral and Brain Sciences*, 41, pp. 1–65. doi:10.1017/S0140525X17001960.

Brennan, G. and Lomasky, L. (1997) *Democracy and Decision: The Pure Theory of Electoral Preference*. Cambridge: Cambridge University Press.

Brennan, J. (2016) *Against Democracy*. Princeton: Princeton University Press.

Caplan, B. (2008) *The Myth of the Rational Voter: Why Democracies Choose Bad Policies*. New edition. Princeton: Princeton University Press.

Caplan, B. (2009) 'Majorities Against Utility: Implications of the Failure of the Miracle of Aggregation', *Social Philosophy and Policy*, 26(1), pp. 198–211. doi:10.1017/S0265052509090086.

Caplan, B. (2012) 'The Myth of the Rational Voter and Political Theory', in Landemore, H. and Elster, J. (eds) *Collective Wisdom: Principles and Mechanisms*. Cambridge; New York: Cambridge University Press, pp. 319–337.

Christiano, T. (2011) 'An Instrumental Argument for a Human Right to Democracy: An Instrumental Argument for a Human Right to Democracy', *Philosophy & Public Affairs*, 39(2), pp. 142–176. doi:10.1111/j.1088-4963.2011.01204.x.

Conly, S. (2012) *Against Autonomy: Justifying Coercive Paternalism*. Cambridge: Cambridge University Press.

Dafoe, A., Oneal, J.R. and Russett, B. (2013) 'The Democratic Peace: Weighing the Evidence and Cautious Inference', *International Studies Quarterly*, 57(1), pp. 201–214. doi:10.1111/isqu.12055.

Dasgupta, P. and Maskin, E. (2008) 'On the Robustness of Majority Rule', *Journal of the European Economic Association*, 6(5), pp. 949–973. doi:10.1162/JEEA.2008.6.5.949.

Dowding, K. (2005) 'Is it Rational to Vote? Five Types of Answer and a Suggestion', *The British Journal of Politics and International Relations*, 7(3), pp. 442–459. doi:10.1111/j.1467-856X.2005.00188.x.

Downs, A. (1957) *An Economic Theory of Democracy*. First edition. Boston: Harper and Row.

Dufek, P. (2018) 'Democracy as Intellectual Taste? Pluralism in Democratic Theory', *Critical Review*, 30(3–4), pp. 219–255. doi:10.1080/08913811.2018.1560669.

Dufek, P. and Holzer, J. (2013) 'Democratisation of Democracy? On the Discontinuity Between Empirical and Normative Theories of Democracy', *Representation*, 49(2), pp. 117–134. doi:10.1080/00344893.2013.816189.

Elster, J. (2008) *Reason and Rationality*. Translated by S. Rendall. Princeton University Press.

Estlund, D.M. (2008) *Democratic Authority: A Philosophical Framework*. Princeton: Princeton University Press.

Feddersen, T., Gailmard, S. and Sandroni, A. (2009) 'Moral Bias in Large Elections: Theory and Experimental Evidence', *American Political Science Review*, 103(2), pp. 175–192. doi:10.1017/S0003055409090224.

Feldman, A.M. and Serrano, R. (2005) *Welfare Economics and Social Choice Theory*. Second edition. New York: Springer.

Gelman, A., Silver, N. and Edlin, A. (2012) 'What Is the Probability Your Vote Will Make a Difference?', *Economic Inquiry*, 50(2), pp. 321–326. doi:10.1111/j.1465-7295.2010.00272.x.

Goodin, R.E. and Spiekermann, K. (2018) *An Epistemic Theory of Democracy*. Oxford: Oxford University Press.

Graeber, D. (2011) *Debt: The First 5,000 Years*. Hoboken: Melville House.

Green, D.P. and Shapiro, I. (1994) *Pathologies of Rational Choice Theory: A Critique of Applications in Political Science*. New Haven: Yale University Press.

Grofman, B., Owen, G. and Feld, S.L. (1983) 'Thirteen Theorems in Search of the Truth', *Theory and Decision*, 15(3), pp. 261–278. doi:10.1007/BF00125672.

Hayek, F.A. (1945) 'The Use of Knowledge in Society', *The American Economic Review*, 35(4), pp. 519–530.

Hillman, A.L. (2010) 'Expressive Behavior in Economics and Politics', *European Journal of Political Economy*, 26(4), pp. 403–418. doi:10.1016/j.ejpoleco.2010.06.004.

Hong, L. and Page, S.E. (2004) 'Groups of Diverse Problem Solvers Can Outperform Groups of High-Ability Problem Solvers', *Proceedings of the National Academy of Sciences of the United States of America*, 101(46), pp. 16385–16389. doi:10.1073/pnas.0403723101.

Jacobs, A.J. (2018) *Thanks A Thousand: A Gratitude Journey*. New York: Simon & Schuster.

Jones, G. (2020) *10% Less Democracy: Why You Should Trust Elites a Little More and the Masses a Little Less*. Stanford: Stanford University Press.

Kinder, D.R. and Kiewiet, D.R. (1981) 'Sociotropic Politics: The American Case', *British Journal of Political Science*, 11(2), pp. 129–161.

Landemore, H. (2012) *Democratic Reason: Politics, Collective Intelligence, and the Rule of the Many*. Princeton: Princeton University Press.

Landemore, H. (2014) 'Yes, We Can (Make It Up on Volume): Answers to Critics', *Critical Review*, 26(1–2), pp. 184–237. doi:10.1080/08913811.2014.940780.

Landemore, H. (2020) *Open Democracy: Reinventing Popular Rule for the Twenty-First Century*. Princeton: Princeton University Press.

Landemore, H. and Page, S.E. (2015) 'Deliberation and Disagreement: Problem Solving, Prediction, and Positive Dissensus', *Politics, Philosophy & Economics*, 14(3), pp. 229–254. doi:10.1177/1470594X14544284.

Lazear, E.P. (2000) 'Economic Imperialism', *The Quarterly Journal of Economics*, 115(1), pp. 99–146. doi:10.2307/2586936.

Lepoutre, M. (2020) 'Democratic Group Cognition', *Philosophy & Public Affairs*, 48(1), pp. 40–78. doi:10.1111/papa.12157.

Levitsky, S. and Ziblatt, D. (2018) *How Democracies Die*. First edition. New York: Crown.

Lucas, G. and Tasić, S. (2015) 'Behavioral Public Choice and the Law', *West Virginia Law Review*, 118, pp. 199–266.

Mackie, G. (2012) 'Rational Ignorance and Beyond', in Landemore, H. and Elster, J. (eds) *Collective Wisdom: Principles and Mechanisms*. Cambridge; New York: Cambridge University Press, pp. 290–318.

Mas-Colell, A., Whinston, M.D. and Green, J.R. (1995) *Microeconomic Theory*. First edition. New York: Oxford University Press.

Mueller, D.C. (2003) *Public Choice III*. Third edition. Cambridge; New York: Cambridge University Press.

Mulligan, C.B. and Hunter, C.G. (2003) 'The Empirical Frequency of a Pivotal Vote', *Public Choice*, 116(1), pp. 31–54. doi:10.1023/A:1024244329828.

Nordhaus, W.D. (2013) *The Climate Casino: Risk, Uncertainty, and Economics for a Warming World*. New Haven: Yale University Press.

Olson, M. (1971) *The Logic of Collective Action: Public Goods and the Theory of Groups, Second printing with new preface and appendix*. Revised edition. Cambridge, MA: Harvard University Press.

Page, S.E. (2008) *The Difference: How the Power of Diversity Creates Better Groups, Firms, Schools, and Societies*. Princeton: Princeton University Press.

Petersen, M.B. (2015) 'Evolutionary Political Psychology: On the Origin and Structure of Heuristics and Biases in Politics: Evolutionary Political Psychology', *Political Psychology*, 36, pp. 45–78. doi:10.1111/pops.12237.

Posner, E.A. and Weyl, E.G. (2018) *Radical Markets: Uprooting Capitalism and Democracy for a Just Society*. Princeton: Princeton University Press.

Riker, W.H. and Ordeshook, P.C. (1968) 'A Theory of the Calculus of Voting', *American Political Science Review*, 62(1), pp. 25–42. doi:10.1017/S000305540011562X.

Rizzo, M.J. and Whitman, G. (2019) *Escaping Paternalism: Rationality, Behavioral Economics, and Public Policy*. Cambridge; New York: Cambridge University Press.

Rubin, P.H. (2003) 'Folk Economics', *Southern Economic Journal*, 70(1), pp. 157–171.

Sandel, M.J. (2020) *The Tyranny of Merit: What's Become of the Common Good?* First edition. New York: Farrar, Straus and Giroux.

Sen, A. (2000) *Development as Freedom*. New York: Anchor Books.

Sen, A. (2017) *Collective Choice and Social Welfare*. New York: Penguin Random House.

Singer, D.J. (2019) 'Diversity, Not Randomness, Trumps Ability', *Philosophy of Science*, 86(1), pp. 178–191. doi:10.1086/701074.

Slovic, P. *et al.* (2007) 'The Affect Heuristic', *European Journal of Operational Research*, 177(3), pp. 1333–1352. doi:10.1016/j.ejor.2005.04.006.

Somin, I. (2013) *Democracy and Political Ignorance*. Redwood City: Stanford University Press.

Sugden, R. (2018) *The Community of Advantage: A Behavioural Economist's Defence of the Market*. New York: Oxford University Press.

Surowiecki, J. (2004) *The Wisdom of Crowds*. New York: Anchor Books.

Thaler, R.H. (2015) *Misbehaving: The Making of Behavioral Economics*. Kindle edition. New York: W.W. Norton & Company.

Thompson, A. (2014) 'Does Diversity Trump Ability?', *Notices of the American Mathematical Society*, 61(09), p. 1024. doi:10.1090/noti1163.

Vermeule, A. (2012) 'Collective Wisdom and Institutional Design', in Landemore, H. and Elster, J. (eds) *Collective Wisdom: Principles and Mechanisms*. Cambridge; New York: Cambridge University Press, pp. 338–367.

3   The Republic of Misinformation

The previous chapters have examined the role of rationality and its bounds in analyzing democracy's epistemic and instrumental promise. An especially salient aspect of the conundrum is that democratic citizens find themselves in a situation that does not encourage investment in gathering political information and unbiased assessment thereof. Given the arguments that uphold the epistemic virtues of democracy—often advertised under the label of the wisdom of crowds—hinge on the assumption that citizens' mistakes in assessing alternatives subject to collective choice are random, the latter problem appears especially bothersome.

We have also seen that neoclassical irrationality makes the agents vulnerable to exploitation. Chapters 1 and 2 have demonstrated this phenomenon on agenda-setting when a third party can take advantage of the shortcomings of people's rationality. Still, the scope of my attention has been heretofore limited to the problems of ignorance and irrationality concerning *information*. Down's analysis of democracy that I have discussed in some detail even explicitly assumes that no false information exists (Downs, 1957, p. 46). However, citizens' beliefs decisive for their democratic choice are increasingly shaped in an environment highly saturated by *misinformation* or even *disinformation*.[1] Fanciful claims about Donald Trump's struggle with sinister "deep state"—a cabal that prevents the people from legitimately exercising their political will and even engages in horrendous crimes including pedophilia—gave rise to QAnon conspiracy movement with millions of followers threatening the peaceful transition of power in the US. Extravagant theories about the origin, properties, and cures of COVID-19 proved at least equally damaging when they hindered an effective collective response to the greatest public health emergency in a century. How should these phenomena be assessed through the lens of behavioral political economy and democratic theory?

To explore whether disinformation is becoming potent enough to disturb the equilibrium in which the liberal democratic regimes operate, I shall consider a particular species of online disinformation which became renowned as *fake news*, that is, deliberately false reports disguised as news (cf. Fallis and Mathiesen, 2019). While fabricated reports are as old as the news industry itself, since the *annus horribilis* of 2016, fake news has risen to prominence among

DOI: 10.4324/9781003274988-4

public concerns. The extent of its media coverage and the intensity of scholarly debates surrounding it suggest that it became perceived as a threat to the established political order, perhaps even a harbinger of a brand new "post-truth situation" (Vacura, 2019). Fake news' current incarnation has been spawned by the digital revolution that transformed—and keeps transforming—the epistemic situation of every society on Earth: it relies on advanced information technologies as a mode of transmission, and its content is often openly political (Lazer *et al.*, 2018; Grinberg *et al.*, 2019). Some studies suggest that false information spreads through social media, such as Facebook or Twitter, as fast as or even faster than true information (Vosoughi, Roy and Aral, 2018). Many fear that the public not only views and shares it but also believes it with enough force to sway the electoral outcomes.

However, is fake news potent enough to upset the democratic equilibrium of liberal democracy? Can it unleash the powers of our political irrationality to the extent that the democratic government in its habitual forms will no longer be viable? Given the dynamics of the recent political developments in many countries, these questions need to be addressed urgently.

So far, the proposed answers were most frequently built around the assumption that the public consists of passive victims of manipulation, whose cognitive biases are being exploited by unscrupulous deceivers for political or monetary gains. In other words, the mainstream explanations of the democratic crisis rely on the hypothesis that the bounds of their rationality trigger democratic citizens' politically irrational choices. I shall call this explanation *the Victim Narrative*. While it may be correct—or mostly correct since we are not dealing with an either/or situation—it does not represent the only possible explanation of the fake news menace. In Chapter 2, I have set bounded rationality apart from rational irrationality. The context of fake news will now enable me to highlight the substantive difference between these two views on the sources of political irrationality. The Victim Narrative sees the public as passive sufferers who are at the mercy of their cognitive limitations. In contrast, rational irrationality-based explanation preserves the public's agency and examines the incentives that motivate people to *choose* political irrationality. Building on a concise analysis by Dan Kahan (2017a, 2017b), I shall suggest a model of the fake news exchange that considers its consumers as rational opportunists who pursue non-epistemic goals, such as signaling their loyalty to an in-group. The main emphasis of this alternative model is on the implications of the social embeddedness of fake news exchange, especially on the prevalence of motivated, rather than epistemically rational, reasoning. As we shall see, rational irrationality is possibly more harmful to liberal democracy than bounded rationality. In addition to undermining the independence assumption of the wisdom of crowds, rational irrationality also threatens its sincerity assumption leading a democratic citizen to embrace beliefs and policies for reasons of signaling in-group allegiance, not for the sake of their substantive merit.

Yet more importantly, the difference between bounded rationality and rational irrationality also matters for how the democratic crisis should be counteracted. As Chapter 2 has suggested, institutional reform may well be necessary to enable democracy's adaptation to digital revolution. In this context, the Victim Narrative often motivates the acceptance of paternalist avenues toward alleviating the misinformation problem. The public is to be helped by a benevolent third-party intervention that will train its members to deliver the proper cognitive response to fake news or diminish their exposure to it. However, I shall argue that the mainstream policy proposals cannot be expected to save the day as far as the fake news exchange is driven by rational irrationality. Unfortunately, the policymakers' prospects to subjugate the tide of disinformation may not be quite as bright as painted by the Victim Narrative, implying the need for a more radical rethinking of democracies' institutional design.

The Victim Narrative

As is the case with any concept that turns into a buzzword, definition of fake news and its explanatory value is contested (European Commission, 2018). One source of confusion is that the label "fake news" has been freely employed to discredit uncomfortable reports independent of their veracity (Levi, 2018). Even if we ignore this kind of frivolous name-calling and limit our attention to fake news as a specific literary genre, it may remain too broad, diluted by many innocuous cases, such as news satire or native advertising (cf. Tandoc, Lim and Ling, 2018).

However, there is an emerging consensus regarding the differences between harmless news imitations and the truly subversive kind. The prominent studies in the field increasingly turn their attention from individual instances of fabricated pseudo-news to the process of their serial production and dissemination: "The attribution of 'fakeness' is (…) not at the level of the story but at that of the publisher" (Grinberg *et al.*, 2019, p. 374). With this more process-oriented approach, three telltale signs of the "actual" fake news have been asserted (Egelhofer and Lecheler, 2019, p. 99):

1 Low facticity: the report is fabricated or misleading.
2 Journalistic format: the report is structured to correspond with actual news in form.
3 Intention to deceive: the report's producers knowingly strive to deceive and manipulate their audience (i.e., fake news represents a species of disinformation).

Although a full-fledged theory to explain fake news' potential to disturb the democratic equilibrium is still in its nascent phase, these definitional efforts reveal the extent of the discourse's preoccupation with fake news producers. The producers share the center focus with technological enablers of their growing success, the digital platforms. In contrast, consumers' role is assumed to be fairly passive. True, suppliers must find an audience willing to click, read, and spread the message further. However, the public tends to be portrayed not

Figure 3.1 Fake news exchange according to the Victim Narrative.

as accomplices but as victims of deception. So, as the mainstream story goes, democratic crisis results from the truth-seeking citizens being manipulated by malicious deceivers who abuse the opportunities presented by the ongoing transition of democratic discourse into the digital sphere to exploit and misguide the public.

This *Victim Narrative* implies a model of the fake news exchange as an interaction among a Deceiver, who produces fake news, an Enabler, who allows the spreading of the message and locates a suitable audience, and a Victim who is tricked into mistaking fake news for actual news (Figure 3.1).

The Deceiver can be portrayed as controlling an online outlet that offers fabricated or misleading information masquerading as news. In line with the emerging mainstream definition of fake news, they deceive intentionally and maliciously. They might be led by ideological reasons and strive to achieve a political change. However, advertising revenues generated by the traffic on their webpage represent an equally probable motive. In that case, posting fake news just happens to be instrumental to money-making (Allcott and Gentzkow, 2017; Gelfert, 2018). Be that as it may, the Deceiver will strive to achieve a wide circulation of the noxious content. To increase the chance of success, the Deceiver may parasitize the existing news brands by mimicking their design and even domain. Minimizing outright fabrication and mixing fake news with other content can be an attractive strategy too (Bakir and McStay, 2018). It is also increasingly simple for the Deceiver to automatize or semi-automatize the sharing using bots or "cyborgs" (Grinberg *et al.*, 2019). The maliciousness of these actions lies in persuading the victims to establish erroneous beliefs about politically relevant facts.

Still, no degree of the Deceiver's sophistication can explain the recent fake news emergency on its own. If the democratic equilibrium in advanced liberal democracies were fragile enough to be shattered by a band of clever disinformers, democracy would never have taken root, let alone survived and conquered large swaths of the world. Thus, we need to contemplate that it has been the traditional news dissemination methods with their numerous gatekeepers and crude audience targeting that kept fake news at bay. The most probable key to its ascent is cheap, accurate, and largely autonomous dissemination among the intended addressees. In short, the upsurge in the subversive impact of fabricated information on the democratic process can be understood only after pairing the Deceiver's efforts with the Enabler's reproduction and amplification capabilities. Fake news owes its viral potential to the digital information revolution and social media above all. Social media platforms, such as Facebook or Twitter, provide the catalyst necessary for turning fake news into a scourge capable of swinging an election or a referendum: "we now find ourselves in an informational environment where technology enables psychometric targeting, information floods, and filter bubbles (…)" (Levi, 2018, p. 236). Spreading the message and targeting the right audience have become exponentially less costly with easy sharing and networked online communities doing most of the work for the Deceiver.

Social media represent an ideal carrier of fake news due to their employment of individualized content optimization. Their interface is finetuned to maximize user engagement, that is, to keep as many people as possible watching, clicking, liking, sharing, or commenting for as long as possible. Given the volume of readily available information, this can only be achieved by carefully selecting the content presented to a particular user based on their observed past behavior (liking, sharing, click-through). The selection of content is managed through algorithmic filtering. Hence, the newsfeed becomes *the Daily Me*, that is, a personalized information source composed of content that closely reflects the user's revealed preferences (Sunstein, 2017). The purpose of the Daily Me is, of course, to maximize the platform's revenue generated by ads or sponsored links, striving against the constraint of the user's available attention.

The Victim Narrative's complaint against social media is that their efforts to maximize user engagement trigger the emergence of epistemic bubbles that discreetly filter out the views and facts that challenge the users' beliefs and create an illusion of consensus.[2] Epistemic bubbles exacerbate the dangers of group polarization and create an opportunity for fake news to thrive. Essentially, the Deceiver is piggybacking on the Enabler's business model; epistemic bubbles represent an ideal environment for misinformation cascades in which content is shared and liked due to the perceived endorsement by online peers and escapes independent verification (Rini, 2017; Sunstein, 2017). According to one prominent study, "homogeneous social networks (…) reduce tolerance for alternative views, amplify attitudinal polarization, boost the likelihood of accepting ideologically compatible news, and increase closure to new information" (Lazer *et al.*, 2018, p. 1095).

Finally, the Victim. As already observed, the Victim Narrative considers the public to be passive recipients of whatever content happens to land on their newsfeed. They care for the truth but cannot discern it. Their epistemic vulnerability is exploited by the Deceiver, who relies on social media's sophisticated content optimization techniques. When false beliefs about the facts become widespread among the public, democracy's epistemic and instrumental performance suffers.

Indeed, it is essential for the Victim Narrative that fake news shifts the public's beliefs in a politically impactful manner. Otherwise, its suggested link between fake news and democratic crisis would break. Nevertheless, many successful fake news stories do not appear particularly sophisticated (Gilbert, 2019). Should we not be more skeptical regarding their persuasive power? Are the people indeed so easily manipulated? The Victim Narrative needs to highlight the Victim's epistemic vulnerability and explain its sources. In doing so, it reveals its embeddedness in the behavioral economics' perspective on human behavior.

Notably, the Victim Narrative appears dysfunctional from the neoclassical perspective. One can attempt to explain the success of fake news based on information asymmetry between news producers and news consumers—after all, there would never be any news exchange if the providers were not presumed to possess an information advantage over the recipients. But this explanatory strategy will fail unless consumers' irrationalities are introduced into the model. Let me show why.

If the prospective parties in exchange know they do not have well-aligned interests, information asymmetry undermines their mutual trust, as far as they cannot rely on credibility-enhancing mechanisms, such as reputation tracking (Akerlof, 1970). In short, a situation of information asymmetry dictates "epistemic vigilance" (Sperber *et al.*, 2010). The more spectacular the claim made by a news producer, the more unshakable evidence needs to support it, and the more substantial reputational bet needs to hinge on its veracity. Suppose the producer does not have any valuable reputation contingent on their truthfulness. In that case, they will be strongly tempted to fabricate information without examining the facts to reduce the production costs or to make up spectacular claims likely to catch the audience's eye. Therefore, reports based on uncertain motivations, informational advantages, and no credible reputational signal are unworthy of attention, let alone trust (cf. Little, 2018). Fake news producers neither back their often-outlandish claims with proofs nor provide a credible reputational signal. Therefore, a rational news consumer cannot trust them.

Accordingly, the Victim Narrative takes a behaviorally informed perspective on the fake news exchange. While fake news would not mislead a neoclassically rational agent, boundedly rational people who are prone to systematic mistakes may well be susceptible to its appeal. In other words, it is our biases in information processing and attention allocation that make us vulnerable. As Gelfert (2018, p. 84) puts it, fake news "manipulates the audience's cognitive processes."

Many empirically documented failures of rationality can be summoned to fortify the Victim Narrative's foundations (Britt *et al.*, 2019). However, the most frequently mentioned cause of the human epistemic vulnerability is the *confirmation bias*, that is, a propensity to preferably search and believe information that aligns with our preexisting beliefs while being asymmetrically skeptical toward the opposing information (Sunstein, 2017; Gelfert, 2018; McIntyre, 2018). Under its influence, people tend to verify their views rather than testing them and, by extension, find others more credible if they share the same beliefs than if they challenge them. For instance, suppose Rob believes that nuclear energy must be prohibited while Martha favors expanding its production. If they debate the issue, epistemic rationality demands that both Rob and Martha update their beliefs based on an unbiased evaluation of the available evidence.

However, confirmation bias may easily preclude any such development. Rob googles "dangers of nuclear energy" and among the many thousands of results obtained he selects the alarmist ones, perhaps dismissing the authors of less grim reports as nuclear industry shills. At the same time, Martha searches for "benefits of nuclear energy" and finds the most cornucopian accounts most credible. The discussion leads nowhere, and both participants may leave it with an even greater confidence in their original views' correctness.

It is not hard to see how confirmation bias could be bolstered by social media's personalized epistemic bubbles, which automatically filter the world based on our preferences to an unparalleled extent. Relying on the Enabler's targeting abilities, the Deceiver can freely feed conservative stories to people with conservative beliefs and progressive stories to progressives. Unconstrained by facts, quality standards, or ethical principles, the narrative can always be finetuned to fit and further cement the divergent perceptions of competing cultural groups. Where actual news frequently reminds people that they live in a world of shared factual reality, fake news is free to create imaginary worlds that affirm various audiences' prejudice. As Downs (1957, p. 139) presciently warns: "whether democracy can lead to stable government depends upon whether the mass of voters is centrally conglomerated, or lumped at the extremes with low density in the center; only in the former case will democracy really work." Alas, under the influence of the Deceiver, the perceptions of the different cultural groups may grow ever more detached from each other until the critical degree of polarization is reached and the current democratic equilibrium disintegrates.

To summarize, the Victim Narrative views the representative democratic citizen as a character who seeks the truth but gets tripped by his biases. The predictable nature of the Victim's epistemic vulnerability, exemplified by the confirmation bias, enables the Deceiver to achieve financial or political gain by spreading predictably believable falsehoods. Accordingly, it has been suggested that fake news spreads false beliefs "by manipulating their consumers' emotions and tapping into deeply held partisan beliefs" (Gelfert, 2018, p. 93). Reliance on the Enabler's capabilities allows the Deceiver to precisely target the message and keep the dissemination costs low. Social media's networked nature makes this exceptionally easy, especially as the Victim who falls for fake news is likely to contribute to their community transmission through likes, shares, and comments. As a result, democracy's epistemic performance falters. Individual voters' perspectives become ever more precisely aligned with one of the several incompatible and mutually isolated worldviews. In this context, let us note that the independence assumption behind the wisdom of crowds does not require the voters to form their views independent of reality but independent of each other (Goodin and Spiekermann, 2018). Perversely, fake news cuts people's ties to reality and bolsters their ties to others. The more precisely one's views on policy issues can be predicted based solely on one's political allegiance, the lesser epistemic advantage stems from large numbers. If we care about democracy's long-term sustainability, growing polarization should worry us greatly (Klein, 2020).

A Question of Agency

Admittedly, the Victim Narrative offers a compelling explanation of democracy's misfortunes in the digital age. However, upon closer inspection, not each of its foundational claims regarding the Victim's character and behavior is equally persuasive. While the presence of democratic citizens' political irrationality is required to explain why fake news may shatter the democratic equilibrium, we must beware of underestimating public's agency. After all, the question of human behavioral adaptiveness has emerged as particularly important in Chapter 1. The Victim Narrative suggests that fake news represents a danger to democracy because it manages to exploit the public's epistemic vulnerabilities. How far does the public's passivity reach, though?

In behavioral economics, cognitive biases are often described as unavoidable, emphasizing that even experts are not immune to them (e.g., Kahneman, 2011, chap. 30). Sometimes, they are compared to optical illusions (e.g., Thaler and Sunstein, 2021, chap. 1). However, we have already seen that their flexibility remains an open question; their elasticity vis-à-vis incentives and learning is far from settled. This is also apparent in the debate enveloping fake news. While the Victim Narrative literature agrees that limits to rationality are at the root of the public's plight, their plasticity remains controversial. The controversy is not inconsequential when it comes to policy implications. Can people learn how to defend themselves against disinformation or must third parties—such as the government—protect them from it?

Let me introduce the following terminology: where the victims of disinformation cannot increase their resistance to cognitive biases, I shall call them *gullible*; where they can learn debiasing techniques—such as new, more effective heuristics—I shall call them *naïve* until they have mastered them. Gullibility stems from the Victim's cognitive makeup and thus represents a universal, stable feature of behavior. Naivety poses a temporary challenge that will be resolved once our cognitive defense mechanisms adapt to the novel environment of the digital infosphere. In short, naivety can be unlearned; gullibility cannot.

Social media offer endless opportunities to get bamboozled. For a gullible person, the cornucopia of the available digital content exacerbates the influence of the immovable bounds of their rationality. As Hills (2019, p. 2) puts it: "The more rapidly that people can access, select, and reproduce preferred information, the more readily will that information reflect the cognitive biases of its users." If there are too many rabbit holes, one becomes destined to fall into some. Especially as the algorithms actively push the public toward them in their effort to "increase user engagement."

For a naïve person, however, there is also an opportunity to shape their rationality's bounds. Naivety does not stem from a built-in deficiency in one's epistemic vigilance but from the fact that adaptation to novel circumstances requires time and effort. The habitual cognitive strategies to deal with information selection are ineffective or even counterproductive if a person is transplanted into an information environment that follows a different set of rules. In short, one may be a keen reasoner in a familiar context and an utter dupe in an unfamiliar one. Successful behavioral adjustments are thus conditional on updating our cognitive defense mechanisms.

So, is the public gullible or naive? That, of course, is a difficult empirical question yet unsettled in the behavioral sciences. Nonetheless, few scholars appear ready to commit to a pure-gullibility-based explanation of the observed epistemic irrationality when it comes to fake news. Deliberate effort or willingness to engage in analytic thinking are routinely recognized as determinants of the ability to recognize fake news (Britt *et al.*, 2019; Bronstein *et al.*, 2019). A key role of learning has often been emphasized. For instance, McIntyre (2018, p. 95) considers the close resemblance between a newsfeed of the Daily Me and a traditional newspaper as one of the significant problems of fake news on social media. Despite the superficial similarity between the two information sources, the principles of their operation differ fundamentally. Cognitive strategies optimized for evaluating a newspaper's credibility fail when applied to the Daily Me because one cannot judge the quality of the content based on the medium through which one receives it but needs to track it toward the original source. However, McIntyre (2018) also believes that a relatively marginal adjustment of the cognitive strategies would resolve the issue. Following a simple checklist may suffice:

1. Look for copyright.
2. Verify from multiple sources.
3. Assess the credibility of the source (e.g., how long has it been around?).
4. Look for a publication date.
5. Assess the author's expertise with the subject.
6. Ask: does this match my prior knowledge?
7. Ask: does this seem realistic?

(McIntyre, 2018, p. 121)

The popularity of the naivety explanation suggests that the cause of the public's failure to discern the quality of sources and reliability of claims is perhaps less the fundamental limits to human rationality than a simple lack of effort in critical thinking or use of misplaced but malleable heuristics. If so, victimhood is hardly the public's fate but rather a path of least resistance. If it is indeed possible for the alleged Victim to flexibly respond to their predicament, the road toward the restoration of their agency seems open. If people can adjust to circumstances and adapt, learn, and consider the cost of their mistakes, it is too rash to ascribe the blame for the democratic crisis chiefly to the Deceiver's manipulation techniques projected through social media. The required explanation for democracy's current plight needs to be more complex and nuanced.

As we have seen, reference to cognitive biases enables the Victim Narrative to explain how the public can fall for the often ludicrous and easily debunkable fake news produced by obviously dubious sources. However, the Victim Narrative also employs a specific assumption about the Victim's motivation: one is not just an irrational agent but an irrational *truth-seeker* (cf. Kahan, 2017c). One's "search for truth" (Britt *et al.*, 2019, p. 99) fails on account of the exploitable gullibility or naivety that undermines it. When extended to the area of political choices, the Victim Narrative's truth-seekers are irrational if they form their beliefs in an epistemically suspect fashion.

However, as already suggested in Chapter 2, a potential problem with these explanations is that their perspective on rational behavior is relatively narrow in what they consider admissible goals. More broadly, rationality lies in finding the proper means to achieve our ends (see Chapter 1). Therefore, assessing the degree of an agent's rationality requires the observer to judge the agent's goal correctly. If such a judgment is faulty to start with, even a hyperrational agent ends up diagnosed as a fool. As our considerations of the paradox of voting and its implications have revealed, there usually exist little to no incentives to be rational in a political context. If political rationality is costly, it is rational to avoid it. The same holds for truth-seeking.

On the face of it, the claim that rationality and truth-seeking are separate phenomena appears uncontroversial. We scarcely view a person who starves to death while ensuring that their white shirt is indeed white as a paragon of rationality. From an evolutionary perspective, there is just one safe assumption about rationality: namely, its opportunism. For humans as beings shaped for eons by the biological and cultural evolution forming true beliefs about the state of the world simply cannot be the ultimate objective. Our bodies and minds have evolved to maximize fitness in the environment of evolutionary adaptation, and excessive truth-seeking is maladaptive (Mark, Marion and Hoffman, 2010). Even the "intellectualist" view of confirmation bias, which represents the Victim Narrative's prime example of how biases derail truth-seeking, appears incoherent in evolutionary terms:

> In particular, a defender of the intellectualist approach should accept the following three claims: (1) reason has a confirmation bias, (2) the confirmation bias makes it harder for reason to help the lone reasoner arrive at better beliefs and better decisions, and (3) the main function of reason is to arrive at better beliefs and better decisions.
>
> (Sperber and Mercier, 2017, p. 216)

Whatever psychological propensities that have spread broadly among humans— which is arguably the case of the confirmation bias—need to be perceived as adaptive, that is, increasing our fitness in the ancestral environment. However, understanding human reason as a tool for deriving true beliefs from the available evidence precludes any possibility of explaining how confirmation bias could have taken root. Perhaps the correct answer is that our reason serves less to derive true beliefs than to manage our social relations for the sake of successful cooperation. Accordingly, Sperber and Mercier (2017, p. 8) suggest confirmation bias would better be called *myside bias*. It remains a bias as far as it is considered from the perspective of truth-seeking. But it has an adaptive function since it enables one to play social games more effectively as it enhances one's position in any negotiation. By investing cognitive resources into supporting only our side of the story, we can make our case stronger than if we wasted effort on formulating a neutral view that could show us in unfavorable light.

Thus, there arises an intriguing possibility that fake news consumers—while *epistemically* irrational as far as disinformation influences their beliefs—are ultimately rational if *instrumental* rationality provides the benchmark. True, they seek the truth not quite as zealously as the defenders of democracy's epistemic virtues might prefer, but perhaps gullibility and naivety are less to blame than the Victim Narrative suggests. Let me consider the seemingly paradoxical concept of rational irrationality in more depth.

Proposed by Bryan Caplan (2000, 2008), rational irrationality seeks to highlight the possible tension between truth-seeking (epistemic rationality) and broader pragmatic concerns (instrumental rationality). It suggests that people converge toward neoclassical rationality where erroneous beliefs come costly but neglect it where erroneous beliefs are free or encouraged by the agents' non-epistemic interests. From its perspective, people tend to be more careful in evaluating available information and forming true beliefs where "the material costs of error" are high. Of course, being pivotal is one of the conditions for that. The aggregate costs of an erroneous collective decision may be horrendous. But for an individual, the cost of mistakes is primarily borne by other agents, and therefore one may rationally neglect them:

> [...] errors with drastic real-world repercussions can be cheap for the individual who makes them. How? When most or all of the cost of the error falls upon strangers. One person messes up, but other people live with the aftermath.
>
> (Caplan, 2008, p. 121)

Bounded rationality suggests biased reasoning is a passive response to triggers. From its perspective, naïve or gullible agents cannot help themselves when the right cognitive levers are pulled. In contrast, rational irrationality stresses that people actively—even if nonconsciously—optimize the degree of epistemic rationality in a forward-looking manner, assessing the expected costs and benefits. Despite this difference, rational irrationality is no "anti-behavioral" concept: its position in the theoretical apparatus of the behavioral political economy is actually quite prominent (Lucas and Tasić, 2015; Schnellenbach and Schubert, 2015). Rational irrationality does not claim that biases are infrequent or insignificant. It just predicts that they will be much more heavily present where the investment into rational information-gathering and information-processing is not worth making.

Specifically, what incentives can be expected to clash with truth-seeking? Caplan (2000, pp. 201–205) gives three examples. First, one may benefit from self-fulfilling positive illusions, the most famous example being the placebo effect. Second, "moral constraints" (such as "do not drink hard liquor") can create self-imposed limits on one's behavior and thus provide incentives for rationalizing one's way around them. Third, social pressure exists that leads one to conform with the signature beliefs of a social group if he wants to cooperate with its members without unnecessary friction. Elsewhere, Caplan (2008) also hints at the positive feelings—that is, intrinsic benefits—provided by certain beliefs: they trigger the rationally irrational voters' preference for "feel-good" policies.

In the following, I adopt Caplan's concept of rational irrationality with one important caveat. I put aside any intrinsic benefits irrational beliefs might provide and concentrate on social incentives: a variable most emphasized by the relevant psychological research.

Victims and Opportunists

The psychologist Dan Kahan (2017a, 2017b) suggests understanding fake news as a demand-driven phenomenon based on his research on politically motivated reasoning and "identity protective cognition," that is, the empirically demonstrated tendency to evaluate information not in the light of its reliability but of people's commitments to various competing social groups. Resonating with the core hypothesis of rational irrationality, reasoning in the politically loaded context tends to be unconstrained by epistemic objectives because—from an individual perspective—they are of low practical relevance. Does it truly matter whether an individual is right about the causes of climate change or about a political candidate's competence? In line with the logic of the paradox of voting, Kahan suggests otherwise. Since a single person's beliefs have a negligible influence on how large-scale social issues play out, their veracity is less important than concerns regarding one's social commitments.

Much of one's social capital can be saved or gained in relationships with family, friends, acquaintances, coworkers, or even strangers if one avoids confrontation of cherished views or engages in their active affirmation. In short, where the truth has few practical implications while the group membership has many, it is instrumentally rational for the people to deviate from truth-seeking for the sake of maintaining their identity and status among their peers (Kahan, 2015a). Reconsidering one's social identity in the light of new evidence promises few benefits given the practical unimportance of most political beliefs. At the same time, its expected costs are considerable: "failing to adopt the stance that signals who she is–whose side she is on–could have devastating consequences for a person's standing with others whose support is vital to her well-being, emotional and material" (Kahan, 2015b, p. 4). Therefore, Kahan's theory suggests that people opportunistically dismiss identity-threatening information and embrace identity-confirming information with little regard for its veracity. In short, they rationally choose to be irrational.

Still, one may object that such an assumption implies an unrealistic degree of "doublethink." It seems odd that people could desire certain beliefs despite being somehow aware that they are false (cf. Bennett and Friedman,

2008). And without knowing which of our beliefs are false, how else could we opportunistically decide to sideline them when acting upon them would cost us dearly? Evolutionary psychology proposes a solution to this problem. As in the case of "myside bias," it suggests that social interactions shape human reason to act as an advocate for one's cause. It searches for socially acceptable reasons that may justify our actions in others' eyes and maintain our positive reputation. Human reason is less a rational faculty than a rationalizing one. Our mind is compartmentalized—*modular*—and our conscious self has only a limited approach to whatever is going on beneath the surface (Kurzban, 2010; Carruthers, 2011). The actual causes of our actions remain hidden from us.

However, that is more of an opportunity than a hindrance from the individual perspective (Simler and Hanson, 2018). Agents who are fully aware of their motivations would need to lie every time they prefer to hide their intentions from others' prying eyes. For agents oblivious of their motivations, it is simpler to manage their public relations. The problem with outright lies is their cognitive cost. They require constant effort on the liars' side to avoid detection, such as keeping their story straight and telling everyone the same thing. Self-deception, enabled by the modular character of mind, is cognitively less demanding than lying. As Robert Trivers (2011, p. 3) puts it: "… we deceive ourselves the better to deceive others."

Thus, in the rational-irrationality-based model of fake news exchange (Figure 3.2), the prime mover of the democratic crisis is not the suppliers' manipulative schemes but rather the demand-side dynamics. The consumers find themselves locked in an interplay with other in-group members. In large-scale issues where one's voice is not pivotal, one's primary motivation is orthogonal to truth-seeking: here, people care about maintaining their social identity and managing their social status instead. Believing in human-caused climate change or a particular politician's competence may be just incompatible with

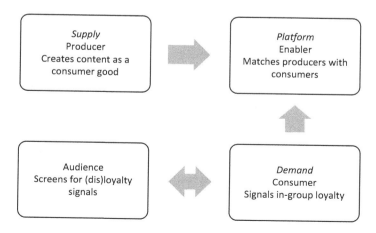

Figure 3.2 Fake news exchange with rationally irrational public.

belonging to a social group that equals a display of such beliefs to waving an enemy flag. If so, the looming threat of status loss has more painful practical implications for a person than a factual error. Therefore, the model of fake news exchange with a politically motivated public predicts that pragmatically insignificant beliefs adjust to the social expectations independent of the evidence available to support them (or a lack thereof).

Still, democratic equilibrium must be stable enough to handle a degree of belief conformity, right? It is not like people only started caring about their reputation recently. Quite to the contrary, it could be suggested that the modern liberal society characteristic for the advanced democracies enforces conformity much less than any preceding social formations did. However, this is where the technological element enters the equation. The world where the information seeped into people's minds through mass and legacy media under the elite gatekeepers' oversight witnessed an unprecedented spread of democracy. Now it is gone, however. Increasingly, democratic citizens filter their perceptions through digital platforms that do not follow the same principles of operation, as described above. Liberal democracy is resilient toward the manifestations of group cognition and conformity usual in the old information economy: "watch the TV, read the news, listen to the radio." But the solutions appropriate for this now antiquated information environment may not be sufficiently effective anymore.

Social media's algorithmic maximization of user engagement makes identity concerns particularly salient. While politically relevant information is, of course, available on Facebook or Twitter, these platforms are not optimized for its easy localization and disinterested assessment: quite the opposite, they strive to direct one's attention toward status considerations instead. Numbers of likes, shares, and followers can be used as precise quantitative measures to establish a social hierarchy in essentially any affinity group. Creating a post that is "merely informative" and ignoring the number of likes and shares it receives is nearly impossible for the ultrasocial *Homo sapiens* psyche adapted to obsess over reputation and status. And rightly so: social media de-anonymize the social exchange and hinder its compartmentalization that otherwise keeps family affairs, work affairs, and exchange relations neatly separated in modern social life. Increasingly, virtual interactions cannot be kept separate from the "real" ones. As an increasing share of personal relationships is established and managed online, the importance of maintaining the right kind of one's digital presence becomes ever more essential (Lieberman and Schroeder, 2020).

A critical aspect of the rational-irrationality-based model is the interaction between an individual (the Consumer) and their peers (the Audience). In Jeremy Bentham's famous Panopticon, a few guards—themselves unseen—can monitor many prisoners. Zygmunt Bauman (2000), who wanted to highlight the role celebrities play in the constant shifting of social norms, introduced an opposite concept of Synopticon where the many watch the few. Social media is different yet: here, everybody watches everybody. In this context, the model suggests that the Audience screens the Consumer for signs of (dis)loyalty. Those perceived loyal to the group's values get rewarded by a stronger position in their peer group; the disloyal get punished through reproach or ostracism. One may be called out, blocked, unfriended, or even "canceled" if their transgressions come to be considered severe enough to deserve coordinated retribution. These sanctions are not merely virtual. Being digitally unfriended and canceled increasingly leads to a tangible real-world loss of friends, social event invitations, jobs, and career prospects.

The Audience's vigilant, even punitive, approach based on the perceived beliefs is necessary for the model's coherence. Without it, the rationally irrational Consumer would lack incentives for careful belief management in identity-sensitive areas. However, why would the Audience bother to perform its monitoring duty? A possible answer is that humans have an innate propensity for "moralistic punishment" (Turchin, 2015). To escape the Hobbesian outcome where cooperation falls apart to a universally disastrous effect, humans establish norms of proper behavior and punish both the norm violators and those who neglect their duty to punish norm violators. How to recognize if wannabe members are reliable allies represents a fundamental problem that social groups must resolve. Because important characteristics of agents—such as the degree of in-group loyalty—are not directly observable, anyone can claim allegiance to any group that may currently benefit them and turn their coat once a more attractive alliance presents itself. Talk is cheap, and individuals have incentives to fake their conformity pretending to share the group's defining beliefs to gain an advantage in cooperation. Such dissimulation is not benign from the Audience's point of view: cooperation tends to be a sequential game where a degree of trust is necessary. Therefore, a rational Audience will screen the Consumer for credible signals of loyalty. Such a signal must be costly to produce and even costlier to fake.

From this perspective, promoting fake news is one possible method of generating such a loyalty signal (cf. Mercier, 2020, chap. 13). To see that, we need to remind ourselves about the specific nature of both fake news and social media used for its dissemination. Here, publicly professing a belief in the unbelievable is a credible proof of loyalty. Simler and Hanson (2018) use the following anecdote for illustration:

> Zhao Gao was a powerful man hungry for more power. One day he brought a deer to a meeting with the emperor and many top officials, calling the deer a "great horse." The emperor, who regarded Zhao Gao as a teacher and therefore trusted him completely, agreed that it was a horse—and many officials agreed as well. Others, however, remained silent or objected. This was how Zhao Gao flushed out his enemies. Soon after, he murdered all the officials who refused to call the deer a horse.
>
> (Simler and Hanson, 2018, p. 83)

In short, just about anyone can say that they believe something which sounds reasonable or probable. However, only true loyalists will publicly profess absurd beliefs for the sake of their team. By rejecting what is in plain sight, they can demonstrate their genuine commitment to the in-group by tarnishing their reputation with the outsiders. Because the true loyalists methodically burn bridges to outsiders, they can be expected never to break away from the group, and their value as allies is exceptionally high. Here, the trademark hyper-partisanship and extravagance of the fake news stories neatly fit the bill.

In contrast with the typically mundane actual news, fake news offers an opportunity to put one's loyalty badge on display. The innovative features of social media are of the essence here, again. Perhaps most importantly, they make it difficult to limit the audience to the in-group. In the "real" world, one can discreetly tell different people different things or modify the tone to fit the occasion. However, online exchanges are always potentially public and context-free. They are also searchable and remain forever on the record. Whatever a user posts can become general knowledge now or at any time in the future, making the mark on their reputation indelible. So, in the signaling game between the Consumer and the Audience, the veracity of the content one shares and likes matters less than its coherence with the in-groups' signature beliefs. True allies are supposed to show their colors ostentatiously and burn bridges to reconciliation with "the enemy." Fake news represents a convenient instrument for such loyalty signaling.

Do note that the success of signaling behavior hinges on the signal being legible for the Audience. I want my peers to think: "He is truly one of us. He shares our core values," not something like: "How can he be so stupid to believe such nonsense?" In other words, every group tends to establish a specific way in which the signals need to be coded to ensure their legibility. Therefore, it is unsurprising that fake news seems more prevalent in some groups than in others if the signaling hypothesis is correct. Indeed, a greater prevalence of expressed trust in fake news has been recorded on the political Right, where it correlates with lower trust in the legacy media. The political Left seems to have been more reluctant to embrace fake news (Grinberg *et al.,* 2019). The difference may owe to the distinct ways in which different cultural groups encode the loyalty signals. While right-wing loyalists prove their allegiance by sharing hyper-partisan fake news, left-wing loyalists may opt for inciting a Twitter mob to cancel a perceived traitor to the progressive cause. Just the coding of the signal is different, not its content.

In any case, it is immediately apparent that the group's "belief coordination" undermines the independence assumption of the wisdom of crowds. The better the within-group belief coordination, the lesser is the advantage for the collective decision-making that stems from inviting more group members to participate. In the extreme case of perfect in-group coordination, ten individuals selected from ten different groups would deliver the same epistemic performance as 10,000 individuals selected from these same groups. Worse yet, the widely distributed default cognitive biases provide convenient focal points for such coordination. The in-group bias makes it simpler to coordinate on an anti-immigration stance than for-immigration stance, the same holds for anti-trade versus pro-trade in the international setting. Due to status quo bias, NIMBY is more intuitively attractive than YIMBY. The examples could be multiplied.

To attract voter support, democratic politicians need to cater to the signature beliefs. If the signature beliefs serve a performative function of allegiance signaling rather than relate to what the voters consider the most pressing pragmatic issues, these dynamics undermine democracy's performance. The recent disaster of the COVID-19 pandemic illustrates the point at hand. Arguably, pandemic prevention is a matter of great practical importance for any democratic citizen. However, the limited say an individual has regarding what policies will be enacted to resolve the practical issue means that the collective choice may end up at the mercy of the second-order considerations of the particular beliefs' symbolic connotations. For example, should face masks be made compulsory? The practical issues of their effect on disease transmission can be overshadowed by concerns of what they may signify concerning the relative status of the competing social groups (cf. Uscinski *et al.,* 2020). To some extent, such dynamics are inevitable. However, fake news proved highly instrumental in feeding the fire of the partisan discord by readily supplying identity-aligned "facts" and using them to feed an interpretation in terms of fundamental values, such as liberty and solidarity, each of them being emphasized by some of the rival alliances. Be that as it may, the beliefs regarding mask-effectiveness ended up being elevated to signature beliefs, much to the collective detriment.

With growing polarization, the conformity pressure and the in-group belief homogeneity grow (Klein, 2020). Thus, also the sincerity assumption is endangered by politically motivated reasoning. Above, I have suggested that self-deception probably plays a vital role in the observed behavior's psychological underpinning. This means that the individuals who express their political preferences in a rational pursuit of their nonpolitical goals—that is, those who are rationally irrational—dissimulate their political preferences. Therefore, they undermine the validity of the sincerity assumption made by the arguments supporting the wisdom of crowds. If I advocate progressive taxation not because I genuinely want it but because my vote is not pivotal and I am motivated by status considerations, the consequences are similar to preference falsification in strategic voting (see Chapter 2). When voting strategically, I remain transfixed with a particular political outcome, at least. If I misrepresent my political preferences for nonpolitical reasons, I may entirely neglect the substance of the collective decision at hand. True, there is no external force in a secret ballot to prevent one from voting inconsistently with one's public utterances. However, such a move would be difficult to rationalize to maintain self-deception (Epley and Gilovich, 2016) and is generally not worth the trouble because one vote does not matter anyway. As Caplan (2008, p. 150) quips: "voting to raise your taxes by a thousand dollars when your probability of decisiveness is 1 in 100,000 has an expected cost of a penny."

One substantive implication of these dynamics is that we should expect a reluctant stance of the digital platforms toward taking steps to reign in disinformation. The social media platforms are profit-oriented and need to compete for the users' attention. If disinformation provided purely negative value to the public—as the Victim Narrative implies—a lukewarm attitude to its eradication would make little sense. Why let third-party parasites degrade your product in a way that leads to bad PR and attracts the regulators' unwanted attention? Would it be so costly and impractical to undertake steps to protect your clients from disinformers' exploitation? However, if fake news is a valuable consumer good, its elimination would diminish, not improve, the users' social media experience. In such a case, it is not hard to see why the platforms would eschew stepping into the editorial role and enforce quality standards which will inevitably elicit the users' discontent.

Also, note that as far as the Consumer–Audience interaction drives the fake news exchange, the influence of the fake news producers is diminished. The Victim Narrative preoccupies itself with the sinister fake news peddlers and their supposed uncanny ability to shift public opinion via social media's technological capabilities. However, to the extent public is politically motivated and engages in active status management, the Deceiver's influence must be considered more constrained. Gullible or naïve people can be systematically bamboozled to act against their self-interest; rationally irrational people cannot. As a result, disinformation lacks the ability to persuade the rationally irrational to switch sides in the political game with dire consequences for their social standing.

The model Producer responds to an open market niche in an entrepreneurial fashion: compared to the market for quality reporting, which is already saturated, the market with custom-made reports that disregard mainstream ethical constraints has lower barriers to entry and lower production costs. However, there are only two ways for fake news producers to succeed with the front lines of the "culture war" already drawn in many topics. The first possibility for the producer is to create the content in the topics with an already well-established partisan divide. A prominent fake news report about Pope Francis endorsing Donald Trump's bid for the presidency is an instance of this. In such a case, the rational irrationality model predicts no influence over political outcomes since the support for the prominent political candidates is pre-determined by social concerns. Fake news is thus reduced to an essentially harmless "infotainment." The second possibility is to work on the margin and provide a partisan twist to newly emerging topics where the group perceptions are not yet cemented. This strategy, instantiated by the COVID-19 political interpretations (including disinformation-based interpretations), presents a far greater danger for the democratic equilibrium (cf. Kahan *et al.,* 2017). Worryingly, it is perhaps also a more commercially attractive one because people seek novelty (Vosoughi, Roy and Aral, 2018).

Democracy contra Disinformation

The model of fake news exchange as driven by rational irrationality provides a coherent alternative to the Victim Narrative. Which of the models is better supported by evidence, though? The possibility of providing an answer is conditional on distinguishing motivated reasoning from biases, especially confirmation bias. Bénabou and Tirole (2016, pp. 144–146) suggest three "telltale markers" to recognize one from the other: (1) motivated beliefs are directed toward some end, while biases skew information processing in general; (2) biases tend to result from inattention or lack of effort, motivated reasoning does not: as a result, more cognitively sophisticated agents have a greater tendency toward it; and (3) challenging motivated beliefs provokes an emotional response because it threatens the motivated reasoner's purpose, challenging biases does not.

If we apply these markers in the case of fake news, the current evidence is admittedly inconclusive. On the one hand, it is uncontested that fake news is designed to resonate with political identities. The research of fake news outlets even suggests that "providing a partisan layer of interpretation" is a more important feature of their business model than outright confabulation (Mourão and Robertson, 2019, p. 14). This happens against a background of the already emotionally heated political debate in the digital space (Coe, Kenski and Rains, 2014). Also, the ideological alignment of news with their preexisting views matters more for heavy media users with more segregated social networks (Allcott and Gentzkow, 2017), suggesting that the people for whom the group identity is especially salient are perhaps more influenced. On the other hand, the hypothesis of greater sophistication of fake news consumers clashes with the available evidence, at least as far as competence can be reduced to analytic thinking (Pennycook and Rand, 2019). The more dogmatic and delusional people or generally the "reflexively open-minded" people, that is, those with a faulty "bullshit detector," appear to believe in fake news more frequently (Bronstein *et al.*, 2019; Pennycook and Rand, 2020).

To summarize, the use of fake news for partisan purposes and to fuel the emotional fire of the debate is coherent with the case for motivated reasoning; the lower performance of the professed fake news believers on some measures of cognitive sophistication contradicts it. There is still much ground to cover, however. The empirical papers show a relatively modest explanatory power of variance in analytical thinking and other traits with respect to belief in fake news. It also remains unclear if traits, such as reflexive open-mindedness, represent fixed cognitive characteristics, instead of learned behavior or even voluntarily chosen personal identity expressions.

Unfortunately, since the fake news exchange in both the Victim Narrative model and the rational-irrationality-based model may produce effects strong enough to disintegrate the democratic equilibrium, democratic societies cannot afford the luxury of waiting for a broader consensus on their relative explanatory power to emerge. Model uncertainty cannot shield us from making policy choices that will influence how detrimental digital disinformation ends up being for liberal democracy.

What difference does it make whether democratic citizens are boundedly rational or rationally irrational in their treatment of fake news? The policy implications depend on the causal mechanism that connects the fake news exchange to the democratic crisis. From the perspective of the Victim Narrative, the danger lies in citizens being deceived into basing their political judgments on false premises. In other words, it suggests that the pool of information from which the citizens draw guidance for their political choices gets polluted by misrepresentations of the empirical realities that succeed due to their ability to exploit the public's cognitive biases. The extent of the danger depends on the ratio of the correct versus incorrect information at the citizens' disposal and on their epistemic vulnerability that prevents them from adequately evaluating the reliability of various sources and rationally updating their beliefs.

With rationally irrational public, the story is more subtle. Given the wisdom of crowds perspective analyzed in Chapter 2, each citizen's epistemic rationality produces spillover effects in terms of marginally better collective choice. However, individuals lack private incentives to consider these spillovers, as we have seen. Especially where beliefs become badges of group identity, a straightforward cost-benefit calculus—even if nonconscious—leads the citizens to abandon a disinterested search for the truth for the sake of their other concerns, status management particularly salient among them. Here, the number and reach of fake news themselves are not of prime importance. What matters is that fake news facilitates turning previously neutral themes into arenas of symbolic political conflict (Kahan *et al.*, 2017). In short, fake news is dangerous to democracy because it broadens and deepens intergroup conflict. If it draws an ever more extensive set of vital issues into the ever-fiercer culture wars and diverts attention from the topics of substance to zero-sum status races, democracy's performance declines.

What is the two models' influence over the public policy then? Table 3.1 provides an overview of the most prominent policy proposals. They can be assigned to two broad categories—*Competence Building* and *Access Restriction*—that roughly correspond with the perspective one takes upon the plasticity of rationality's bounds: the former category of interventions targets naivety, to latter category is consistent with presuming the public's gullibility.

Table 3.1 Policies to battle digital disinformation

Competence Building	Education: critical thinking, information literacy (European Commission, 2018; Lazer *et al.*, 2018; McIntyre, 2018; Britt *et al.*, 2019) Transparency: fact-checking, reputation-tracking (Rini, 2017; European Commission, 2018; Grinberg *et al.*, 2019) Quality media empowerment (European Commission, 2018; Levi, 2018)
Access Restriction	Content selection: quality adjustment, serendipity (Sunstein, 2017; European Commission, 2018; Lazer *et al.*, 2018; Grinberg *et al.*, 2019) Content restriction: demonetization, deplatforming (Bakir and McStay, 2018; Britt *et al.*, 2019)

Competence Building aims at strengthening the public's cognitive defense mechanism. It strives to turn people into "digital natives" via several avenues. Perhaps the most conservative possibility is to teach people information literacy and critical thinking, preferably in the regular course of their education. Another is to aid recognition of the quality of the content encountered by providing additional context. Reputation tracking of sources or even individual users by the platforms is one option. The platforms would provide information on whether the source is suspect, whether other users or independent fact-checkers contest its content, or perhaps even track individual users' "reliability reputation" based on their past shares and likes. The third road toward Competence Building aims at empowering the legacy media outlets to survive and successfully compete in the digital information market. Here, the effect is indirect: fake news is suspected of crowding out the higher quality sources due to its significantly lower production costs, and the financial or institutional support awarded to the latter may revert the trend. These measures mainly aim to dispel the public's naivety and train the democratic citizens into more competent judges of what and whom to trust in the digital infosphere.

In contrast, Access Restriction aims at limiting the prevalence of digital disinformation. Many of its measures target the content selection algorithms: if they currently contribute to disinformation's success, they can also be tweaked to suppress it. For instance, the algorithms may be altered to emphasize reputable, non-partisan sources or just "serendipity" where the users would be gently led out of their epistemic bubbles through exposition to content that can be expected to collide with their established views. More forcible tools on the menu include demonetization of suspect content as well as deplatforming of its producers. The producers could be prevented from benefiting financially by cutting their access to the advertising revenue or banned from the platform on account of "violating the community standards."

Note that subscribing to the Victim Narrative does not resolve all tensions inherent in these measures. For instance, if people are gullible—that is, if their epistemic character prevents them from discerning the reliability of the information encountered—they need to be shielded from these encounters. However, if they are just naïve, encounter-prevention may degrade their learning curve and prevent them from becoming independent critical reasoners cognitively adapted for the digital age. Nonetheless, there are yet greater concerns that stem from considerations rooted in the behavioral political economy of democracy. The first pertains to the policies' paternalism, the second to their expected efficacy. Let me address them in turn.

Although the proposed measures tend to be shrouded in the language of "transparency," "empowerment," or "diversity and sustainability" (European Commission, 2018, pp. 5–6), many of them tread a treacherous ground. Free speech and free information exchange are the cornerstones of liberal democracy. The Victim Narrative paints a public in need of a helping hand that would shield it against making choices incoherent with its own best interest. Naturally, if one gets exploited by bad actors, regulation or (re-)education can easily come with positive net benefits. Thus, the Victim Narrative provides a rationale to conceive the anti-disinformation policies paternalistically, effectively reining in these freedoms on account of the public's incompetence to avoid their self-destructive use. Although the proposals are careful to frame the government intervention as politically neutral and outsource anything that resembles censorship to presumably disinterested third parties, the situation is inherently delicate. Perhaps, it is not a far-fetched concern that government subsidies for legacy media may exploit or introduce a pro-government bias in their reporting. Political biases of the fact-checkers are also an issue that has been frequently raised. Moreover, pressure on the platforms to take a more active editorial stance intensifies their arbitrary power over the content right as they are turning into dominant fora for framing the issues of the day and setting the political agenda.

Additionally, the Victim Narrative creates an expectation of a voluntarily cooperating public, which will be disappointed to the extent the hypothesis of rationally irrational public has any merit. Members of such a public know what they want, and they are getting it. Because they are neither harmed nor exploited, they are not interested in third parties educating them, verifying the information's reliability, offering them content different from the one they like, or preventing them from enjoying the content they seek. Policies that are supposed to offer help and prevent harm will thus be deemed overbearing. The empirical research provides a glimpse of the seriousness of the problem.

For many, fact-checking has been the flagship policy against disinformation. Nevertheless, the evidence on its efficacy is mixed at best (Chan *et al.*, 2017; Colliander, 2019). Not only are the consumers resistant to heed the fact-checkers' warnings, but they also strive to undermine their credibility, often by charging them with partisan bias. Perhaps, this skepticism can be countered by greater transparency of fact-checking (Humprecht, 2020). However, it may also represent a straightforward response to unwanted meddling with the users' business. More coercive policies, such as deplatforming and demonetization, can perhaps diminish the prevalence of loyalty-signaling via disinformation if they make it more costly or reduce its benefits. Being kicked out of Twitter for trying to impress your friends too hard is arguably not worth the risk for many users. Nonetheless, there remains a significant risk that these policies will trigger backlash: for instance, they can delegitimize the platforms in the users' eyes or stimulate the emergence of alternative platforms less willing to intervene. Tellingly, the accounts of fake news exchange that emphasize the role of politically motivated reasoning come up somewhat short on policy recommendations. Perhaps the most prominent advice is to reduce the salience of cultural identities (Kahan, 2017a). Unfortunately, such advice is too vague and probably impractical. If people use social media to emit and monitor partisan loyalty signals—the more extravagant the claim, the more credible the signal—they will always stimulate the supply side to deliver the requisite material.

In the light of these findings, I shall dedicate the rest of this book to examining whether a democratic society should rely on paternalist solutions when battling political irrationality, and whether any non-paternalist avenues to its containment appear passable.

Conclusion

The Victim Narrative, a story that portrays the public as the prey of unscrupulous deceivers, shapes thinking about digital disinformation and its danger for democracy. Most policy recommendations to counter fake news' dissemination follow its path. However, the Victim Narrative is not the only viable explanation of how the current technological challenges may disturb the democratic equilibrium. Its foundational assumptions about the public's epistemic character may be too narrow in their relevance to inform a successful policy solution. In the context of fake news exchange, the public's bounds of rationality—that is, its naivety and gullibility—may ultimately be proven less important than its orientation toward non-epistemic ends. A failure to appreciate the extent to which news consumption and belief formation are embedded in the symbolic conflict among the competing cultural groups can lead to an overoptimistic assessment of the policy options. It is unlikely that politically motivated reasoning and conspicuous displays of in-group loyalty are safely ignored in the digital age.

A major challenge to the mainstream view of the fake news exchange can be formulated based on the theory of rational irrationality wedded to politically motivated reasoning. From its perspective, the danger of digital disinformation lies in dragging the emerging themes of the public discourse swiftly amidst the most intense partisan struggles, which preclude a reasoned appraisal of the alternatives at hand.

The empirical support for the two models is mixed so far. Too little is currently known about the fake news exchange to determine their relative explanatory power. The situation is vexing because both models agree that fake news may represent an imminent danger to the liberal democracy, but their policy implications do not overlap. The Victim Narrative motivates an upbeat assessment of the policymakers' prospects to counter fake news because it expects a cooperating public. In line with this expectation, resources are being invested in fact-checking and other interventions to protect the public from fake news and strengthen its cognitive defense mechanisms. However, to the extent the public is rationally irrational, the efficacy of such interventions is doubtful. They will be perceived as unwanted meddling and resisted with charges of manipulation or censorship: the evidence is already mounting that this problem is substantial.

Beyond its questionable factual merit and the possible inefficacy of policy solutions that follow in its path, it is also worrisome that the Victim Narrative—all too conveniently—lays the blame for the democratic crisis on "the bad guys" from whom an honest citizen needs protection. The paternalist theme of the fragile public that needs its keepers should not be presumed innocuous. It accentuates the division between epistemic elites expected to preside over the proposed interventions and the gullible or naïve crowd whose capacities for rational action are lacking: a trope that any supporter of democracy should consider suspect. Chapter 4 examines the paternalist promise to deal with the irrationality problem in broader terms.

Notes

1 To set the terminology straight, disinformation is a subspecies of misinformation where false information is spread knowingly, with malicious intent.
2 Epistemic bubbles that emerge spontaneously are not to be equated to echo chambers that arise as a result of an active effort to discredit out-group sources (Nguyen, 2020).

Bibliography

Akerlof, G.A. (1970) 'The Market for "Lemons": Quality Uncertainty and the Market Mechanism', *The Quarterly Journal of Economics*, 84(3), pp. 488–500. doi:10.2307/1879431.

Allcott, H. and Gentzkow, M. (2017) 'Social Media and Fake News in the 2016 Election', *Journal of Economic Perspectives*, 31(2), pp. 211–236. doi:10.1257/jep.31.2.211.

Bakir, V. and McStay, A. (2018) 'Fake News and The Economy of Emotions: Problems, Causes, Solutions', *Digital Journalism*, 6(2), pp. 154–175. doi:10.1080/21670811.2017.1345645.

Bauman, Z. (2000) *Liquid Modernity*. Cambridge; Malden: Polity.

Bénabou, R. and Tirole, J. (2016) 'Mindful Economics: The Production, Consumption, and Value of Beliefs', *Journal of Economic Perspectives*, 30(3), pp. 141–164. doi:10.1257/jep.30.3.141.

Bennett, S.E. and Friedman, J. (2008) 'The Irrelevance of Economic Theory to Understanding Economic Ignorance', *Critical Review*, 20(3), pp. 195–258. doi:10.1080/08913810802503418.

Britt, M.A. *et al.* (2019) 'A Reasoned Approach to Dealing with Fake News', Policy Insights from the *Behavioral and Brain Sciences*, 6(1), pp. 94–101. doi:10.1177/2372732218814855.

Bronstein, M.V. *et al.* (2019) 'Belief in Fake News Is Associated with Delusionality, Dogmatism, Religious Fundamentalism, and Reduced Analytic Thinking', *Journal of Applied Research in Memory and Cognition*, 8(1), pp. 108–117. doi:10.1016/j.jarmac.2018.09.005.

Caplan, B. (2000) 'Rational Irrationality: A Framework for the Neoclassical-Behavioral Debate', *Eastern Economic Journal*, 26(2), pp. 191–211.

Caplan, B. (2008) *The Myth of the Rational Voter: Why Democracies Choose Bad Policies*. New edition. Princeton: Princeton University Press.

Carruthers, P. (2011) *The Opacity of Mind: An Integrative Theory of Self-knowledge*. Oxford; New York: Oxford University Press.

Chan, M.S. *et al.* (2017) 'Debunking: A Meta-Analysis of the Psychological Efficacy of Messages Countering Misinformation', *Psychological Science*, 28(11), pp. 1531–1546. doi:10.1177/0956797617714579.

Coe, K., Kenski, K. and Rains, S.A. (2014) 'Online and Uncivil? Patterns and Determinants of Incivility in Newspaper Website Comments', *Journal of Communication*, 64(4), pp. 658–679. doi:10.1111/jcom.12104.

Colliander, J. (2019) '"This Is Fake News": Investigating the Role of Conformity to Other Users' Views when Commenting on and Spreading Disinformation in Social Media', *Computers in Human Behavior*, 97, pp. 202–215. doi:10.1016/j.chb.2019.03.032.

Downs, A. (1957) *An Economic Theory of Democracy*. First edition. Boston: Harper and Row.

Egelhofer, J.L. and Lecheler, S. (2019) 'Fake News as a Two-dimensional Phenomenon: A Framework and Research Agenda', *Annals of the International Communication Association*, 43(2), pp. 97–116. doi:10.1080/23808985.2019.1602782.

Epley, N. and Gilovich, T. (2016) 'The Mechanics of Motivated Reasoning', *Journal of Economic Perspectives*, 30(3), pp. 133–140. doi:10.1257/jep.30.3.133.

European Commission (2018) *A Multi-dimensional Approach to Disinformation*. Luxembourg: Publications Office of the European Union. Available at: https://ec.eur opa.eu/digital-single-market/en/news/final-report-high-level-expert-group-fake-news-and-online-disinformation (Accessed 19 July 2021).

Fallis, D. and Mathiesen, K. (2019) 'Fake News Is Counterfeit News', *Inquiry*, pp. 1–20. doi:10.1080/0020174X.2019.1688179.

Gelfert, A. (2018) 'Fake News: A Definition', *Informal Logic*, 38(1), pp. 84–117. doi:10.22329/il.v38i1.5068.

Gilbert, B. (2019) *The 10 Most-viewed Fake-news Stories on Facebook in 2019 Were just Revealed in a New Report, Business Insider*. Available at: www.businessinsider.com/most-viewed-fake-news-stories-shared-on-facebook-2019-2019-11 (Accessed 27 July 2020).

Goodin, R.E. and Spiekermann, K. (2018) *An Epistemic Theory of Democracy*. Oxford: Oxford University Press.

Grinberg, N. *et al.* (2019) 'Fake News on Twitter During the 2016 U.S. Presidential Election', *Science*, 363(6425), pp. 374–378. doi:10.1126/science.aau2706.

Hills, T.T. (2019) 'The Dark Side of Information Proliferation', *Perspectives on Psychological Science*, 14(3), pp. 323–330. doi:10.1177/1745691618803647.

Humprecht, E. (2020) 'How Do They Debunk "Fake News"? A Cross-National Comparison of Transparency in Fact Checks', *Digital Journalism*, 8(3), pp. 310–327. doi:10.1080/21670811.2019.1691031.

Kahan, D.M. (2015a) 'The Politically Motivated Reasoning Paradigm, Part 1: What Politically Motivated Reasoning Is and How to Measure It', in Scott, R.A. and Kosslyn, S.M. (eds) *Emerging Trends in the Social and Behavioral Sciences*. Hoboken: John Wiley & Sons, pp. 1–16. doi:10.1002/9781118900772.etrds0417.

Kahan, D.M. (2015b) 'The Politically Motivated Reasoning Paradigm, Part 2: Unanswered Questions', in Scott, R.A. and Kosslyn, S.M. (eds) *Emerging Trends in the Social and Behavioral Sciences*. Hoboken: John Wiley & Sons, pp. 1–15. doi:10.1002/9781118900772.etrds0418.

Kahan, D.M. *et al.* (2017) 'Motivated Numeracy and Enlightened Self-government', *Behavioural Public Policy*, 1(1), pp. 54–86. doi:10.1017/bpp.2016.2.

Kahan, D.M. (2017a) *Misconceptions, Misinformation, and the Logic of Identity-Protective Cognition*. SSRN Scholarly Paper ID 2973067. Rochester, NY: Social Science Research Network. Available at: https://papers.ssrn.com/abstract=2973067 (Accessed 10 July 2020).

Kahan, D.M. (2017b) 'Misinformation and Identity-Protective Cognition', *Yale Law & Economics Research Paper No. 587*. doi:10.2139/ssrn.3046603.

Kahan, D.M. (2017c) 'The Expressive Rationality of Inaccurate Perceptions', *Behavioral and Brain Sciences*, 40, pp. 26–28. doi:10.1017/S0140525X15002332.

Kahneman, D. (2011) *Thinking, Fast and Slow*. London: Allen Lane.

Klein, E. (2020) *Why We're Polarized*. New York: Avid Reader Press/Simon & Schuster.

Kurzban, R. (2010) *Why Everyone (Else) Is a Hypocrite: Evolution and the Modular Mind*. Princeton: Princeton University Press.

Lazer, D.M.J. *et al.* (2018) 'The Science of Fake News', *Science*, 359(6380), pp. 1094–1096. doi:10.1126/science.aao2998.

Levi, L. (2018) 'Real Fake News and Fake Fake News', *First Amendment Law Review*, 16, pp. 232–326.

Lieberman, A. and Schroeder, J. (2020) 'Two Social Lives: How Differences between Online and Offline Interaction Influence Social Outcomes', *Current Opinion in Psychology*, 31, pp. 16–21. doi:10.1016/j.copsyc.2019.06.022.

Little, A. (2018) 'Fake News, Propaganda, and Lies Can be Pervasive Even if They Aren't Persuasive', *Fake News and the Politics of Misinformation, Comparative Politics Newsletter*. Edited by M. Golder and S. Golder, 28(2).

Lucas, G. and Tasić, S. (2015) 'Behavioral Public Choice and the Law', *West Virginia Law Review*, 118, pp. 199–266.

Mark, J.T., Marion, B.B. and Hoffman, D.D. (2010) 'Natural Selection and Veridical Perceptions', *Journal of Theoretical Biology*, 266(4), pp. 504–515. doi:10.1016/j.jtbi.2010.07.020.

McIntyre, L.C. (2018) *Post-truth*. Cambridge, MA: MIT Press.

Mercier, H. (2020) *Not Born Yesterday: The Science of Who We Trust and What We Believe*. Princeton: Princeton University Press.

Mourão, R.R. and Robertson, C.T. (2019) 'Fake News as Discursive Integration: An Analysis of Sites that Publish False, Misleading, Hyperpartisan and Sensational Information', *Journalism Studies*, 20(14), pp. 2077–2095. doi:10.1080/1461670X.2019.1566871.

Nguyen, C.T. (2020) 'Echo Chambers and Epistemic Bubbles', *Episteme*, 17(2), pp. 141–161. doi:10.1017/epi.2018.32.

Pennycook, G. and Rand, D.G. (2019) 'Lazy, not Biased: Susceptibility to Partisan Fake News Is Better Explained by Lack of Reasoning than by Motivated Reasoning', *Cognition*, 188, pp. 39–50. doi:10.1016/j.cognition.2018.06.011.

Pennycook, G. and Rand, D.G. (2020) 'Who Falls for Fake News? The Roles of Bullshit Receptivity, Overclaiming, Familiarity, and Analytic Thinking', *Journal of Personality*, 88(2), pp. 185–200. doi:10.1111/jopy.12476.

Rini, R. (2017) 'Fake News and Partisan Epistemology', *Kennedy Institute of Ethics Journal*, 27(2S), pp. E-43–E-64. doi:10.1353/ken.2017.0025.

Schnellenbach, J. and Schubert, C. (2015) 'Behavioral Political Economy: A Survey', *European Journal of Political Economy*, 40, pp. 395–417. doi:10.1016/j.ejpoleco.2015.05.002.

Simler, K. and Hanson, R. (2018) *The Elephant in the Brain: Hidden Motives in Everyday Life*. New York: Oxford University Press.

Sperber, D. *et al.* (2010) 'Epistemic Vigilance', *Mind & Language*, 25(4), pp. 359–393. doi:10.1111/j.1468-0017.2010.01394.x.

Sperber, D. and Mercier, H. (2017) *The Enigma of Reason: A New Theory of Human Understanding*. London: Allen Lane.

Sunstein, C.R. (2017) *#Republic: Divided Democracy in the Age of Social Media*. Princeton; Oxford: Princeton University Press.

Tandoc, E.C., Lim, Z.W. and Ling, R. (2018) 'Defining "Fake News": A Typology of Scholarly Definitions', *Digital Journalism*, 6(2), pp. 137–153. doi:10.1080/21670811.2017.1360143.

Thaler, R.H. and Sunstein, C.R. (2021) *Nudge: Improving Decisions about Money, Health, and the Environment*. Final edition. New York: Penguin Books.

Trivers, R. (2011) *The Folly of Fools: The Logic of Deceit and Self-deception in Human Life*. New York: Basic Books.

Turchin, P. (2015) *Ultrasociety: How 10,000 Years of War Made Humans the Greatest Cooperators on Earth*. Chaplin: Beresta Books.

Uscinski, J.E. *et al.* (2020) 'Why Do People Believe COVID-19 Conspiracy Theories?', *Harvard Kennedy School Misinformation Review*, 1(3). doi:10.37016/mr-2020-015.

Vacura, M. (2019) 'Emergence of the Post-truth Situation: Its Sources and Contexts', *Disputatio*, 9(13). doi:10.5281/ZENODO.3567162.

Vosoughi, S., Roy, D. and Aral, S. (2018) 'The Spread of True and False News Online', *Science*, 359(6380), pp. 1146–1151. doi:10.1126/science.aap9559.

4 The Conceit of Behaviorally Informed Paternalism

Whatever principal vulnerabilities democracy has, political irrationality—be it triggered by gullibility, naivety, or pursuit of non-epistemic goals—exacerbates them. It hinders emergence of the wisdom of crowds and impairs democracy's performance. Can democracy be designed in a way that mitigates the threat of political irrationality? I have argued that resilience against political irrationality is a necessary condition democratic institutions must fulfill if the democratic equilibrium is to be maintained. So far, democratic societies have been successful in this regard. However, as illustrated in Chapter 3, the current transition of democracy's underlying information economy into the digital sphere may catalyze political irrationality, overwhelming the existing defense mechanisms.

As we have seen, the mainstream policy proposals to battle digital disinformation, which I have associated with the Victim Narrative, tend toward a paternalist route when striving to fortify democracy. As a result, supposedly benevolent third parties, such as the government, are called upon to limit the vulnerable citizens' contact with disinformation or improve their critical thinking competence.

Some caveats of this approach have already been apparent in the context of the war on disinformation: noncoercive interventions are ineffective vis-à-vis rational irrationality, and coercive interventions clash with democratic commitments to free speech. Nonetheless, the behavioral paternalist program deserves a more systematic assessment since its influence is not limited to considerations of how to defuse fake news. Essentially any situation where cognitive biases and the resulting systematic mistakes are suspected can become a fair target for paternalist intervention. Such assessment is conditional on a focused engagement with the elusive concept of welfare. This exercise requires us to delve more deeply into the realm of normative social science, more specifically *behavioral welfare economics*.

I shall argue that behavioral welfare economics in its paternalist guise fails to deliver on a promise to uncover people's "true preferences" in a politically neutral fashion. As a result, whenever behavioral-paternalist interventions get implemented, they require the citizens' watchfulness and thus add to the burden of the democratic social choice instead of making it lighter. The cheap and effective behaviorally informed tools of choice manipulation present a

DOI: 10.4324/9781003274988-5

temptation for the incumbent politicians to strengthen their grip on power.[1] As such, they underscore the need for the citizens' oversight: a troubling outcome in the context of the suspected growing threat of their political irrationality. I shall elaborate on these themes to build a general case against behaviorally informed paternalism as the appropriate answer to the current predicament of democratic countries. Throughout, I shall analyze and defend what I call the Sovereignty Principle: an umbrella term that unites the normative notions inherent in more standard concepts of consumer sovereignty and citizens' sovereignty.

(Ir)rationality, Sovereignty, and Welfare

What do people want? This question has been obsessively examined by anyone interested in the human condition since the dawn of history. As always, I shall dedicate special attention to how economists have treated the issue. We have already seen in Chapter 1 that the neoclassical approach is both subjectivist and individualist. What people want is based on how they subjectively value alternatives (alternative bundles of goods, or, more broadly, alternative states of the world) relative to each other, that is, on their individual preferences. Preferences, in turn, are assumed to be integrated: internally consistent, stable in time, and context-independent (Sugden, 2018, p. 7). Under these conditions, the question after people's wants has a straightforward answer, although one might not find it especially profound at first sight: what people want is revealed by the choices they make.

Accordingly, a neoclassical economist feels justified to avoid the grueling and uncertain task of uncovering what goes on in an individual's mind: recovering preferences from choices has nothing to do with stating hypotheses about one's mental states and the like. An economist just connects the observed input (i.e., a set of available alternatives) with the observed output (i.e., an alternative chosen) via a mathematically tractable utility function that ranks any alternatives in the order of the individual's preference. Every choice one makes reveals a bit of information about what they want, or more precisely, their preference ranking of alternatives. The exact shape of their utility function is not determined by psychological evaluation, focus group, or an fMRI scan, but estimated based on observation of the actual choices made in various (observable) conditions.

I have already discussed the shortcomings of the neoclassical picture of human behavior at length: it excludes the possibility that people make systematic mistakes. So, it runs into the face of voluminous evidence amassed by behavioral scientists. As far as the neoclassical rationality assumption provides a foundation for the presumed choice-preference relation, its implications are often problematic. Part of the issue is pragmatic, as we have already seen; rationality-based predictions will be less precise than those that take biases into account. But there is also a normative dimension to consider. In neoclassical economics, the concept of welfare is grounded in the idea of preference satisfaction through choice. If choices can be systematically mistaken, how are we to treat their relation to welfare?

Welfare is a notoriously elusive concept for economists and philosophers alike. However, if one believes that the agents' preferences are integrated, it seems its precise meaning can be left unspecified. As McQuillin and Sugden (2011, p. 555) argue, there is not much sense in distinguishing whether we understand welfare as happiness, as preference satisfaction, or as a realization of freedom of choice because it makes no pragmatically significant difference which of these views we decide to embrace. Welfare is individually subjective, and a definitive account of its substance is neither necessary nor possible. This "open" view of welfare is characteristic of neoclassical normative economics, usually called just *welfare economics*.

The open view of welfare can be illustrated with the help of the most elementary and pervasive normative criterion economists use, that is, the Pareto efficiency. As its standard definition has it, an economy is Pareto efficient if and only if the resource allocation is such that no one's welfare can be further increased without diminishing someone else's welfare. There is no free lunch in terms of welfare in a Pareto efficient situation. Symmetrically, whenever there is a possibility of a Pareto improvement—that is, such a shift in resource allocation that would make some agent better off without anyone else having an incentive to veto it—an efficient allocation has not been reached (yet).

The standard interpretation of Pareto improvements connects them directly to choices. Voluntary exchange is considered the prime example of a Pareto improvement. A welfare gain has been realized whenever two parties agree on a deal, for example, a cup of coffee for €1.50. Such a view is uncontroversial if several conditions hold: for instance, the participants must be informed about the nature of the transaction, and no spillover effects (externalities) that would afflict third parties exist. Crucially, however, the voluntary exchange example of a Pareto improvement also relies on the neoclassical assumption that the individuals possess integrated preferences revealed through their choice to accept the transaction. In line with the open view of welfare, a third-party intervention cannot increase welfare by meddling with people's choices if externalities or other "market failures" do not hinder the Pareto optimal outcomes.

Arguably, the foundational claims of neoclassical welfare economics can be summarized with three premises (Bernheim, 2016, p. 16, italics in the original)[2]:

Premise 1: Each of us is the best judge of our own wellbeing.
Premise 2: Our judgments are governed by coherent, stable preferences.
Premise 3: Our preferences guide our choices: when we choose, we seek to benefit ourselves.

While the latter two premises have already been explored in the previous chapters, the first one deserves close attention. I shall identify it with the principle of consumer sovereignty, which is routinely emphasized as the guiding normative light of welfare economics that connects it to the humanist philosophical tradition (Tresch, 2014, pp. 5–6). The actual genesis of principle is not as straightforward, though, and the complaints about its vagueness and ambiguity have been raised for a long time (Rothenberg, 1962). The principle often becomes tied to the "neoliberal" ideology (Olsen, 2018). This interpretation covers only part of the ground, however. While consumer sovereignty has indeed been frequently summoned to the defense of the markets (often as an alternative to command economies of the Soviet Bloc), it can also be understood independent of such ideological connotations.

Consumer sovereignty has been coined by a South African economist W. H. Hutt (1936) in his book *Economists and the Public: A Study of Competition and Opinion.* His original meaning relates to the claim that the final say belongs to the consumer in a free-market economy. Thus, however wealthy and resourceful are "the captains of the industry," their success remains conditional on satisfying the wishes and desires of the choosy and capricious consumers. In short, the rise and fall of business empires depend on the consumers' whims.

Consumer sovereignty as a hypothesis about a laissez-faire economy has been later embraced by libertarian-leaning authors, such as Ludwig von Mises, who used it to a powerful rhetorical effect:

> Capitalists, entrepreneurs, and landowners can only preserve and increase their wealth by filling best the orders of the consumers. They are not free to spend money which the consumers are not prepared to refund to them in paying more for the products. In the conduct of their business affairs, they must be unfeeling and stony-hearted because the consumers, their bosses, are themselves unfeeling and stony-hearted.
>
> (Mises, 2010, pp. 270–271)

Of course, the problem with such a notion of consumer sovereignty is that its underlying hypothesis about a division of power in a free-market economy may be false. Perhaps the producers ultimately "call the shots" and gain the upper hand in the exchange relations. After all, even Mises (2010, p. 681) admits that consumer sovereignty may be limited in the situations, such as natural monopoly, although he largely blames the government for the empirical prevalence of monopoly power.

Be that as it may, the notion of consumer sovereignty invoked here is different. Instead of targeting the distribution of power between the producers and the consumers in a competitive economy, it addresses a normative question. Namely, who decides upon the *value* of the alternatives at hand. Here, the principle of consumer sovereignty proclaims an individual—that is, *any* individual, no qualification requirements added—the ultimate authority. Although the individuals are free to seek whatever technical advice that they consider helpful, the binding act of valuation is their own to perform. In the spirit of Protagoras' famous dictum ANTHOROPOS METRON PANTON—a human being is a measure of all things—it is each and every person whom the principle of consumer sovereignty calls upon to express their evaluative stance without being required to provide reasons and justifications to substantiate it.

Of course, the parallel to political democracy readily comes to mind. Little wonder Farrar (1989, p. 77) proclaims Protagoras "the first democratic political theorist in the history of the world." The alignment between consumers' and citizens' sovereignty has certainly not been lost upon Hutt (1936), who drew an analogy between market and democracy from the start. In a democracy, individual valuations are considered binding when deciding what is "socially preferable" to something else. Society's values are determined neither by the powers that be nor by experts but by the aggregation of the people's preferences. In a clear analogy to Arrow's condition that values are not to be imposed (see Chapter 2), whatever valuation of alternatives occurs, there is no other source of such valuation than an individual, a regular person in the role of a consumer *or a citizen*. Thus, the normative principle that brings together the consumers' and the citizens' sovereignty can be called *the Sovereignty Principle*: there is no such thing as an exogenous normative authority to which individuals would owe deference.

Still, even if we agree on the Sovereignty Principle as the normative guideline, its proper implementation remains debatable. The market-democracy parallel is impure. Democratic politics presumes equality usually incorporated in the "one person, one vote" principle. But market exchange is unequal because those with more resources possess a stronger voice (Persky, 1993). Also, even if the individuals represent ultimate normative authorities, it is not necessarily the case that they are also the most competent in implementing their valuations through their choices. Democratic citizens alone may determine the policy goals, but they may still benefit from third-party expertise in their implementation. A consumer can similarly benefit from third-party intervention: being the best judge of what one's well-being consists in does not imply being the best judge of how specifically to achieve it. In short, deference to the Sovereignty Principle does not preclude doubts about individuals' instrumental competence. Therefore, empirical evidence regarding the systematic mistakes in choices retains its relevance. In their presence, one's welfare is not best served by consumer sovereignty if the sovereignty is considered—in line with the open view of welfare—coextensive with freedom of choice.

One convenient starting point for any critique of the neoclassical normative framework from the behavioral perspective are time-inconsistent preferences in the background of self-control problems many people struggle with. As Oscar Wilde once quipped: "I can resist anything except temptation." Most of us can relate. Therefore, it is unsurprising that self-control issues tend to be treated as paradigmatic cases where neoclassical inadequacies are manifest. For example, Thaler (2015) offers the following scenario as one of the prominent examples where people "misbehave," that is, they do not follow the precepts of neoclassical rationality:

> Some friends come over for dinner. We are having drinks and waiting for something roasting in the oven to be finished so we can sit down to eat. I bring out a large bowl of cashew nuts for us to nibble on. We eat half the

bowl in five minutes, and our appetite is in danger. I remove the bowl and hide it in the kitchen. Everyone is happy.

(Thaler, 2015, loc. 404–406)

Although the account is merely anecdotal, it certainly does not sound overly fanciful. What kind of trouble does it signify for the neoclassical approach on a normative level? From its perspective, it is impossible to make anyone better off by taking away their most preferred alternative. The people in the vignette have revealed their preference for eating cashews over not eating cashews by *choosing* to eat them. There is no more reliable proof of preference—or, more precisely, no other proof of preference—than the actual choice. Consider the possibility that Thaler and his friends *say* they would like to stop eating cashews, yet they continue eating them. Should the verbally stated preference count for anything? The neoclassical answer is a resounding no. Their cheap talk bears no information on the "real" preference regarding eating cashews. It reveals a preference for "eating cashews while complaining about it" over, say, "eating cashews while chatting about the weather," but that is all. Their choice is the sole proof of preference. For *homo economicus* as a utility maximizer, it is impossible *from definition* to choose an alternative that is not the most preferred among the available ones.

Problems, such as those with self-control, thus put a neoclassical welfare economist into a somewhat awkward position. Two defensive stratagems seem available. One is to deny that situations like Thaler's cashew example are empirically prevalent: if self-control problems are rare, there is no pressing issue to address. Another is to summon the difference between utility and happiness. Because utility is not identified with any specific mental state in neoclassical economics, one can say that the people might have been happy that cashews were removed, but that does not preclude the possibility that they were nevertheless made worse-off in terms of welfare. However, neither stratagem seems powerful enough to dispel the normative significance of self-control problems.

On the one hand, the evidence of these problems—both anecdotal and experimental—appears far too widespread to discard them as marginal (de Ridder *et al.*, 2012). If they were, the billion-dollar industry of self-help literature would not prosper quite as much, after all. On the other hand, while the divorce between utility and happiness is, of course, analytically permissible, one needs to beware of a disconnection between the economic notion of welfare and its commonsense notion: remember that economists can claim no more authority in the normative area than laypeople do.

It is therefore not surprising that Thaler (2015, loc. 4191–4192) finds himself at odds with the principle of consumer sovereignty, which he defines as "the notion that people make good choices, and certainly better choices than anyone else could make for them" (see also Sunstein, 2014, p. 4). It appears that if it is no longer possible to assume that people's choices reveal what they truly want, at least on average, the normative appeal of the neoclassical choice-based view of welfare vanes. Of course, in relation to Arrow's Impossibility Theorem, we have already seen there is no such thing as a straightforward translation of individual preferences to collective welfare. But the current problem is yet more pressing: any cognitive bias creates a wedge between choices and welfare, and there seems to be plenty of such biases. Given the economists' preoccupation with efficiency, what is welfare-maximization if it cannot be viewed neoclassically as preference satisfaction via choice? The standard tools of cost-benefit analysis certainly seem compromised unless the possible presence of irrationality is explicitly accounted for and steps to clean our data from its influence are undertaken (cf. Sunstein and Thaler, 2006, p. 253). Politically, the issue is no less daunting: how should the democratic government respond to irrationality?

In Our Best Interest

The extent to which the divorce between choices and preferences on account of the systematic mistakes justifies a third-party intervention has been one of the prime causes of controversy in normative economics over the last decades. In response to experimental findings that document instances of misbehaving, we have witnessed a widespread revival of interest in paternalism, now frequently associated with *behavioral public policy*. The "behavioralists" argue that neoclassical welfare economics ignores the human reality where choices occur under conditions of limited willpower, limited memory, and limited cognitive ability. Thus, it disregards human cognition's inherent weaknesses, which frequently lead people to choices that undermine their welfare instead of promoting it. Contrary to a *homo economicus*, that is, an "Econ" (Thaler and Sunstein, 2008), we humans often act against our best interest: we save too little for retirement, we gorge on junk food, we do not exercise as much as we would like to, we waste resources, we procrastinate. In its quest to help humans avoid self-destructive choices, the behavioral public policy takes explicit guidance from both the methods and the findings of behavioral sciences that experimentally demonstrate how "supposedly irrelevant factors" (Thaler, 2015, 2016), such as defaults or frames, are potent enough to alter human choices across many domains (see Chapter 1).

Today, the approach to behavioral public policy that is most successful in challenging the position of neoclassical welfare economics is Thaler's *libertarian paternalism* which he proposed together with Cass Sunstein (Sunstein and Thaler, 2003; Thaler and Sunstein, 2003, 2008). Well-aware of the apparent oxymoron inherent in the libertarian paternalist label, they seek ways to make people's choices better aligned with their well-being without resorting to coercive measures. In their view, coercion is not a must since it is not just the old-school changes in "hard" costs and benefits of alternatives, such as taxes or subsidies, that can be used to influence the choosers in a predictable direction. Soft interventions, such as unobtrusive changes in the environment of choice—that is, in the "choice architecture"—are often enough to influence people's choices. Accordingly, libertarian paternalists favor the employment of *nudges*, subtle tweaks in choice architecture. Noncoercive tampering with choice architecture does not change the availability of alternatives, only the way they are arranged and presented. In a paradigmatic example, Carolyn, a benevolent cafeteria manager, thus fine-tunes the choice environment in her shop to encourage healthy food choices (Thaler and Sunstein, 2008, 2021).

As an innovative policy tool, nudges have received broad acclaim in the academia and beyond, often presented as a third way between *laissez-faire* and coercive regulation. Conservatives praise it as a freedom-preserving alternative to more intrusive measures, while progressives see it as a promising way to gently implement their policy agenda in areas, such as sustainability (Button, 2018, p. 1036). Nudges also seem quite popular among the regular democratic citizens who cannot be suspected of any firm ideological commitment (Sunstein, Reisch and Rauber, 2018). It is thus unsurprising that an increasing number of governments and international organizations have become keenly interested in using nudges as policy tools that are highly effective in terms of their economic and political costs (Schubert, 2017).

In short, libertarian paternalism marks one of the great successes in popularizing academic ideas. However, much of its rhetorical success may owe to its ambiguity (Sugden, 2017, pp. 115–116). Used equivocally to start with, once nudge turned into a brand name, its meaning expands and dilutes, sometimes beyond recognition, exemplifying a rather severe case of a "concept creep" (Haslam, 2016). The original definition by Thaler and Sunstein (2008, pp. 6, 8) states that a nudge is "any aspect of the choice architecture that predictably alters people's behavior without forbidding any option or significantly changing their economic incentives," or "any factor that significantly alters the behavior of Humans, even though it would be ignored by Econs [that is, neoclassically rational agents]." There are multiple problems with both the definition and the actual use of the concept of nudge, as the resulting voluminous academic debate suggests (e.g., Hausman and Welch, 2010; Rebonato, 2014; Oliver, 2015; Mongin and Cozic, 2018).

Perhaps most importantly, many prominent interventions that have been put forward as examples of nudges do not target any aspects of what is standardly understood as bounded rationality. For instance, Sunstein (2018b) frequently asserts a GPS as a prominent example of a nudge. However, it is not entirely clear how GPS alleviates a rationality failure. Its core function, that is, changing people's behavior by providing information that would be otherwise inaccessible or costly to acquire, is perfectly understandable from the perspective of neoclassical economics. Similarly, "educative nudges" that attempt to inform people (e.g., Sunstein, 2015, p. 427) cannot be counted as nudges as far as they work through rational channels.

To avoid as much conceptual confusion as possible, I shall draw on Hansen's (2016) meticulous efforts to provide a more precise delimitation of a nudge:

> A nudge is a function of (I) any attempt at influencing people's judgment, choice or behaviour in a predictable way, that is (1) made possible because of cognitive boundaries, biases, routines, and habits in individual and social

decision-making posing barriers for people to perform rationally in their own self-declared interests, and which (2) works by making use of those boundaries, biases, routines, and habits as integral parts of such attempts.

(Hansen, 2016, p. 174)

At the same time, adds Hansen (2016, p. 174), nudges must not forbid or add options, change incentives, provide information, or employ rational persuasion. Thus, as far as there is a genuine policy innovation behind the idea of nudging, it is that of "exploiting people's cognitive and motivational deficiencies in ways that help them to make decisions that their better self (or superego) would make" (Hertwig and Grüne-Yanoff, 2017, p. 153). For an intervention to count as a nudge, it must rely on the existence of bounded rationality in two distinct ways. First, it presumes systematic deviations of the individuals' behavior from neoclassical rationality that are detrimental to her welfare. Second, it employs means that are assumed ineffective from the neoclassical standpoint because they do not influence the costs and benefits of the available alternatives.

By now, it is probably apparent that behavioral public policy offers a much broader set of tools than those associated with the nudging proper (cf. Loewenstein and Chater, 2017). What binds it together is not the vague "libertarian" idea that its interventions should not "significantly" alter costs and benefits but the notion that policy design may benefit from systematic employment of behavioral sciences' findings regarding the limits of human rationality. Oliver (2015, 2018) proposes a three-dimensional model of the possible behaviorally informed policies. It includes a liberty-regulation axis, an internalities-externalities axis, and a behavioral-rational axis. Accordingly, the policies may differ in how coercive they are, whether they target instances of harm to self or harm to others, and whether they appeal to rational faculties. In such a space, nudges constitute merely one of the possibilities. There are also "shoves," coercive interventions that target instances of irrationality-induced self-harm, or "budges," that is, coercive interventions to stem externalities that result from the exploitation rationality's bounds by third parties (Oliver, 2018, p. 274). Moreover, one can also consider the employment of debiasing techniques, or "boosts" (Grüne-Yanoff and Hertwig, 2016; Hertwig and Grüne-Yanoff, 2017), to empower the decision-makers to make better choices without additional third-party intervention.

Given the breadth of these possibilities, many consider behavioral public policy a breakthrough toward sophisticated science-based government interventions. As Jones, Pykett, and Whitehead (2013) assert, an era of the Psychological State is upon us. There is already ample evidence that behaviorally informed interventions—including the nudges proper—influence human behavior and tend to be more cost-effective than other measures (e.g., Benartzi *et al.*, 2017).

But how about the normative problem of welfare and sovereignty? In its context, the relationship between behavioral public policy and paternalism is of prime interest. While there is no *necessary* connection between the behavioralist approach to policy design and paternalism as the arguments for budges or boosts testify, the paternalist options (both "libertarian" and coercive) have overshadowed the other alternatives so far. As a result, behavioral public policy has acquired a paternalist overtone. So, do the findings that compromise neo-classical welfare economics also testify to the suitability of paternalist solutions?

There has been an extensive debate on whether paternalism can be liber-tarian (e.g., Grüne-Yanoff, 2012). But while "libertarianism" can make pater-nalism more attractive because it precludes many concerns about personal autonomy, the real conundrum runs deeper. It is the challenge to consumer sovereignty, which is perhaps the most significant contribution of behavioral paternalists. As we have seen, Thaler (2015) is dissatisfied with the notion that people are the best judges of their own well-being. What paternalism is all about, normatively speaking, is a suggestion that third-party intervention can improve the quality of people's choices for the sake of their welfare. After all, how can we conceive of systematic mistakes in choices without feeling the urge to limit their prevalence? In short, paternalism presumes a third party—such as a behaviorally informed choice architect—can influence one's choices to make them better aligned with her ultimate goals than the choices she would make independently.

According to its arguably most famous definition, formulated by Gerald Dworkin (1972, p. 65), paternalism is an "interference with a person's liberty of action justified by reasons referring exclusively to the welfare, good, happiness, needs, interests or values of the person being coerced." Although the defin-ition appears too narrow as it connects paternalism directly with coercion and thereby precludes any possibility for it to be "libertarian," it is valuable for the present discussion because it highlights the paternalists' interest in the welfare of the persons in their care.[3] The paternalists' guiding normative principle, which they draw much legitimacy from, states that the aim of their interventions is "to influence choices in a way that will make choosers better off, *as judged by themselves*" (Thaler and Sunstein, 2008, p. 5, emphasis in the original). Thus, paternalists do not impose values on people but merely help them with their implementation. Paternalism only aims at helping the agent—be it through "hard" or "soft" means—to realize what she truly wants in situations where achieving it may be precluded by her systematically mistaken choices. In other words, people's ability to choose the right means to satisfy their preferences is doubtful for the paternalist, but these preferences are ultimately respected as a normative benchmark. Paternalism may reject consumer sovereignty as a hypothesis about people's instrumental abilities. Nonetheless, it still subscribes to the Sovereignty Principle as its normative guideline.

So, a peculiar problem pushes itself to the center stage of the discussion enveloping behavioral public policy. Essentially, paternalists want to keep the open view of welfare, but in their commitment to nudge (or shove) people for their own good, they do not identify welfare with the satisfaction of preferences revealed via choices. Frequently, choices manifest systematic mistakes. As such, their normative worth is questionable. The actual normative significance belongs to mistake-free preferences hidden somewhere beneath the actual choices. Suppose Tatiana, a smoker with a history of unsuccessful quitting efforts, chooses to purchase a pack of cigarettes instead of a healthy snack. Nela, a benevolent paternalist, doubts the normative worth of such revealed preference. Still, she cannot just overrule Tatiana since that may violate the Sovereignty Principle: perhaps Tatiana genuinely prefers the cigarettes to the snack, after all. Nela must first find a way to reconstruct Tatiana's mistake-free preferences using a method that avoids value imposition. In short, before she proceeds with an intervention, she must uncover Tatiana's "true preferences."[4]

Searching for True Preferences

The paternalist playground can be staked out in the following way. People do make choices; that much is obvious. However, many of these choices are caused by systematic mistakes triggered by cognitive biases. Therefore, an opportunity exists to increase people's welfare by helping them make choices more closely corresponding with whatever they actually want to achieve. Importantly, an "internality" (Allcott and Sunstein, 2015), that is, harm to self, is supposed to provide legitimacy for third-party intervention in the same way neoclassical market failures do. Nonetheless, to fulfill the value non-imposition requirement of the Sovereignty Principle, such legitimacy can only stem from the ultimate approval of the interventions by the target population.

As already explained, paternalism is not preference-independent. Accordingly, paternalist solutions are cast in technocratic light promising that people's own objectives will be promoted impartially (cf. Sugden, 2018, p. 19). For that purpose, some of their preferences—namely, the true ones—must be taken seriously and considered normatively binding. Otherwise, the concept of a mistake is meaningless because there is no benchmark against which the hits and misses could be told apart. Therefore, the most fundamental question is the following: given a set of preferences, observably revealed, how can a third-party committed to the Sovereignty Principle determine the true preferences?

In general, there are two possible roads to reconstruct the true preferences: one may either ask people to state them explicitly or design a method to launder them from the observed choices. Unfortunately, each of them runs into serious pitfalls.

Consider the former option first. In neoclassical economists' eyes, asking people for an explicit statement of their preferences amounts to eliciting cheap talk. And for a good reason: if the respondents have nothing at stake—no skin in the game—the informational content of the answers is dubious. Even where general information about people's goals or values is available (people want health, status, and riches), it is the trade-offs between these values that are practically important, not the absolute magnitudes. "What is your willingness to pay for an increase of your life expectancy by one year?" is a policy-relevant question. "Do you want to be healthy?", not so much. At the same time, it is perhaps easy to get a reliable answer on the second question but very difficult to get it on the first one. Also, as considered in Chapter 3, noninstrumental motivations, such as status management, may frequently shape the answers. Our very ability to access our own motivations is doubtful (Simler and Hanson, 2018). Thus, instead of sharing our innermost preferences, we say things we are expected to say, presenting a narrative that is supposed to show us in a favorable light.

Can we launder the true preferences directly from choices instead? Mainstream paternalist proposals indeed prefer this route toward true preferences. So, Sunstein and Thaler (2006) suggest three elementary rules of thumb for benevolent choice architects to identify the "true" welfare-maximizing choices. They may rely on what *"the majority would choose if explicit choices were required and revealed"* (Sunstein and Thaler, 2006, p. 257, emphasis in the original); they may require people to make their choice actively instead of using a default; or they may strive to minimize the number of people who opt-out from the preselected default.

Unfortunately, each of the three suggested routes leaves a lot to desire (Qizilbash, 2012). A hypothetical majority's explicit, active choices create one-size-fits-all solutions that are often inappropriate where private—rather than public—goods are under consideration. Moreover, there is the risk that the wisdom of crowds fails on account of the widespread cognitive biases (see Chapter 2): the majority choice can end up revealing systematic mistakes rather than true preferences, as Sunstein and Thaler (2006) themselves recognize. At the same time, there is no guarantee that an active choice will be less biased than a passive one. After all, it is usually the active choices that experimentally reveal the biases (Kahneman, 2011). Lastly, minimizing the number of opt-outs is a weak criterion, too. True, people may stick with the preselected options because they genuinely prefer them. But irrational influences, such as the status quo bias, that is, the tendency to hold to things as they stand, are also probable.

Also, suppose one decides to opt-out from a default choice. Do the libertarian paternalists consider such a revealed preference sufficient proof that the default was not aligned with one's true preferences? Not necessarily. They may also try to apply a different intervention to make one stick to the "right" choice. It is, after all, a common feature of experimental studies to test which of the tweaks in the choice architecture works best, that is, has the strongest influence upon the choosers. The opt-out minimization rule makes it questionable whether there is *any* sufficient proof of true preference, whose sufficiency is not determined by an arbitrary decision of an external authority. There is a thin line indeed between recovering people's values and imposing values exogenously.

Certainly, Sunstein's and Thaler's (2006) suggestions are not the only ones on the table. Neither are they the most recent. But other proposals on how to recover true preferences do not fare much better. For instance, Beshears *et al.* (2008) present a list of "red flags" to highlight circumstances that make the normative content of preferences revealed through choices doubtful. They find choices suspect if they are passive (choosing the default), complex, intertemporal, made with limited personal experience, or influenced by third-party marketing.

Or consider Allcott and Sunstein (2015), who enumerate rules the choice architects should follow to identify true preferences:

1. Use well-informed choices.
2. Use considered choices. Here, "considered" means choices where the individual evaluates all relevant facets of a product or activity.
3. Use active choices. (...)
4. If individuals are present-biased, use long-run instead of present-biased (impulsive) choices.

(Allcott and Sunstein, 2015, p. 702)

These proposals are intuitively appealing, and empirical studies can be enlisted to support the suggested criteria. However, one is left to wonder if they are not a tad too stringent. How many choices would pass as normatively significant if such a filter were strictly applied? Is there any choice that could not be disqualified as "influenced by third-party marketing" in an advanced capitalist economy? A choice where "all relevant facets" of the alternatives have been evaluated? In short, it appears all too simple for paternalists to doubt the normative significance of human choices wholesale.

Besides the filter being too demanding, there are other worrisome features of such proposals. Consider the vagueness of the criteria. "Complexity" or "personal experience" do not represent binary variables but come in many shades of grey. It is difficult to imagine a nonarbitrary cut-off level at which a person qualifies to be experienced enough to make a choice that counts, or a choice qualifies simple enough that even unsophisticated decision-makers can be trusted with it. Similarly, any objective standard for identification of the "relevant" facets of the decision-making problem seems difficult to come by. Note the clash with the value-subjectivism implied in the Sovereignty Principle: the paternalists do not know the correct values beforehand; they are supposed to recover valuations from people's preferences. But unless the valuations have already been recovered, how can the paternalists identify the alternatives' relevant aspects or establish normative precedence for expert choices?

Let me stick with the expert precedence a while longer. The underlying assumption is that less experienced choosers would benefit from the emulation of the more experienced choosers, who tend to be more consistent (Goldin, 2015, p. 258). However, there is the same problem we have encountered in Chapter 2 with the reconstruction of "enlightened preferences." An expert is not "just like me but with more experience;" she is a different person along indefinitely many dimensions (cf. Lepoutre, 2020). The criteria that put normative preference on well-informed or experienced choices presume a homogeneity of the true preferences between the experienced choosers and the naïve choosers. Nonetheless, one does not need to subscribe to extreme subjectivism to see flaws in this assumption which—if it were correct—would probably preclude any instrumental argument for democracy over epistocracy, that is, the rule of the knowledgeable (Brennan, 2016). Let us consider a straightforward example: would I be better off emulating an expert in my investment decisions? Prima facie, the answer is perhaps affirmative. To maximize the return on my investment, it seems mimicking somebody else's more informed and more considered choices is prudent. However, there is more than a single dimension to the investment choice. How about my risk preferences? Are they the same as those of the experts? Quite possibly not because the experts tend to self-select for their specializations based on their peculiar traits. Most situations are more complex yet. Often enough, growing expertise changes the nature of the subjective experience. A connoisseur will rank wines systematically differently from someone, who can barely tell red from white by taste, not just because of their expertise but also because they experience the taste differently.

At the same time, the normative preference for expert choices is not the only paternalist suggestion that reeks of value imposition. The idea instantiated in Allcott's and Sunstein's (2015) fourth guideline, namely that long-run preferences should be prioritized over short-run ("present-biased") preferences if a clash occurs between the two is another instance of the same issue (Rizzo and Whitman, 2019). In this context, behaviorally informed paternalists like to draw normative implications from the dual process theory (cf. Kahneman, 2003, 2011) that distinguishes between *System 1*, the intuitive, effortless, automatic, emotional processing, and *System 2*, which is tied to controlled, effortful reasoning. However, while Kahneman uses the distinction as a convenient functional metaphor, paternalists endow it with a distinct normative twist.

Considering how cautiously economics handles the prospect of any interpersonal utility comparisons, one would expect that a clash between two competing sets of preferences is a cause for concern. Instead, the conflict is discreetly resolved by eliminating one of the sets from consideration (Rebonato, 2014, p. 363). System 1 is detracted as a "knee jerk system" (Grüne-Yanoff and Hertwig, 2016, p. 152) whose preferences have no normative weight, and System 2's preferences are treated as revelatory of an individual's true interests and equated, without much further ado, with preferences that a neoclassical rational agent, an Econ, would have. Such a stratagem is clearly suspect, however. Individual people, even whole cultures, may prefer the effortless flow of an unreflected "living in the moment" (cf. Bernheim, 2016, pp. 38–39). And even if they were not, it seems a strong argument is necessary to justify a decisive elimination of short-term preferences from normative consideration.

One specific problem deserves closer attention here. Namely, the "reasonable" long-run preferences—especially to the extent we rely on people's explicit confirmation of their existence—are particularly likely to be influenced by the considerations pertaining to social status management (Chapter 3). Thus, their authenticity and strength can be easily overstated. From the perspective of evolutionary psychology, it appears probable that the "reasonable self" is less a disinterested observer than a weaver of a narrative of our life whose purpose is to present us in a favorable light to our prospective allies and mates (Sperber and Mercier, 2017; Simler and Hanson, 2018). Normative priority to the long-run preferences thus perhaps unduly prioritizes the rationalized preferences of our embellished public persona. It is not quite certain that pushing people toward living the industrious, healthy, and moral lives pictured in their narratives created for public consumption would represent a welfare-increasing move and bring us any closer to solving the problem of true preferences.

To underscore the extent of the challenge to recover people's true preferences, let me summarize the problems discussed so far:

1   *An exceedingly demanding filter.* The classification criteria may set standards very difficult or even impossible to fulfill in realistic situations. If we understand true preferences as such that people would have if they had "complete information, unlimited cognitive abilities, and no lack of self-control" (Sunstein and Thaler, 2003, p. 1162; see also Thaler and Sunstein, 2008, p. 5), they can never be found through the study of mere mortals (Qizilbash, 2012).

2   *Vagueness and arbitrariness of the criteria*: It is easy to muster intuitive support to claim that some choices are better qualified and have a lower probability of being mistaken than others. Nevertheless, the real problem for the paternalists is how the competence criteria could be stated with any degree of precision and how a competence cutoff at which the revealed preferences become normatively binding (i.e., considered "true enough") could be set in a nonarbitrary way.

3   *Third-party value imposition*: From the suggestions proposed so far, it is apparent that paternalists have difficulties avoiding value imposition inconsistent with the Sovereignty Principle. Prominently, the normative priority for expert choices and long-term preferences is put forward as either a neutral criterion or as self-evidently justified, while neither is the case.

Fair enough, perhaps a purely technocratic fix cannot resolve the welfare conundrum of the true preferences. After all, Sugden (2018, chap. 4) argues that there are few reasons to believe in existence of any latent integrated preferences to uncover, whatever laundering method we might envisage. If so, it is impossible to decode a clear normative signal from the mess of people's choices unless its content is at least partially imposed using an exogenous evaluative standard.

Still, behaviorally informed paternalists have gathered much support across the political spectrum and gained influence over the applied policy through "Nudge Units" active in many countries with strong democratic credentials and prominent international organizations (cf. Grüne-Yanoff and Hertwig, 2016, p. 153). Thus, it is vital to consider the possibility that deference to the Sovereignty Principle incorporated in the "better off as judged by themselves" standard can be preserved by obtaining a people's consent either individually or via the political channel. If "the people"—as individuals or as a collective— themselves require expertise is rewarded and impatience is punished, then the paternalist program is perhaps all fine and well, after all.

Democratic Preference Laundering

As Sunstein (2015, p. 432) explains, "if people think, on reflection, that the nudge is directing them in a way that they endorse, then the 'as judged by themselves' standard is met." Let me distinguish two ways the "endorsement" can be given. I shall call them *direct* and *indirect* way. The direct way requires the person under the paternalist influence to agree with the intervention to increase her welfare. The indirect way is political: here, the consent with policy objectives and means is obtained via democratic social choice (presumably filtered through the mechanism of representation and subject to the customary checks and balances). Note that the direct way appears more in line with the paternalist commitment to advance the individual's well-being on her own terms. Nonetheless, the "better-off as judged by themselves" standard (AJBT standard, for short) can also be interpreted on collective terms to mean that an intervention does not represent value imposition if it has been accepted via democratic channels relying on elections and representatives.

First, consider Sunstein's (2018a) defense of the AJBT standard, which promotes the direct way of consent acquisition. His defense relies on hypothetical cases rather than real ones, which is peculiar given the advanced stage of many behavioral-paternalist policies' deployment. Anyway, how is the AJBT standard observed in Sunstein's vignettes? Notably, the agents are not being described as giving explicit consent at some stage of the process. Instead, the presumed welfare improvements are always related to their internal mental states. Thus, the agents are "very glad" to be subject to interventions which they "like a lot," as well as "happy and possibly grateful" to have received them (Sunstein, 2018a). Unfortunately, such defense of the AJBT standard requires an epistemically privileged observer with access to the contents of the agents' minds. As Rizzo and Whitman (2019) put it:

> We know that Jones ordered the fish tacos out of habit (and not for some other reason), and also that he didn't enjoy them, because the example says so. We know he's happy with his GPS because the example says so. We know he likes the more and less fuel-efficient cars equally well because the example says so.
>
> (Rizzo and Whitman, 2019, p. 409)

However, this assumes away the gist of the AJBT problem: namely, how do the paternalists know whether they have avoided value imposition. From the above-discussed guidelines for choice architects (esp. Sunstein and Thaler, 2006), it is apparent that they are occasionally content with an implicit consent which they presume in cases where the individuals decide not to opt-out.[5] Such strategy is deficient because it equates an effective intervention with a beneficial one: if the intervention works—that is, people change their behavior instead of opting out—they are also presumed better off than before. There remains no space to entertain the possibility of effective but injurious intervention. Since there is a consensus that tweaks in choice architecture can also be used to exploit the agents' cognitive biases to their detriment—constituting nudges' evil twin, that is, "sludges" (Thaler, 2018)—the solution relying on tacit consent is inadequate.

Given no indication that the problem of consent acquisition via the direct route has been successfully resolved appears at sight, let me turn toward how it could be addressed via the indirect route. Gerald Dworkin, in his remarkably current classic piece on paternalism, examines the social—or *political*—route toward justifying paternalism and proclaims it passable: "An electorate may mandate its representatives to pass legislation which when it comes the time to 'pay the price' may be unpalatable" (Dworkin, 1972, p. 77). And indeed, plenty of paternalist legislation apparently leaves democratic citizens content. Is that not enough? Why would it be illegitimate for the citizens to bind their own hands via a democratic process, at least if their fundamental rights remain protected? Alas, there is a devil in the details.

While the legitimacy of the indirect way of providing consent represents a rather thorny issue, I have no intention to attack it *in principle*. Even so, it still matters how specifically it is to be utilized. Remarkably, Dworkin does not preoccupy himself with restrictions that some actual flesh-and-blood citizens agree to have imposed upon them. Instead, he is concerned about the possible consent by hypothetical fully rational individuals. In his thought experiment, these entities lay down a constitutional system that enables restrictions of people's liberty in cases that constitute self-harm. Dworkin then arrives at the suggestion that the legitimate areas of paternalist intervention include an insurance policy against risky choices with irreversible far-reaching consequences; choices made under "extreme psychological and sociological pressures" (Dworkin, 1972, p. 81); and choices that involve "dangers which are either not sufficiently understood or appreciated correctly by the persons involved" (Dworkin, 1972, p. 82). The last class encompasses situations of limited self-control, such as the cashew case discussed above, or irrational work with facts, such as wishful thinking about the health hazards of smoking. At the same time, Dworkin (1972, pp. 83–84) urges the rational constitution-givers to require the government to back any paternalist intervention with a substantial burden of proof and implement the intervention in the least restrictive way possible.

How is all this relevant for the current debate? As suggested above, behavioral paternalists may rhetorically flaunt the AJBT standard as directly justified, but its actual justification is indirect, at best, with little promise of improvement. Whether the consent necessary for preserving the commitment to the Sovereignty Principle can be given via democratic politics thus represents the real question that must be answered. On the political interpretation of the Sovereignty Principle (i.e., the Sovereignty Principle as incorporated in *citizens'* sovereignty), the ultimate normative authority rests with the collective body of the citizens. Perhaps we can relax knowing that the decision regarding the people's true preferences is safely in the hands of the people themselves and that the democratic procedure lets the society sidestep the problem of true preferences by tasking its representatives to achieve specific goals and requiring them to rely on specific means along the way. In other words, maybe it suffices that behavioral paternalism gets implemented by democratically elected governments.

Unfortunately, behavioral paternalists tend to avoid addressing this issue directly. Instead, they rely on an audacious idealization. As we have seen, Dworkin searches justification for paternalist intervention hypothesizing a collective of perfectly rational constitution givers. The behavioral paternalists go even further and direct their advice to a perfectly rational, endlessly powerful, and impeccably benevolent individual—*a social planner* (Sugden, 2018, chap. 2). Thus, for all its reformational, even revolutionary aspirations, behavioral welfare economics simply follows the line set by its neoclassical predecessors, who subscribed to the public finance approach to policy advice. The hypothetical social planner is an agent who aims at maximizing society's welfare and possesses all the necessary political means to carry out her agenda. For economists, she represents a conveniently simplified model addressee that allows them to wrap the analysis up just before the gates of the actual politics and provide the policy recommendations in the most neutral, scientific way.

The justificatory road via a benevolent despot assumption is well-paved but treacherous nevertheless. As public choice scholars have been relentlessly repeating over the years, the government's benevolence is not a given, and as far as it can be even achieved, its maintenance requires sustained effort. The "public choice problem" (Sunstein, 2014), that is, the possibility that the government officials will misuse their power, requires a credible and robust solution.

Still, behaviorally informed paternalism is often considered just one more tool to achieve the conventional policy goals (cf. Oliver, 2019, p. 173). So why worry if the governments add a few fancy ingredients into the policy mix, making it more "behaviorally-informed," that is, more effective and cheaper? Why cannot we presume that the democratic equilibrium will prove as robust to the common pathologies of politics as it was in the past? Well, the behavioral political economy of democracy has much to say on this account.

The proposals addressed to the benevolent social planner are ultimately accepted (or rejected) by Humans, not Econs. Thus, the closest thing to an actual "as judged by themselves" moment comes on an election day. Accordingly, the concern that a broad application of paternalist measures ostensibly directed at diminishing the harm of cognitive biases in consumption will ultimately endanger the democratic equilibrium grows from two main roots. First, given the incentive setup of mass democratic politics (see Chapter 2), people's political preferences are probably less rational than their consumption preferences (cf. Glaeser, 2006). And worse: the ascendant digital age may be broadening the gap (see Chapter 3). Second, paternalism does change the scope of policy interventions considered justified on welfare grounds. It also provides novel policy tools whose availability may alter the nature of the political game in ways aggravating the public choice problem. Let me elaborate.

If humans are systematically misguided as consumers, can we expect them to be any less misguided as citizens? It appears that the same empirical evidence that undermines neoclassical welfare economics in the area of consumption is no less relevant for people's political choices (cf. Kelly, 2012, pp. 39–43; Lucas and Tasić, 2015). Perhaps we could argue that an irrational consumer can be transformed into a rational (or at least less irrational) voter because the political choices are more reflected than the choices in consumption. However, the evidence on voters' lack of political information and interest in unbiased political reasoning should make us cautious about this exegesis.

As already discussed at length, a democratic citizen's political choice is insignificant in the narrow instrumental sense because of one's essentially zero probability of being pivotal. So, the voter's incentives are less supportive of instrumental rationality than the consumer's incentives. A voter's instrumental errors generate costs that overwhelmingly accrue to third parties (i.e., represent externalities). Thus, even if the cognitive biases represented just a weak default that can be overcome with a modest exertion of effort, the voter has no reason to make the necessary investment. For the same reason—namely the meager incentives for political rationality—voters can easily enable a free reign of non-epistemic motivations, such as status management. In contrast, a consumer's voice tends to be decisive when it comes to the composition of purchases, with the costs and benefits accruing chiefly to the choosers themselves and those personally close to them.

Even if you remain unpersuaded that rational irrationality matters greatly in the political realm, things become no more cheerful if cognitive biases are attributed to citizens' naivety or gullibility. In particular, there is the sheer immensity of the choice problem under their consideration. On Thaler's (2015, loc. 872–879) view, if learning matters, our choices tend to be most rational when it comes to small-scale, oft-repeated decisions with rapid and reliable feedback, such as selecting the best flavor of yogurt for breakfast. With complicated, infrequent, large-scale choices, the probability of making a predictable mistake is growing. The same understanding is incorporated in the various sets of laundering criteria discussed above. From this perspective, there can hardly be a choice that raises more red flags (Beshears *et al.*, 2008) than the one we make in an election booth every four years or so: the complexity of political issues, people's inexperience with dealing with them, as well as temporarily distant and nonobvious consequences of collective choices loom large. At the same time, political marketing is arguably even more vicious than commercial marketing (cf. Simons, 2020).

Moreover, there is the concern voiced in Chapter 3 that in the content-rich environment of the hyper-social digital platforms, rationality's bounds can be more easily exploited, and our non-epistemic motives become more pronounced. We are not living in a stasis where we can be confident that our hereditary political institutions will contain political irrationality for the foreseeable future. The checks and balances, as they stand, are not built to account for social media. There is a sizable probability that the ground is disintegrating under our feet with the revolutionary digital technologies transforming our democratic discourse. If an argument for endowing political preferences with primary normative significance can nonetheless be made, the behavioral paternalists are yet to supply it.

To make things worse, behaviorally informed paternalism opens the Pandora's box of intervention justified not by harm to others but by self-harm. Interventions legitimized by externalities require at least an identification of the third-party victims or beneficiaries. Interventions that address internalities have a far broader potential scope: they can be summoned wherever a case can be made that people suffer from self-defeating incompetence in their choices. Combine this with an inattentive, cognitively biased electorate often driven in its political participation by noninstrumental motives, add self-interested politicians in pursuit of reelection by any means available, and you have a recipe for trouble.

From the perspective of behavioral political economy, it comes as no surprise that the incumbent politicians welcome behavioral paternalist proposals without being too worried if abstract concerns, such as the proper mechanism of true preference identification, have been resolved. The nudge units around the world were not instituted to sit around idly until a proper method of preference laundering became available. The government tasks them to achieve specific goals, such as increased retirement savings, by any means that do not require rewriting the existing laws (cf. Alemanno and Spina, 2014). The resulting style of intervention is pragmatic, not principle-based (Cartwright and Hight, 2019). Noting the situation, Hansen (2018) describes the haphazard way in which multiple treatments are thrown at a problem and evaluated with little regard for any theoretical background as a "shotgun approach."

In all likelihood, the shotgun approach is not an accidental lapse on the side of the governmental choice architects but an all-but-inevitable outcome of the democratic politics' business as usual. It is here to stay. The Psychological State—as far as it evolves in the framework of the current democratic institutions—appears destined to employ a piecemeal approach to behavioral policy intervention, not a comprehensive strategy. However, this leaves little space for the hope that the behavioral paternalist agenda will be salient enough for the voters already overwhelmed by the more prominent themes of the public debate and prone to voting based on their identity concerns and coarse-grained clues, such as the overall satisfaction with the perceived government's performance (Achen and Bartels, 2016).

Thus, ample reasons exist to worry that implementing behaviorally informed paternalism weakens the democratic control over government policies, giving it a considerable leeway in directing its choice architects to serve its own ends. In this vein, Edward Glaeser (2006, p. 156) points out that nudging means "an increased role of an incumbent government as an agent of persuasion," which carries the risk that the governments will use the enhanced persuasive powers to retain power instead of helping the citizens to achieve their own goals. He also argues that public monitoring of "soft," that is, noncoercive paternalism is more difficult than the more traditional policies based on material incentives. To this concern, it must also be added that implementing fine-tuned micro-interventions many behavioral paternalists fancy is conditional on the availability of a large quantity of personal data. Much has been written about surveillance capitalism lately (Yeung, 2017; Zuboff, 2020). However, enhanced government surveillance is not necessarily any more appealing. In the wake of the recent pandemic, the surge of interest in stimulating compliance with public health measures, even at the expense of suspending fundamental liberties, underscores these concerns regarding behavioral regulation.

Again, the government's benevolence is not a given. It represents an outcome of the political game with all its complexities. The availability of behavioral paternalist tools may ultimately make it harder for the government to maintain the degree of benevolence customary in advanced democracies. In short, the threat is that "new policies create new politics," as Button (2018, p. 1035) has succinctly put it. Worryingly, very little is currently known about how the new and shiny policy tools can be expected to change the political equilibria (Schubert, 2017). Especially so if these tools are discrete and nonintrusive like nudges: where coercive measures easily become focal points for coordinating opposition, "libertarian" ones usually appear too benign to ignite the passions necessary to trigger any mass political dissent.

The tools of preference manipulation currently under development by "nudge units" are of general use. With more data and a more personalized approach, their effectiveness will probably grow. They can be implemented to influence the preferences that voters reveal at the election booth—and not only in an amateurish fashion, such as making the vote for incumbent the default option (Sunstein, 2014). Take, for example, Sunstein's (2017) own proposal for introducing the "architecture of serendipity" as a cure to the ills of the voters' polarized worldview. Its purpose is to alter the selection of content encountered by social media users on their newsfeed. In place of the current model, where the users encounter content aligned with their likes and interests, the architecture of serendipity would increase the share of information for which they would probably not search themselves. Thus, it is supposed to penetrate their epistemic bubbles. However, given the vast amount of content unrelated to the users' known likes, such a strategy must be either ineffective if pursued randomly or dangerous if the newsfeed is manipulated with a particular agenda in mind. In short, if the architecture of serendipity is fully outsourced to the digital platforms, their arbitrary power over one of the most prominent stages of the democratic discussion increases significantly. If the government were to choose a more hands-on approach, it may find it difficult to resist the temptation to push the information mix in a direction serendipitous relative to its reelection prospects.

Can behavioral paternalists dispel the concern that their favored policies intensify the toxic mix of politicians' misuse of power (i.e., the public choice problem) and voters' irrationality? Unfortunately, they tend to discard the former issue as orthogonal to their agenda and avoid addressing the latter one. As Sunstein maintains:

> The most objectionable cases reflect not unacceptable paternalism but an altogether different problem: impermissible motivations. Indeed, many of the strongest intuitive objections to paternalism, even in its soft form, involve examples, real or imagined, in which government is acting on the basis of impermissible factors (…). The objections are right, but the real problem has nothing to do with paternalism.
>
> (Sunstein, 2014, p. 158)

Accordingly, Sunstein (2013, 2015, 2016, and elsewhere) is convinced that implementing relatively mild structural requirements or ethical guidelines can preclude the public choice problem. Given his prominence as a promoter of the "libertarian" variety of behaviorally informed paternalism, it is perhaps unsurprising that he advertises nudges as the safest possible means of behavioral intervention (cf. Sunstein, 2014, p. 16). Essentially, his structural safeguards boil down to *transparency* and *easy opt-out*.

However, if we limit attention to nudges proper (i.e., those that fit Hansen's [2016] definition) and exclude mere information provision, there is the problem that the interventions are not transparent for the individual chooser in the particular situation of choice. As Bovens (2009, p. 216) points out, there is a difference between *type interference transparency* and *token interference transparency*. Token interference transparency may be impractical or even undermine the effect of nudging (Grüne-Yanoff, 2012), although the jury is still out given the empirical intricacies surrounding the issue (Ivanković and Engelen, 2019, pp. 47–50). Be that as it may, for Sunstein, transparency pertains to the type of intervention, not its specific instance. Transparent equals non-secret on the level of a general rule, not "obvious" in the given instance where one encounters a nudge. The transparency requirement thus relies on the indirect justification of paternalist intervention via politics. If one likes, they can find information on what interventions are being used and resort to political action if they are not content. Even if the pertinent information is easily accessible—which would probably require introducing a legal registry of nudges (Lepenies and Małecka, 2015)—such a safeguard does little to tame the menace of misuse of power and political irrationality. If anything, it increases the burden on the citizens who are now expected to monitor additional government activities whose nature makes the monitoring especially costly. Even the demands posed by Ivanković's and Engelen's (2019) imminently modest and sensible democratic conception of citizen's watchfulness toward the paternalist interventions imply a significant institutional reform to create new channels to enhance the citizens' control over to government's actions (Ivanković and Engelen, 2019, pp. 66–67).

True, the easy opt-out requirement presents an alternative to political action. It (nominally) preserves the freedom of choice. If the choice architects are considered corrupt or, less dramatically, do not live up to the AJBT standard, it is supposed to be simple to resist their interventions. Can an opt-out save the day? There are some reasons to be skeptical about its potency. People tend to be overoptimistic about their own rationality (Pronin, Lin and Ross, 2002) and underestimate how likely they are to be influenced by the nudge (Schubert, 2017). This may partially explain the enthusiasm for behavioral paternalist intervention among the public. Still, it increases the probability that the manipulation—which the overoptimistic individuals consider a priori impossible to influence them—will succeed, and the opt-out will not be used. Besides, many interventions will not be noticed beforehand, if at all (Ivanković and Engelen, 2019). Betting all on the opt-out as a foolproof safety measure thus appears imprudent.

Ethical requirements, for their part, represent a prima facie problematic answer to the public choice problem. If we could rely on public officials' adherence to moral virtues, there would be no public choice problem in the first place. Functional democracy cannot be built on blind faith that the policymakers will self-regulate for ethical reasons. In a democratic society, government's benevolence must be grounded in institutions that provide its credible guarantee. Democratic citizens must always beware of incumbents' temptations to use any means available to extend and fortify their grip on power. It is just a slight exaggeration that democracy remains forever one election away from dictatorship. New policy tools that promise cheap, effective, and possibly covert tools of behavioral regulation can shift the existing political equilibria in a way detrimental for liberal democracy, especially as far as they provide the government with new tools to forge the citizens' consent with their actions. Any "bad people do bad things" narrative ignores the question of incentives. In contrast to the moralist view, the standard economic assumption is that politicians maximize the expected number of votes. Therefore, it remains crucial if and how does the availability of the advanced tools of behavioral manipulation change the incentives that the vote-maximizing politicians face.

All in all, it appears that behaviorally informed paternalism lacks a persuasive answer to the problems of voters' irrationality and politicians' misuse of power. While I have singled out Cass Sunstein as a prominent target of my criticism, the problem goes far beyond his writings. For instance, Conly (2012), who presents a case for coercive paternalism, or Loewenstein and Chater (2017), who discuss all the possibilities of behaviorally informed regulation, also dedicate little attention to the issues under consideration here. Therefore, it does not seem unfair to conclude that implementation of the behavioral paternalist program appears capable of making democracy's imperfections more pronounced. In the stormy waters of the current democratic crisis, this is a particularly disconcerting possibility.

Conclusion

Although the neoclassical notions of the relationship between choice and welfare appear untenable, behavioral paternalists struggle to provide a viable alternative to neoclassical welfare economics. They count on the possibility to identify situations where people make systematic mistakes so the behaviorally informed choice architects could intervene with people's choices while avoiding value imposition. Accordingly, the interventions—be they coercive or not—would enable the choosers to achieve better outcomes as judged by themselves. This means, normatively speaking, that behavioral paternalists cast doubt upon consumer sovereignty as far as it equals an assumption that people always choose the best alternative. At the same time, however, they keep allegiance to a more general Sovereignty Principle that considers people's preferences the ultimate source of any valuation if they are recovered by proper methods. However, the existing proposals on how to launder the observed choices to obtain the underlying, normatively binding preferences suffer from numerous shortcomings, including vagueness and arbitrariness of the criteria. Uncovering the "true preferences" to which the choices should converge remains a formidable challenge. Their very existence is doubtful if they are supposed to be integrated in the neoclassical sense.

Perhaps the issue of the true preferences could be sidestepped if people welcome the paternalist interventions. However, I have shown that behavioral paternalists do little to obtain a direct consent of individuals in their paternal care with the interventions hurled their way. Instead, they try to do justice to the Sovereignty Principle by relegating approval to democratic politics. However, citizens' sovereignty is no less tainted by the suspicion of irrationality than consumers' sovereignty is. In fact, there are strong reasons to expect that political choices are, on average, more irrational than consumption choices on account of their greater complexity, lower frequency, or the problematic incentives that the voters face. Even worse, against the background of the democratic crisis, which probably relates to the technological upheavals changing the nature of the democratic discourse, the paternalist avenue to policymaking broadens the scope of political interventions and intensifies the public choice problem of how the government's benevolence can be credibly guaranteed.

What is to be done? In Chapter 5, I shall examine the non-paternalist possibilities of fortifying democracy against the tides of the citizens' political irrationality. Although the idea of purely technocratic, neutral intervention to fix people's choices to align with true preferences is probably a mirage, there still seems much can be done to utilize the behavioral insights in fortifying democracy against the imperfections of human reason. In short, the indirect way toward observing the Sovereignty Principle is perhaps not impassable, after all. But a safe passage—especially in the digital era—requires a non-paternalist approach.

Notes

1 In a historically stable democracy, it is easy to take a significant degree of government's benevolence for granted. One may forget that does not represent a necessary, let alone "natural," feature of a political order. The containment of the government's coercive powers has been difficult to achieve and can be undone. A step toward authoritarian

populism fond of manufacturing consent by any means available remains uncomfortably short (Levitsky and Ziblatt, 2018).
2 Throughout the text, welfare and well-being will be used as synonyms (cf. Fletcher, 2016, p. 10).
3 For a more extensive set of paternalism's definitions see Dworkin (2015).
4 The literature also often uses adjectives such as "rational," "informed," "normative," or "laundered" to denote the normatively binding preferences (cf. Hausman, 2012, p. 79). Note that the true preferences do not pose a problem for neoclassical welfare economics. Due to its reliance on consumer sovereignty—that is, the Sovereignty Principle extended by an empirical assumption that a person "always knows best"— neoclassical welfare economics is implicitly anti-paternalist. Agents with integrated preferences already optimize in any imaginable situation. It makes little sense to distinguish the preferences revealed in their choices from true preferences because there can be no meaningful difference between the two.
5 Note that this avenue is limited to libertarian paternalism as the more coercive kinds of behavioral intervention do not include opt-outs.

Bibliography

Achen, C.H. and Bartels, L.M. (2016) *Democracy for Realists: Why Elections Do Not Produce Responsive Government*. Princeton: Princeton University Press.
Alemanno, A. and Spina, A. (2014) 'Nudging Legally: On the Checks and Balances of Behavioral Regulation', *International Journal of Constitutional Law*, 12(2), pp. 429–456. doi:10.1093/icon/mou033.
Allcott, H. and Sunstein, C.R. (2015) 'Regulating Internalities', *Journal of Policy Analysis and Management*, 34(3), pp. 698–705. doi:10.1002/pam.21843.
Benartzi, S. *et al.* (2017) 'Should Governments Invest More in Nudging?', *Psychological Science*, 28(8), pp. 1041–1055. doi:10.1177/0956797617702501.
Bernheim, B.D. (2016) 'The Good, the Bad, and the Ugly: A Unified Approach to Behavioral Welfare Economics', *Journal of Benefit-Cost Analysis*, 7(1), pp. 12–68. doi:10.1017/bca.2016.5.
Beshears, J. *et al.* (2008) 'How Are Preferences Revealed?', *Journal of Public Economics*, 92(8), pp. 1787–1794. doi:10.1016/j.jpubeco.2008.04.010.
Bovens, L. (2009) 'The Ethics of Nudge', in Grüne-Yanoff, T. and Hansson, S.O. (eds) *Preference Change: Approaches from Philosophy, Economics and Psychology*. Dordrecht: Springer Netherlands, pp. 207–219. doi:10.1007/978-90-481-2593-7_10.
Brennan, J. (2016) *Against Democracy*. Princeton: Princeton University Press.
Button, M.E. (2018) 'Bounded Rationality without Bounded Democracy: Nudges, Democratic Citizenship, and Pathways for Building Civic Capacity', *Perspectives on Politics*, 16(4), pp. 1034–1052. doi:10.1017/S1537592718002086.
Cartwright, A.C. and Hight, M.A. (2019) '"Better off as Judged by Themselves": A Critical Analysis of the Conceptual Foundations of Nudging', *Cambridge Journal of Economics* [Preprint]. doi:10.1093/cje/bez012.
Conly, S. (2012) *Against Autonomy: Justifying Coercive Paternalism*. Cambridge: Cambridge University Press.
Dworkin, G. (1972) 'Paternalism', *The Monist*, 56(1), pp. 64–84.
Dworkin, G. (2015) 'Defining Paternalism', in Schramme, T. (ed.) *New Perspectives on Paternalism and Health Care*. Cham: Springer International Publishing, pp. 17–29. doi:10.1007/978-3-319-17960-5_2.

Farrar, C. (1989) *The Origins of Democratic Thinking*. Cambridge: Cambridge University Press.

Fletcher, G. (2016) *The Philosophy of Well-being: An Introduction*. London; New York: Routledge.

Glaeser, E.L. (2006) 'Paternalism and Psychology', *University of Chicago Law Review*, 73(1), pp. 133–156.

Goldin, J. (2015) 'Which Way to Nudge? Uncovering Preferences in the Behavioral Age', *Yale Law Journal*, 125(1), pp. 226–270.

Grüne-Yanoff, T. (2012) 'Old Wine in New Casks: Libertarian Paternalism Still Violates Liberal Principles', *Social Choice and Welfare*, 38(4), pp. 635–645. doi:10.1007/s00355-011-0636-0.

Grüne-Yanoff, T. and Hertwig, R. (2016) 'Nudge Versus Boost: How Coherent Are Policy and Theory?', *Minds and Machines*, 26(1–2), pp. 149–183. doi:10.1007/s11023-015-9367-9.

Hansen, P.G. (2016) 'The Definition of Nudge and Libertarian Paternalism: Does the Hand Fit the Glove?', *European Journal of Risk Regulation*, 7(1), pp. 155–174. doi:10.1017/S1867299X00005468.

Hansen, P.G. (2018) 'What Are We Forgetting?', *Behavioural Public Policy*, 2(2), pp. 190–197. doi:10.1017/bpp.2018.13.

Haslam, N. (2016) 'Concept Creep: Psychology's Expanding Concepts of Harm and Pathology', *Psychological Inquiry*, 27(1), pp. 1–17. doi:10.1080/1047840X.2016.1082418.

Hausman, D.M. (2012) *Preference, Value, Choice, and Welfare*. Cambridge; New York: Cambridge University Press.

Hausman, D.M. and Welch, B. (2010) 'Debate: To Nudge or Not to Nudge', *Journal of Political Philosophy*, 18(1), pp. 123–136. doi:10.1111/j.1467-9760.2009.00351.x.

Hertwig, R. and Grüne-Yanoff, T. (2017) 'Nudging and Boosting: Steering or Empowering Good Decisions', *Perspectives on Psychological Science*, 12(6), pp. 973–986. doi:10.1177/1745691617702496.

Hutt, W.H. (1936) *Economists and the Public: A Study of Competition and Opinion*. London: J. Cape.

Ivanković, V. and Engelen, B. (2019) 'Nudging, Transparency, and Watchfulness', *Social Theory and Practice*, 45(1), pp. 43–73. doi:10.5840/soctheorpract20191751.

Jones, R., Pykett, J. and Whitehead, M. (2013) *Changing Behaviours: On the Rise of the Psychological State*. Cheltenham: Edward Elgar Publishing.

Kahneman, D. (2003) 'Maps of Bounded Rationality: Psychology for Behavioral Economics', *The American Economic Review*, 93(5), pp. 1449–1475. doi:10.2307/3132137.

Kahneman, D. (2011) *Thinking, Fast and Slow*. London: Allen Lane.

Kelly, J.T. (2012) *Framing Democracy: A Behavioral Approach to Democratic Theory*. Princeton: Princeton University Press.

Lepenies, R. and Małecka, M. (2015) 'The Institutional Consequences of Nudging – Nudges, Politics, and the Law', *Review of Philosophy and Psychology*, 6(3), pp. 427–437. doi:10.1007/s13164-015-0243-6.

Lepoutre, M. (2020) 'Democratic Group Cognition', *Philosophy & Public Affairs*, 48(1), pp. 40–78. doi:10.1111/papa.12157.

Levitsky, S. and Ziblatt, D. (2018) *How Democracies Die*. New York: Crown.

Loewenstein, G. and Chater, N. (2017) 'Putting Nudges in Perspective', *Behavioural Public Policy*, 1(1), pp. 26–53. doi:10.1017/bpp.2016.7.

Lucas, G. and Tasić, S. (2015) 'Behavioral Public Choice and the Law', *West Virginia Law Review*, 118, pp. 199–266.

McQuillin, B. and Sugden, R. (2011) 'Reconciling Normative and Behavioural Economics: The Problems to be Solved', *Social Choice and Welfare*, 38(4), pp. 553–567. doi:10.1007/s00355-011-0627-1.

Mises, L. von (2010) *Human Action: The Scholar's Edition*. Auburn: Ludwig von Mises Institute.

Mongin, P. and Cozic, M. (2018) 'Rethinking Nudge: Not One but Three Concepts', *Behavioural Public Policy*, 2(1), pp. 107–124. doi:10.1017/bpp.2016.16.

Oliver, A. (2015) 'Nudging, Shoving, and Budging: Behavioural Economic-Informed Policy', *Public Administration*, 93(3), pp. 700–714. doi:10.1111/padm.12165.

Oliver, A. (2018) 'Nudges, Shoves and Budges: Behavioural Economic Policy Frameworks', *The International Journal of Health Planning and Management*, 33(1), pp. 272–275. doi:10.1002/hpm.2419.

Oliver, A. (2019) *Reciprocity and the Art of Behavioural Public Policy*. Cambridge: Cambridge University Press. doi:10.1017/9781108647755.

Olsen, N. (2018) *The Sovereign Consumer: A New Intellectual History of Neoliberalism*. New York: Palgrave Macmillan.

Persky, J. (1993) 'Retrospectives: Consumer Sovereignty', *The Journal of Economic Perspectives*, 7(1), pp. 183–191.

Pronin, E., Lin, D.Y. and Ross, L. (2002) 'The Bias Blind Spot: Perceptions of Bias in Self Versus Others', *Personality and Social Psychology Bulletin*, 28(3), pp. 369–381. doi:10.1177/0146167202286008.

Qizilbash, M. (2012) 'Informed Desire and the Ambitions of Libertarian Paternalism', *Social Choice and Welfare*, 38(4), pp. 647–658. doi:10.1007/s00355-011-0620-8.

Rebonato, R. (2014) 'A Critical Assessment of Libertarian Paternalism', *Journal of Consumer Policy*, 37(3), pp. 357–396. doi:10.1007/s10603-014-9265-1.

de Ridder, D.T.D. *et al.* (2012) 'Taking Stock of Self-Control: A Meta-Analysis of How Trait Self-Control Relates to a Wide Range of Behaviors', *Personality and Social Psychology Review*, 16(1), pp. 76–99. doi:10.1177/1088868311418749.

Rizzo, M.J. and Whitman, G. (2019) *Escaping Paternalism: Rationality, Behavioral Economics, and Public Policy*. Cambridge; New York: Cambridge University Press.

Rothenberg, J. (1962) 'Consumers' Sovereignty Revisited and the Hospitability of Freedom of Choice', *The American Economic Review*, 52(2), pp. 269–283.

Schubert, C. (2017) 'Exploring the (Behavioural) Political Economy of Nudging', *Journal of Institutional Economics*, 13(3), pp. 499–522. doi:10.1017/S1744137416000448.

Simler, K. and Hanson, R. (2018) *The Elephant in the Brain: Hidden Motives in Everyday Life*. New York: Oxford University Press.

Simons, G. (2020) 'Policy and Political Marketing: Promoting Conflict as Policy', *Journal of Political Marketing*, pp. 1–28. doi:10.1080/15377857.2020.1724426.

Sperber, D. and Mercier, H. (2017) *The Enigma of Reason: A New Theory of Human Understanding*. London: Allen Lane.

Sugden, R. (2017) 'Do People Really Want to be Nudged Towards Healthy Lifestyles?', *International Review of Economics*, 64(2), pp. 113–123. doi:10.1007/s12232-016-0264-1.

Sugden, R. (2018) *The Community of Advantage: A Behavioural Economist's Defence of the Market*. New York: Oxford University Press.

Sunstein, C.R. (2013) *Simpler: The Future of Government*. New York: Simon & Schuster.

Sunstein, C.R. (2014) *Why Nudge? The Politics of Libertarian Paternalism*. New Haven: Yale University Press.

Sunstein, C.R. (2015) 'The Ethics of Nudging', *Yale Journal on Regulation*, 32(2), pp. 413–450.

Sunstein, C.R. (2016) *The Ethics of Influence: Government in the Age of Behavioral Science.* New York: Cambridge University Press.

Sunstein, C.R. (2017) *#Republic: Divided Democracy in the Age of Social Media.* Princeton; Oxford: Princeton University Press.

Sunstein, C.R. (2018a) '"Better off, as Judged by Themselves": A Comment on Evaluating Nudges', *International Review of Economics*, 65(1), pp. 1–8. doi:10.1007/s12232-017-0280-9.

Sunstein, C.R. (2018b) 'Misconceptions about Nudges', *Journal of Behavioral Economics and Policy*, 2(1), pp. 61–67.

Sunstein, C.R., Reisch, L.A. and Rauber, J. (2018) 'A Worldwide Consensus on Nudging? Not Quite, but Almost', *Regulation & Governance*, 12(1), pp. 3–22. doi:10.1111/rego.12161.

Sunstein, C.R. and Thaler, R. (2006) 'Preferences, Paternalism, and Liberty', *Royal Institute of Philosophy Supplements*, 59, pp. 233–264. doi:10.1017/S135824610605911X.

Sunstein, C.R. and Thaler, R.H. (2003) 'Libertarian Paternalism Is not an Oxymoron', *The University of Chicago Law Review*, 70(4), pp. 1159–1202. doi:10.2307/1600573.

Thaler, R.H. (2015) *Misbehaving: The Making of Behavioral Economics.* Kindle edition. New York: W.W. Norton & Company.

Thaler, R.H. (2016) 'Behavioral Economics: Past, Present, and Future', *American Economic Review*, 106(7), pp. 1577–1600. doi:10.1257/aer.106.7.1577.

Thaler, R.H. (2018) 'Nudge, not sludge', *Science*, 361(6401), pp. 431–431. doi:10.1126/science.aau9241.

Thaler, R.H. and Sunstein, C.R. (2003) 'Libertarian Paternalism', *The American Economic Review*, 93(2), pp. 175–179.

Thaler, R.H. and Sunstein, C.R. (2008) *Nudge: Improving Decisions About Health, Wealth, and Happiness.* New York: Yale University Press.

Thaler, R.H. and Sunstein, C.R. (2021) *Nudge: Improving Decisions about Money, Health, and the Environment.* Final edition. New York: Penguin Books.

Tresch, R.W. (2014) *Public Finance: A Normative Theory.* Third edition. Cambridge, MA: Academic Press.

Yeung, K. (2017) '"Hypernudge": Big Data as a Mode of Regulation by Design', *Information, Communication & Society*, 20(1), pp. 118–136. doi:10.1080/1369118X.2016.1186713.

Zuboff, S. (2020) *The Age of Surveillance Capitalism: The Fight for a Human Future at the New Frontier of Power.* New York: PublicAffairs.

5 Fortifying Democracy for the Digital Age

Liberal democracy is the currently prevailing incorporation of the Sovereignty Principle, which states that there is no such thing as an exogenous normative authority to which individuals would owe deference. A liberal democratic system abates political irrationality by relying on checks and balances that divide the government power, making it more difficult to misuse, and by introducing counter-majoritarian principles such as the inviolability of fundamental rights and judicial review. Over the last two centuries, this institutional setup has achieved enviable success and witnessed unprecedented human flourishing. Yet, this chapter concerns its reform—possibly a rather significant one.

Why reform liberal democracy? If it isn't broken, don't fix it, as they say. However, there are at least two substantive reasons to be wary of complacency. First, it is one thing to claim that the current system has been historically successful in keeping political irrationality contained, and quite another to conclude that the system is optimized to meet the challenges of the current era. In terms of scientific knowledge regarding human behavior available today, modern democracy's founders were groping in the dark. There is no doubt that concerning the intricacies of human nature, their practical wisdom was extensive and their intuition piercing. Yet, humanity has achieved much epistemic progress since. Thus, even if everything were simply splendid in democratic societies, there would still be a reason to explore the possibilities of reform given the expansion of the relevant knowledge to inform it.

Second, all is not in fact splendid, and the situation of liberal democracy worldwide appears to be deteriorating. While numerous possible culprits for this development have been named, it is hardly imaginable that this has nothing to do with the rapid change in the information technologies that facilitate political discourse. In short, the citizens of liberal democracies are currently living in a constitutional system whose central features have been conceived when news traveled at the speed of a galloping horse, and when most people remained ignorant regarding the political realities in a way that would put even today's "know-nothings" to shame. It is already something of a miracle that liberal democracy has proven capable of prosperity in the age of mass media.[1] There is no guarantee that it can deal with the digital age's fractured and anarchic

DOI: 10.4324/9781003274988-6

information environment equally well. Chapter 3 provided ample grounds for concern in this regard.

To sum up, we should ponder reform because we are more knowledgeable than our predecessors and need to adapt to the shift of technological realities constitutive of our society. There is a pull since we have learned a lot about human behavior and may counter political irrationality more effectively. But there is also a push: the unstoppable digitalization of the democratic discourse probably aggravates the situation and creates a sense of urgency about designing new strategies for the institutional containment of political irrationality.

An institutional reform to tackle political irrationality has already been envisioned by Kelly (2012, chap. 5), who emphasizes the need for stimulating competition among the various frames in which the issues of the day can be expressed. However, my examination of behaviorally informed paternalism—and its drawbacks—in Chapter 4 reveals that a broader approach is necessary. Framing effects are only one facet of the issue we face, after all.

The Landscape of Democratic Reform

Although I have argued that the paternalists' solutions are ill-advised against the background of surging political irrationality, their analysis is still valuable because it draws attention to the prominent features of the conundrum ahead. When viewed from the normative perspective informed by the Sovereignty Principle, what are their main strengths and weaknesses?

Let us start with the positives. These primarily have to do with being "behaviorally informed." Paternalist proposals do succeed in bringing into consideration the cutting-edge findings of behavioral sciences. Also, their drive toward application of experimental methods in the policy realm is laudable. Their ability to generate interventions effective in altering people's behavior is thus well-grounded. Let us consider the distinction analyzed in Chapter 3 between gullibility as a "hardwired" form of irrationality, naivety as irrationality that arises from lack of experience in the given choice environment, and rational irrationality, that is, epistemic or political irrationality driven by broader instrumental considerations such as reputation management. Of these, gullibility and naivety certainly appear amenable to paternalism. Paternalists may nudge gullible choosers in a harmless or even beneficial direction. They may also shove people to overcome their naivety faster. Given that shoves change material incentives, they could also target rationally irrational behavior, although the traditional paternalist rationale for intervention, the "as judged by themselves" principle, is even hazier in this area than elsewhere.

At the same time, the risks and failures of the paternalist approach are also instructive. We have seen in Chapter 4 that the behavioral paternalists falter in establishing transparent, general criteria to identify people's true preferences. Also, the implementation of their program concerned with irrational consumption choices does little to alleviate the arguably more fundamental issue of political irrationality. Quite to the contrary, the expanding scope of government intervention, and its growing behavioral sophistication, make the democratic citizens' burden of political choice heavier, and elevate the preference-revelation via politics to a yet more prominent position. Thus, the public choice problem of policymakers' benevolence becomes particularly salient, as the threat of third-party value imposition looms large.

We can learn a lot concerning the design of democratic institutions resilient toward political irrationality from these examinations of behaviorally informed paternalism. On their blueprint, we can orient the assessment of other democratic reforms' promise to alleviate the threat of political irrationality. I suggest the following shortlist of questions to guide the assessment:

1   Is the reform behaviorally informed?
2   What is its predicted efficacy vis-à-vis the various forms of political irrationality?
3   What mechanism does it suggest for recovering people's preferences that will be treated as normatively binding?
4   Does it presume third-party benevolence?

The first question is motivated by the desire to utilize relevant scientific knowledge in the institutional design. The second targets the distinction between gullibility, naivety, and rational irrationality. Each can trigger political irrationality, but they are susceptible to different treatments. As a result, reform may be powerful in dealing with one of them but impotent when it comes to another. The third question is most intimately associated with the Sovereignty Principle as a normative guideline. If the Principle is to be observed, collective choices must be based on people's preferences. That is, some of their preferences need to be considered normatively binding. What mechanism will guide their revelation? The mechanism needs to discourage political irrationality, but not at the price of an inability to harness the dispersed information on people's valuations. Question four relates to the public choice problem: any reform whose success is contingent on third parties—especially the government—avoiding value imposition, without being compelled to do so, needs to be considered suspect.

These questions may be used to structure the evaluation of a prospective reform. However, the landscape of possible reform is immense, and my coverage of the existing proposals cannot be exhaustive. I shall therefore reduce the task to manageable proportions, first, by categorizing the reform proposals as *marginal* or *radical*, and then addressing some of the most recent and prominent specimens in each category.

Calling the reforms in the first category marginal, it is not my intent to belittle them in any way. Drawing on the economic meaning of the concept, I include proposals that are conceived against the background of the institutional status quo and tackle political irrationality by piecemeal interventions, not by rewriting democracy's basic rules. Marginal reforms' guiding principle is that several minor policy tweaks, taken together, may conquer the mountain of political irrationality one bias at a time. Thus, against the static background of the current liberal democratic institutions, the "marginalists" devise targeted policy solutions to increase the odds of their long-term survival. For instance, enhanced education in critical reasoning that inoculates people against believing fantastic claims offered by low-quality sources or support for independent fact-checking—considered in Chapter 3 as a possible cure for the fake news epidemic—belong to the category of marginal reforms.

The fake news problem is just one part of liberal democracy's current predicament, of course. I shall therefore address marginal reform on a more general level, namely in the form of "budges," that is, behavioral regulations to preclude the use of techniques optimized to exploit irrationality (Oliver, 2013, 2015, 2018b), and "boosts," debiasing methods people may utilize to improve their decision-making performance (Grüne-Yanoff and Hertwig, 2016; Hertwig and Grüne-Yanoff, 2017). These methods call for empowering people to make better choices on their own rather than be guided in a specific direction. A significant advantage of such an approach is, among other things, that it does not require the identification of true preferences at any stage of the process.

Yet, whatever its merits, marginal reform can easily prove insufficient to stem the tide of political irrationality. Its principal defect is that it does not address the incentive problem underlying much political irrationality. Thus, a more radical remodeling of democracy's architecture may be required.

This leads me to the second category of democratic reforms where I place the radical proposals. Their radicalism lies in taking a non-deferential stance toward the institutional status quo. They contemplate changes that introduce nontraditional preference aggregators—that is, voting mechanisms significantly different from the majority rule in its usual forms—or even overhaul the traditional concepts of political representation. Of course, the radical approach is not without its perils. The risk of unintended consequences resulting in a counterproductive outcome is high, not to mention the potentially exorbitant costs of such a failure. The problem of democracy's institutional design is complex, and many features of the proposed solutions remain speculative. Nonetheless, some proposals are intriguing enough to deserve a detailed examination, due to their promise of reshaping citizens' incentives in political choices. As we have seen in previous chapters, perverse incentives have a lot to do with political irrationality, which threatens to subvert the current political order: individual citizens have almost no stake in unbiased information processing and can be swayed frequently by considerations orthogonal to the substance of the issue at hand. If radical reform brings hope for alleviating the incentive issue, its prospects must be appraised carefully.

I shall consider two radical proposals that encompass an incentive overhaul. The first is quadratic voting (QV), originally proposed by E. Glen Weyl (2013) to reproduce the allocative efficiency of competitive markets in the area of collective choice. As such, it belongs in the framework of a broader reform agenda of "radical markets," addressing social issues through the lens of what economists call *mechanism design* (Posner and Weyl, 2018). The goal is to engineer institutions so that they incentivize self-interested agents to behave in ways supportive of desirable social outcomes like efficient public good provision. Since QV is rarely contemplated in relation to political irrationality, it will be instructive to ponder its merits here.

I shall also assess Hélène Landemore's (2020) "open democracy," a system of democratic collective choice that combines sortition—that is, selection of representatives through a lot instead of an election (e.g., López-Guerra, 2011)—and deliberation. In the tradition of deliberative democracy, only the preferences recorded (and aggregated) after a properly conducted deliberation carry normative weight: democracy is not about uncovering and counting preexisting preferences but about discovering and shaping them through discourse among fellow citizens (Bächtiger *et al.*, 2018). If deliberation is set up correctly, "an unforced force of a better argument," to quote Jürgen Habermas' famous dictum, is supposed to triumph and carry the day.

The account of the deliberative formation of preferences sounds rather different from the usual economic assumption of stable preferences that is implicitly present also in the QV proposals. Yet, despite this marked difference, even open democracy can be interpreted in terms of mechanism design, as I shall attempt to do. Where QV appeals to the citizens' material self-interest to motivate them to take their political choices with the seriousness they deserve, given their collective impact, open democracy puts emphasis on social incentives. Both reforms might offer ways to eliminate the incentive deficit that democratic citizens experience in their political choices.

One Step at a Time: Marginal Reform

On the markets, behaviorally informed paternalists target the demand side's bounded rationality "for the people's own benefit," that is, to alleviate the problem of suboptimal or counterproductive choices. Their chief concern is with how the consumers can be discouraged or prevented from behaviors inconsistent with their genuine self-interest. So, consumers can be nudged or shoved away from faulty choices. Of course, the requisite interventions affect both sides of the market: sellers can be required to employ certain features of choice architecture, such as unpalatable graphic warnings, or they may face prohibition on the sale of certain kinds of goods. But it is not the sellers at whom the regulators' gaze is directed: whatever effects these interventions might have on the producers, it is the consumers' psychological limitations and quirks that represent their actual target.

The drawbacks of this approach have already been analyzed. However, taking the criticism to justify complacency about empirically documented systematic mistakes in choices (cf. Rizzo and Whitman, 2019) is unnecessary. The large volume of empirical evidence on systematic mistakes in experimental scenarios would be perilous to ignore. While external and ecological validity issues are often intricate, it is rash to dismiss predictable irrationality as a relevant policy concern on account of the problems that paternalists confront when trying to exploit it in democratically acceptable ways. After all, if there is anything like systematic irrationality, the markets will find potent ways to take advantage of it for the sake of profit maximization (Akerlof and Shiller, 2015). Every department store or e-shop already represents a meticulously fine-tuned and relentlessly perfected choice environment that steers consumers behavior to generate profit. In itself, the spread of the methods of choice architecture through the private sector proves that they work well enough to justify the requisite investment.

How does non-paternalist marginal reform fit into all this? Instead of striving to protect people from their follies as the paternalists do, its goal is to empower them to avoid making systematic mistakes on their own. This can be done in two ways: either via teaching people more effective heuristics and increasing their decision-making competence or via shielding them from the most exploitative communication techniques. The former option has been called "boosts," the latter one "budges." As I shall argue, a significant advantage of these measures compared to nudges and shoves is that they can be applied more easily to choices in both consumption *and politics*, given their lower risk of value imposition.

Boosts

Boosts are grounded in the tradition of "fast and frugal heuristics," or "simple heuristics," associated most prominently with Gerd Gigerenzer (Gigerenzer, 2010; Grüne-Yanoff and Hertwig, 2016). In contrast to nudging—which views reliance on cognitive shortcuts, that is, heuristics, critically as the source of systematic mistakes—the boost approach embraces heuristics' inevitability, given the constrained nature of our cognition (cf. Hertwig and Grüne-Yanoff, 2017, p. 975). The answer to systematic mistakes cannot be the elimination or neutralization of cognitive shortcuts. We better notice how well they perform in most circumstances and learn how their failure mode could be avoided. Accordingly, from the boosters' perspective, the key to alleviating systematic mistakes is in updating and redesigning dysfunctional heuristics: "[boosts] aim to improve individuals' skills or decision tools with the purpose of extending the agent's decision-making *competences*" (Grüne-Yanoff, 2018, p. 212, emphasis mine). Thus, in contrast to nudges, boosts do not achieve better performance through the often-unnoticed exploitation of rationality's bounds but strive to enhance their understanding. The active cooperation of choosers is required because they need to decide to utilize a particular heuristic.

What can a boost look like? This issue is somewhat thorny because the boosters enclose several rather different things under one catchall label (cf. Sims and Müller, 2019, p. 220). They claim that the competence improvement can be achieved *either* by expanding and enhancing the repertoire of the choosers' decision-making skills, *or* by changing the choice architecture to better correspond with his existing skills, *or* by teaching people basic facts about the respective domain (Grüne-Yanoff and Hertwig, 2016, p. 162). However, the triplet of the suggested types of interventions appears to possess too few unifying features. Upgrades of choice architecture in line with the boosting approach seem prima facie difficult to distinguish from nudges and may lack many of the advantages that boosts-qua-competence-enhancers otherwise possess, as the choosers' post-intervention competence set remains unaltered. Information provision, in its turn, lacks the ambition of the truly educative approach boosts strive to offer and makes the problem of third-party benevolence more pressing as information-selection can be manipulated more easily than the selection of skills to teach. Moreover, it is not entirely clear, again, how information provision relates to boosting competence since the set of heuristics at the agents' disposal will not be altered by it.

While the preceding concerns may perhaps be dispelled, I shall take the liberty of narrowing down my examination of boosts to those instances in which teaching new or enhanced competencies occurs. So, I shall concentrate on the examples in which the choosers are truly active as competence-builders, instead of being mere trivia-crunchers or passive receivers of choice-architectonic improvements. The suggested reduction in scope appears well in line with the gist of the boost approach's emphasis on agency, transparency, and education (cf. Hertwig, 2017).

What examples are there of boosts, narrowly taken? They include many of the techniques commonly appearing in self-help literature: for instance, support of self-control via "temptation bundling," that is, the coupling of instantly gratifying activities with activities that are currently unpleasant but promise long-term rewards, financial planning techniques such as basic accounting principles, or training in statistical literacy are included (Grüne-Yanoff and Hertwig, 2016, p. 158; Hertwig and Grüne-Yanoff, 2017, pp. 978–979; Grüne-Yanoff, 2018, p. 212). Some techniques are relatively narrow in their aim, representing "short-term boosts" that improve the choosers' performance in a specific domain. Others, called "long-term boosts," expand or enhance the choosers' general competence vis-à-vis a broad set of problems (Hertwig and Grüne-Yanoff, 2017, p. 977).

So, can boosts avoid the problems that plague the behavioral paternalist policy program? The boosters expend much effort to distinguish their approach from nudging (Grüne-Yanoff and Hertwig, 2016, p. 164; Hertwig and Grüne-Yanoff, 2017, p. 974). From the numerous differences between boosts and nudges that they highlight, some appear particularly significant concerning the issue of political irrationality. Most importantly, since a chooser's active cooperation is required for the boost to be effective, there is a diminished threat of value imposition and little need to identify their exact goal. The choosers are free to apply the boost themselves when and if they see fit, enabling them to evaluate the relevant context independently and utilize their personal, dispersed knowledge that the policymakers cannot access directly. If boosts increase statistical literacy, for instance, they do not need to be directed by a clear prior idea of the specific kinds of context in which the choosers will apply their novel competencies or the ends they will pursue in doing so (cf. Grüne-Yanoff and

Hertwig, 2016, p. 166). The inherent freedom to use or not to use a competence does away with the need for policymakers' benevolence, especially for the more general long-term boosts.[2]

From the perspective of political irrationality, boosts suffer from one fundamental limitation, though. The success of their implementation depends on the ability of choosers to detect their systematic mistakes, their capability and willingness to engage in competence training, and their motivation to put the acquired competence to use. There exist several reasons why these requirements are especially problematic when it comes to political irrationality. First of all, their effect is limited to naivety-induced irrationality. Boosts work neither for gullibility nor for rational irrationality. Gullible choosers' competencies just cannot be improved. If appropriate cognitive levers are pulled, they cannot stop themselves from responding in a particular way.[3] With rational irrationality, incentives get in the way. A rationally irrational person lacks incentives to invest effort into eliminating their default systematic mistakes or even faces incentives toward irrationality. In such an unfortunate setup, boosts cannot be effective because they are not bundled with an incentive change. In short, "boosts require people to be motivated to participate in the intervention. Without their active participation, it cannot be effective" (Grüne-Yanoff and Hertwig, 2016, p. 177). As such, they offer no cure to rational irrationality.

Given our findings regarding the situation in which regular democratic citizens find themselves (Chapter 2), it seems that we have hit a dead-end here. Boosts show promise in areas relevant for collective choice, such as inculcating people with heuristics that allow better decision-making in situations of risk and uncertainty (Hertwig and Grüne-Yanoff, 2017, p. 739). However, with the current incentive setup, the citizens-qua-voters lack the motivation to apply them. The maximum we could hope for is an indirect effect. Let us suppose that people improve their competence for the sake of their private transactions, and the increased competence then spills over into the political realm: arguably, if I am better able to compose my own budget, I can also assess the government's budget proposal with more ease. However, such a solution is conditional on strong expectations regarding the efficacy of boosts and the scope of their applicability. Boosts can be predicted to influence the outcomes of the collective choice only to the extent that their use is free—that is, no more effortful than the use of those default cognitive techniques upon which citizens rely when forming their political beliefs—and not counterproductive with respect to politically irrational goals such as loyalty signaling (Chapter 3). At the same time, boosts could represent a more promising answer to political irrationality if combined with a radical democratic reform that reshapes the incentives of citizens. I shall return to this possibility later.

Budges

Perhaps the limitations of boosts could be circumvented by a different kind of behaviorally informed intervention, namely, budges. Budges, or *behavioral regulations*, have been proposed by Adam Oliver (2013, 2015, 2018a) as another alternative to the dominant libertarian paternalism. Oliver suggests that the risks associated with nudges follow from their intention to tackle internalities and from their form as minutely fine-tuned, even personalized, micro-interventions. As discussed in Chapter 4, the introduction of internalities as a policy rationale dramatically expands the potential scope of government intervention. All that in a situation where no transparent set of welfare enhancement criteria is available (cf. Oliver, 2013, p. 794). At the same time, the inconspicuous, nonintrusive nature of nudges makes them less transparent and more difficult to control democratically. In Oliver's view, these problems can be avoided without sacrificing the possibility of using the findings of behavioral science to make people better off. The scope of intervention needs to be rolled back to externalities, albeit with special emphasis on externalities that follow from exploiting the bounds of people's rationality. Hidden, noncoercive interventions should be replaced by visible, coercive ones—that is, by regulations—that target producers, not consumers. Thus, one could circumvent the problem of an uncontrollably broad rationale for policy intervention and avoid any opacity as the regulatory rules could retain their habitual form of abstract legal rules whose generality makes them relatively transparent.

Budges rely on behavioral sciences to identify widespread cognitive biases and strategies that could be used to exploit them. They counter exploitation by regulating problematic marketing stratagems:

> rather than leaving the supply side largely free while attempting to influence demand so that people make "better" choices, the demand side is left largely free but the supply side is shorn of those goods, services and processes that are deemed excessively exploitative.
>
> (Oliver, 2013, p. 697)

Thus, nudges and budges present answers to different questions. For nudges, it is: "What do people really want, and how should the choice architects design the environment of choice to help them achieve it?" For budges: "Which means of communication or products are too deceptive or manipulative to be permissible?" If the paradigmatic example of a nudge is a default, a paradigmatic example of a budge could be the prohibition on subliminal advertising. Oliver's (2013, p. 698) own examples include "excessive and exploitative marketing techniques" that stimulate excessive drinking and smoking, eating of unhealthy food, driving inefficient vehicles, or unsustainable borrowing (see also Oliver, 2015, pp. 711–712, 2018b, pp. 163–164, 2018a, p. 274).

With budges, there is no need to identify positively what people genuinely want beyond a broad identification of a "bias manipulation." The point is to prevent exploitation of bounded rationality, not to direct choices to a specific alternative. So, budges aim to circumvent the problem of true preferences.

But how promising are budges as a cure to *political* irrationality? Oliver's examples are all directed at problematic profit-seeking activities and commercial communication. At the same time, it does not appear prima facie impracticable to transplant budges into the context of political communication. If subliminal advertising promoting alcohol can be prohibited, so can subliminal advertising that promotes a political candidate or a particular stance on an issue subject to collective choice. As the example of subliminal advertising suggests, there are already many precursors of such regulation in place—often connected to limitations on campaign spending or disclosure requirements (cf. Alemanno and Spina, 2014). From this perspective, perhaps the only change required to adopt Oliver's budge approach is to ground such regulations more systematically and explicitly in the findings of behavioral science.

Moreover, the scope of the applicability of budges is not limited to political communication produced by officially recognized political agents such as the registered parties or candidates. They can equally well target the forms that political and other discourse takes in the digital world. As we have seen in Chapter 3, the destructive potential of fake news is conditional on sophisticated content targeting that enables it to be cheaply delivered to those users who are most likely to appreciate it and help its further spread. Thus, we may picture behavioral regulations targeting digital platforms to limit trading of personal data, increase the platforms' responsibility for the content, push for transparent user agreements, or even update antitrust law to avoid the possibility that a particular framing of political issue(s) will become dominant (cf. Kelly, 2012; Yeung, 2017; Véliz, 2021). One can even imagine a strict regulation on A/B testing that enables the gathering of behavioral data for machine learning and, by extension, for user manipulation.

As an instrument against irrationality, budges' effectiveness is unhindered by gullibility. Being coercive, they prevent people from encountering inadmissibly manipulative communication strategies and choice architectures. Thus, irrationality will not be triggered even if it is "hardwired." With rational irrationality, the story may be more subtle, though. True, to the extent that budges succeed in making problematic content less accessible (i.e., more costly to get), they can be predicted to diminish its consumption. However, much depends on the amount of backlash they produce among the rationally irrational. Budges target the supply side and do not consider the buyers' incentives beyond taking away what could otherwise be their chosen option. Having their favorite product taken away, they will search for ways to acquire a close substitute.

There are also other reasons for caution when it comes to budges. With more than 150 psychological biases on the table, it does not appear unlikely that some fault could be found with essentially any kind of communication if one desires to do so. A message that appeals to people to keep to their habitual ways can be suspected of exploiting their status quo bias and loss aversion. But an opposite message which promotes change and novelty fares no better: maybe it targets the action bias. Is there any objective scientific litmus test to set apart persuasion and manipulation? The distinction appears inevitably normative. Budges thus replace the problem of true preference identification with a new one. Namely, what is the necessary burden of proof to be met before a budge is considered a legitimate measure to prevent suspected manipulation?

Given their nature of general rules, not context-specific micro-interventions, budges are more transparent than nudges. Still, the actual degree of awareness and control the democratic public can be expected to wield is uncertain. If the incumbent government can raise the issue of inadmissible manipulation too easily, the introduction of budges will increase the burden of democratic choice without promising to improve the citizen's incentives to monitor the government's actions. Let us consider the possibility that incumbents will utilize budges to increase their chances for reelection, hindering the opposition's political communication under the pretense of suspected manipulation. For instance, imagine a government skeptical toward the threat of climate change that declares "environmental scare-mongering" off-limits. To maintain a scientific ethos of its decision, it references literature on affect heuristic and framing effects. The resulting budge requires that, in political communication, climate change cannot be referred to as climate *crisis*—let alone climate *collapse*—and any connections drawn between, say, climate change and extreme weather events must include a reference to the appropriate peer-reviewed literature. In short, the risk is that budges empower the incumbents to direct the framing of the issues of the day more easily (cf. Kelly, 2012).

For budge enthusiasts, it should serve as a warning sign that liberal democracies are universally committed to the preservation of freedom of speech. And rightfully so. In political communication, any limitation on free speech needs to be viewed with suspicion as it could be used to suppress political competition. Sure, budges are supposed to address the form of communication rather than its content: any message can, in theory, get across; it just cannot be framed in an overly manipulative way. Nonetheless, disentangling form and content is, of course, tricky in practice. Thus, the currently wobbly basis on which illicit manipulation is to be identified deserves much attention. If it can be improved, budges may represent a welcome ingredient in the policy mix to battle political irrationality. If not, they will suffer from a severe case of the benevolence presumption, like the paternalist interventions do.

Democracy Remodeled: Radical Reform

Neither of the examined marginal reforms provides an immediate solution to political irrationality. Let me thus consider more radical ways to address it. Where the marginal reforms chip at political irrationality one step at a time, radical reformists conceive of a more substantive restructuring of democracy's institutional foundation. Since the invention of democracy, there has never been any shortage of such radical proposals, of course. However, I shall consider a limited range of the recent ones from the perspective of mechanism design.

So far, we have seen that the volume of political irrationality may have much to do with citizens' incentives. Liberal democracy's current institutional setup is to be blamed: in the same way that citizens are not motivated to seek political information for instrumental reasons, they remain unmotivated to second-guess their intuitions, to learn more effective heuristics, or to employ their cognitive faculties effortfully to increase the chance of avoiding systematic errors of judgment. Marginal reforms do not address these incentives. Mechanism design, on the other hand, is all about incentive management. Therefore, if the status quo appears too permissive of irrationality against the background of the ascending digital age, let us ponder the radical democratic reforms potential to change this predicament.

Quadratic Voting

QV strives to enhance the ability of social choice to process information regarding people's valuations. From the perspective of its proponents, the current voting rules, such as the majority rule, have one fundamental weakness: the inability to capture the intensity of people's preferences. Their reliance on the hallowed "one person, one vote" principle of political equality—or *1p1v* principle, following Posner and Weyl (2015)—has the unfortunate side effect that it discards any information on *how strongly* the voter prefers the chosen alternative. It simply requires people to mark their favorite option, no further questions asked. Why specifically is this important, though?

Note that Arrow (1963) has intentionally precluded any information beyond the purely ordinal kind from entering the calculus of social choice: in his view, jettisoning intensity was a feature, not a bug of a desirable aggregation rule. And it is certainly true that the measurement of preference intensity is a delicate task—especially if it is to include any interpersonal comparisons. At the same time, significant advantages accrue to any scheme able satisfactorily address the conundrum: for the QV advocates, these advantages are increased efficiency and increased democratic responsivity (Posner and Weyl, 2015).

The paradigmatic problem addressed by QV is the provision of public goods. In economic parlance, a public good is not just any good provided by the public sector, but one that generates an extreme externality due to its constitutive features, namely non-rivalry and non-excludability. Consider national defense as a public good and notice that much of its job consists of deterrence rather than an active engagement in any military conflict. As such, the services of deterring adversaries that it provides have a specific nature. Providing it to one citizen does not in any way diminish the benefits that another citizen receives from it. Also, no one can be prevented from receiving the benefit without being physically removed from the protected territory—that is, usually a country—which tends to be impractical. This leads to a peculiar problem: while public goods can provide people with extensive benefits, private markets cannot supply them in optimal quantities. As everyone receives the benefits no matter what, then, if the good is provided, everyone also has an incentive to become a free-rider, that is, not to pay for its provision but to save their resources for the goods of a private nature, such as sandwiches or cars.

Certainly, payments for public goods can be made compulsory, that is, these goods can be financed via taxation. Provided each citizen's "tax price" is no greater than their willingness to pay for the public good, the tax-based provision represents a Pareto improvement. The solution has a catch, however. How much do the citizens value the given public good? What is their willingness to pay for it? Since public goods are provided to the whole community in a non-rival and non-exclusive fashion, there is never a moment where individuals are directly observed to pay for their part of the benefits. Also, if we just ask an individual how much they are willing to pay for the sake of charging them a tax price, they are incentivized to confabulate a lower willingness to pay to evade the tax burden. Taking their answer at face value means running back into the under-provision problem. Disregarding the answer leaves the government groping in the dark regarding the efficient quantity of the public good to be provided. The typical solution is that the democratic governments try to divine information pertinent for the public goods' provision from polls and electoral outcomes based on mechanisms such as majority rule that discard any information on preference intensity. Thus, the willingness to pay—a key to efficiency—is dropped from the equation.

And there is yet another setback of the 1p1v aggregation rules: a risk of the *tyranny of the majority*. Because both mild preference and intense preference for an alternative are counted equally, namely as one vote in the alternatives' favor, majorities can obtain inefficient victories when they approve proposals that they care little about against an intense minority opposition. Note that "minority" and "majority" are no fixed coalitions but differ for each issue. The same person can be in a minority when it comes to approving gay marriage, but in a majority when expropriation of the rich gets on the table. Since it is easy to see how this problem could lead to a situation where—to everybody's detriment—transient majorities engage in predatory behavior against equally transient minorities, there is a pressing need to address the threat of majority tyranny. The counter-majoritarian features that we have considered in connection to the political irrationality of liberal democracies, such as the judicial review and the constitutional protection of fundamental rights, also serve to preclude this tyranny. However, their presence makes the political system less transparent and less responsive to people's preferences, that is, ultimately less democratic (Posner and Weyl, 2015).

QV promises to solve both issues—inefficiency and tyranny of the majority—via mechanism design. It wants to place the individuals in such an incentive setup, where revealing the true intensity of their preferences is in their best interest. The idea of mechanism design is not new. Unfortunately, the proposals in its tradition—most prominently the Vickrey–Clark–Groves (VCG) auction mechanisms—tend to be rather impractical for mass democratic social choice on account of their complexity and vulnerability to manipulation (Posner and Weyl, 2015, p. 471, 2017, p. 4). The participants need to understand the complicated rules of the mechanism perfectly, and they must be prevented from coordinating to "game the system," that is, from colluding.

QV wants to overcome the limitations of the VCG mechanism. According to its proponents (Posner and Weyl, 2015, 2017; Weyl, 2017; Lalley and Weyl, 2018), it offers a much simpler, more robust, and equally efficient solution to the problem of revealing preference intensity. What does it look like? Awarding victory to the alternative which receives the most votes, its key innovation is that it dismantles the 1p1v principle and enables the voters to purchase as many votes as they desire: the more intense one's preference, the greater one's spending and the stronger one's voice.[4]

However, will a possibility to purchase extra votes not replace the risk of tyranny of majority with the certitude of the "tyranny of wealth" (Archer, Engelen and Ivanković, 2019)? In the QV system, government monopoly on vote-selling and maintenance of an appropriate price schedule is key to the proposals' functionality. The requisite schedule is quadratic. If one vote costs €1, two votes go for €4, three votes for €9, and so on. A quadratic increase in the votes' price represents the middle road between the tyranny of wealth and 1p1v indifference toward preference intensity.[5] The initial votes are cheap enough, but buying additional ones gets very expensive very fast (cf. Posner and Weyl, 2015, pp. 488–489). A thousand votes—hardly an astonishing number as it would seem—would go for €1,000,000.

Moreover, notice that the marginal cost of a vote increases linearly. Why is that important? For rational decision-makers maximizing their utility, the marginal variables are decisive for their choices, not the totals. Accordingly, one chooses to buy three sandwiches not because their *total* value is greater than their total cost, but because one's willingness to pay is above the market price for the third sandwich but below it for the fourth one. As noted, QV strives to introduce an analogical measure of preference intensity into the collective choices upon the supply of public goods. Suppose you buy four votes for €16, and I buy eight votes for €64. Well, then the marginal cost of your fourth vote is €7, and the marginal cost of my eighth vote is €15. That is, if I feel twice as strongly about the given issue, I end up buying twice as many votes (there is some obvious approximation here, but not too sizable). Right?

Well, there is one more issue to consider: the free-rider problem. We must remember that the main problem with the provision of public goods was incentivizing people to reveal their true valuation. Accordingly, one may care about an issue deeply, but he is also tempted to save his money for other things, hoping that the remaining voters will win the issue without his assistance. Therefore, how does the QV system motivate voters to spend money buying votes? The QV proponents, being sophisticated game theorists, do expect people to consider the option of freeriding, of course. However, they also expect people to recognize the possibility that their votes will end up being pivotal in the election. Of course, my favored alternative will probably win or lose, even if I do not purchase an additional vote in its favor. But maybe not! There is necessarily a nonzero probability that the vote will end up being pivotal. Accordingly, the citizens are expected to purchase votes based on their valuation of the alternative at hand weighted by the probability that their next vote will be pivotal.

Valuing a project at €1,000, I shall gladly purchase a vote for €1 if there is a 1% probability that it will prove decisive; someone who only values the project at €50 would not make the purchase on the same terms. If everybody has the same expected probability of their vote being pivotal—which is most likely if the number of voters is large—the resulting spending will precisely mirror the relative intensity of their preferences (Posner and Weyl, 2015, p. 477).

All this sounds intriguing; is there a catch then? Unfortunately, there are quite a few.

Despite being more robust than the VCG mechanism (Weyl, 2017), QV remains vulnerable to collusion. Suppose that like-minded citizens coordinate their voting activity and form a voting bloc, that is, an organized interest group. Instead of buying many votes at high marginal prices, the bloc members with high willingness to pay (WTP)—in other words, those with the highest income or most extreme preferences—will do better if they funnel resources to the members who would themselves buy only a few votes. So, the number of votes purchased can be maximized against the constraint of the block's aggregate WTP, not the individual WTPs: instead of spending €100 to obtain their tenth vote, a high-WTP individual can funnel the resources elsewhere and secure, say, 50 second votes from the low-WTP bloc members. Moreover, each vote on "my side" of an issue increases the probability that my preferred alternative will win. Thus, it creates a positive externality for the other people who share the direction of my preference. As is well known, goods that generate positive externalities end up undersupplied in a competitive marketplace. Collusion decreases the spillover, and it does so more effectively if a greater share of the alternative's supporters become coordinated. Thus, it internalizes the externality and allows the voting block to translate resources into votes more efficiently even if direct money-funneling is precluded.

As it would appear, an asymmetric group mobilization around a signature issue represents no fringe concern (see Chapter 3). In response, Weyl (2017, pp. 81–87) asserts that successful collusion is unlikely because the bloc members face incentives to defect and because the citizens opposing the bloc's agenda would mobilize to thwart its efforts once they became apparent. However, there are at least two problems with such a defense of QV's robustness. Both have to do with the assumptions employed by the most elaborate proofs of QV's superiority over 1p1v systems in terms of efficiency (Lalley and Weyl, 2018). First, democratic citizens are supposed to behave as Econs at their most extreme form: they need to be hyperrational to estimate the probability of being pivotal, and selfish to limit their considerations to their own expected benefits. Second, the information pertaining to pivotality estimates needs to be free or distributed symmetrically across the population: remember that all the citizens are supposed to come to the same estimate (Posner and Weyl, 2015, p. 477). What happens if these assumptions are violated as they almost certainly are in democracy's current setup?

Consider the problem of costly information first. Goodman and Porter (2021) point out organized interest groups' superior ability to gather information and distribute it among their members. Even if interest groups can be prevented from moving resources among their members to maximize the obtained vote count, they cannot be prevented from providing information relevant to the pivotality estimates. Because the probability of being decisive is the key variable in the QV calculus, the groups' information edge allows them to allocate resources more efficiently. Thus, concentrated interests must be expected to obtain an even greater advantage with QV than in 1p1v systems.

Costly information causes trouble even if the assumption of hyperrational citizens is retained. With politically irrational behavior, QV's outlooks are murkier yet. Posner and Weyl (2015, p. 497) argue that "voter irrationality is not a problem for QV as long as the irrationality is approximately uniform across individuals—more specifically, as long as the irrationality is not correlated with the utility that individuals gain from different laws or projects." So, if irrationality uniformly increases participation, it makes no difference or may even prove beneficial because it decreases the probability that extremists' collusion could be successful (Posner and Weyl, 2015, p. 498; Weyl, 2017). However, considering our examinations in Chapters 1 and 2, this is not how political irrationality typically works. Even if we consider just gullibility, that is, "hardwired" irrationality, which is most likely to be uniformly distributed, it works non-randomly by skewing the perception of alternatives' costs and benefits. True, biases would not matter if both the citizens who favor a trade deal and the citizens who oppose it were casting 20% or 200% more votes than an Econ would. But consider the findings regarding the prevalence of folk-economic beliefs (Boyer and Petersen, 2018). In their light, expect the trade deal's benefits to be underestimated systematically and its costs overestimated. Thus, be the participation based on a hyperrational or biased estimate of pivotality, the outcome will be biased anyway. It is not the bias in the estimate of pivotality but the bias in the estimate of the alternative's benefits that undermines the wisdom of crowds here.

Moreover, even irrationality's influence on pivotality estimates is unlikely to be as well-behaved as Posner and Weyl (2015) hope. As Kaplow and Kominers (2017) point out, the technical literature on QV does not ask why the voters bother to show up at the election and posits full participation instead. So, the paradox of voting and all the complications for rational choice that follow in its path (see Chapter 2) are assumed away. With an electorate in the usual size in millions, such a "simplification" produces misleading expectations: as it turns out, the negligible probability of being pivotal matters a lot for QV too. If people were rational and selfish, participation would be a negligible fraction of what is commonly observed in democratic countries. The fact of mass participation thus requires other explanation: quoting people's altruism, non-instrumental motivations, irrationality, or some combination thereof is most common. Is it credible that the same people who participate due to such motives revert to hyperrationality once they whip up their credit cards to purchase votes? Vis-à-vis a realistic pivotality probability, the optimal spending would be nowhere in the realm of multiple € and votes suggested by the above examples. A hyperrational voter in a mass election needs to be expected to spend a fraction of a cent to obtain a tiny fraction of a vote, even if they have intense preferences (Kaplow and Kominers, 2017, pp. 137–139).

For better or worse, hyperrational voters' behavior is perhaps of secondary importance since their very existence is doubtful. Considering what we know about the actual voters, Kaplow and Kominers (2017) emphasize three issues in particular: the same motivations that drive participation will also drive vote-purchasing; the voters will not rely on complex pivotality estimation but on simple rules of thumb to decide the volume of their spending; the organized interest groups will mobilize their members using social—not just material—incentives. For instance, a simple rule of thumb such as "spend €1" or "spend €10" would save much cognitive effort without overextending many voters' budgets. At the same time, if applied, it greatly overshoots efficient spending. Thus, as far as any sophisticated voters vote instrumentally, their tiny vote counts will be insignificant for the outcome of collective choice (Econs should expect this and abstain anyway), and intensity weighting will be all but eliminated from the system. QV also opens an additional avenue of influence by allowing organized interest groups to nudge—maybe even shove—their members toward a focal point of higher spending. As a result, "the battle among focal points across various affinity groups could be the most important determinant of election outcomes" (Kaplow and Kominers, 2017, p. 145).

In the light of these difficulties, does QV bear any promise to quell political irrationality? The current developments around QV suggest that it might. Some of its most troubling aspects have to do with trading votes for money. Suppose instead that QV would utilize an artificial currency—that is, "voice credits" (Posner and Weyl, 2018, chap. 2)—whose use is limited to vote-buying. For instance, Posner and Stephanopoulos (2017, p. 266) suggest that each person obtains 100 credits upon reaching the age of 18. They are then able to spend any fraction of these credits in their first election allocating them among the candidates to purchase votes in the quadratic fashion. The credits that remain unspent can be used in the next election and so on. Each voter's stock of credits may also be replenished periodically. Posner and Stephanopoulos (2017, p. 266) suggest a period of ten years, after which an additional 100 credits are provided.

From the point of view of QV's acceptability as a device of democratic decision-making, it is perhaps most important that the voice credit scheme avoids introducing political inequality. Each citizen is endowed with an equal number of credits that they can dispose of as they see fit. One of the main sources of controversy is thus removed (cf. Ober, 2017). At the same time, the main advantage of QV compared to the 1p1v systems—that is, the possibility to express the intensity of one's preferences—is preserved.

Well, at least to some extent. It is no longer possible to care more about *all* political issues than somebody else, as it was before (Posner and Weyl, 2018, pp. 122–123). Also, the opportunity costs are transformed. In the original proposal, political spending channels resources from private consumption. Spending €1 on votes means giving up €1 in terms of private goods. The introduction of voice credits changes this calculus. Now, the opportunity cost is purely political.

Credits used to obtain votes cast for the sake of one issue mean a weaker voice when it comes to other issues. If Josh allocates most of his credits trying to push forward carbon taxation, he gives up an opportunity to influence social policy, for instance. If Angela spends her endowment in the current election to prevent the victory of a candidate that she finds particularly unsavory, she sacrifices her influence on the outcome of the next election in the row.

The introduced non-translatability between money and votes does not have straightforward implications. It restores the boundary between markets and politics since one no longer spends "real money" but an artificial currency whose usage is restricted to politics. But it is unclear if the opportunity cost of obtaining votes is reduced or increased this way. On the one hand, voters do not sacrifice their private consumption to secure political influence, and one may therefore be tempted to conclude that their incentives to take their political choices seriously are thus reduced. On the other hand, the framing of political choice as "something else" than a mere market transaction promotes the salience of political trade-offs included in spending the vote credits. It is also vital that the voice credits cannot be replenished at will. While in the original proposal one is always free to funnel more resources into politics if the need arises, voice credits fix the amount of the resources available. The political trade-offs forced by this constraint can end up being more painful than the trade-offs implied in the original money-for-votes QV proposals. Where the original strives to address only the issues of allocation (any purely redistributive proposal would be blocked [Posner and Weyl, 2015, p. 483]), voice credits imply expansion beyond the paradigmatic problems of allocation like the public goods provision toward distributional issues. The increased salience and more pressing nature of the political trade-offs, therefore, offer a decent chance that the political choices will be perceived as more serious by the citizens, compared to the original QV proposal. Also, to the extent it is easier to frame a modest outlay of money as a charitable donation for the sake of a common cause—compared to asking people to sacrifice their political voice—the interest groups' outsized influence might be diminished. Nonetheless, collusion remains a significant threat.

Moreover, vis-à-vis a limited endowment of voice credits, the issue of agenda-setting is particularly prominent. Flooding the agenda with irrelevant or extreme proposals becomes a serious challenge to the system. "Crazy" items could be used to pump out the citizen's voice credit budget. This implies a broader point: creating a plan for optimal voice credits spending in the face of uncertainty regarding the agenda—let alone on the time scales anywhere near those suggested by Posner and Stephanopoulos (2017)—is cognitively demanding, if not impossible. As it would appear, the whole agenda would need to be known in advance for the whole period when the votes are valid to allow for proper planning: hardly a realistic possibility given the dynamic nature of politics.

All things considered, the shift toward the voice credits requires a sacrifice of rigor for the sake of experimentation. The proofs of QV's superiority over 1p1v in models with a binary choice, real currency, Econs, and full participation have little to say how well the things will go with, say, multi-contest choice, or multi-candidate election (cf. Kaplow and Kominers, 2017, pp. 145–146; Levine, 2020, p. 480) by mere humans with all their quirks and irrationalities using voice credits. However, experimentation is necessary anyway—the empirical specters of psychological and sociological factors influencing the voters' behavior beyond the narrow bounds of political rationality cannot be otherwise accounted for despite probably being decisive (cf. Posner and Weyl, 2017, p. 21).

From the perspective of behavioral political economy, we must consider how the voice credit QV scheme would function with gullible, naïve, or rationally irrational citizens. Voice credits limit the complexity of the choice situation to political trade-offs and thus save the voters from the necessity to consider what amount of private resources they should sacrifice to further their political goals. Nonetheless, even this simplified setting is far from straightforward and transparent. The political choices remain complex and agenda uncertainty makes it difficult to plan how to distribute one's spending across time. Since we cannot safely presume that the uncertainty is distributed uniformly—with insiders and interest groups being in a better position to foresee the future agenda and actively shape it—this represents another feature of the QV system with hard-to-predict, probably detrimental consequences. Perhaps the greatest shortcoming of the QV system, even with voice credits that increase the saliency of the political trade-offs, is that it does not create significant incentives toward political rationality. Of course, incentives are not a panacea; they leave gullibility untouched. But they would matter for both naïve and rationally irrational voters pushing them toward more effective heuristics and more serious consideration of the political issues' substance relative to their symbolic meaning. Even with voice credits, a single citizen remains a drop in the sea of voices. There is nothing to discourage them from reliance on default intuitions.

In short, the main problems with the voice-credit-based QV system are that it does not go far enough in creating incentives that discourage political irrationality and does not address the issue of agenda-setting. These shortcomings are burdensome, but perhaps not insuperable. I shall take the opportunity to consider QV as a potentially worthy complement of "open democracy," to which I turn next.

Open Democracy

Can a greater emphasis on deliberation cure democracy's ills? There is an ascending stream in democratic theory that replies in the affirmative. From its perspective, the concern about aggregating preferences—that I have adopted as the guiding light of my analysis since Chapter 2—is misguided in limiting its attention to an aspect of the democratic game which is of merely secondary importance. Deliberative democrats reject the notion that preformed preferences should be normatively binding for democratic choice. What happens *before* the citizens get to cast their vote is of the essence. If deliberation did not test the mettle of the preferences-to-be-aggregated, no sophisticated aggregation rule can save the day. In deliberative democrats' eyes, one cannot be considered as having formed the preferences worthy of normative deference prescribed by the Sovereignty Principle, unless one has encountered disagreement and honestly considered the reasons that drive it.

Perhaps most broadly, deliberation can be defined as "mutual communication that involves weighing and reflecting on preferences, values, and interests regarding matters of common concern" (Bächtiger et al., 2018, p. 2). Such a minimalist definition intentionally avoids taking a normative stance, required to justify the above statements on deliberation's virtues, though. Whatever criteria are used to distinguish "good" and "bad" deliberation, both will fit into the definition's confines. On the one hand, minimalism is convenient because deliberative democracy as a school of thought represents a broad stream of ideas which unites authors with varying normative commitments and any more demanding definition would be contested. On the other hand, since this chapter has embarked upon a quest to uncover a democratic reform to blunt the effects of political irrationality more effectively than the current liberal–democratic institutional setup does, it cannot shy away from a normatively thicker definition. Given our considerations in Chapter 3, counting partisan scuffles on social media as cases of deliberation appears inadvisable.

Accordingly, I shall rely on a definition by List (2018) who shares my interest in bringing together the aggregative and deliberative notions of democracy for a thicker account of deliberation. As he puts it:

> deliberation [is] a communicative procedure, typically in the run-up to a collective decision, which is designed to promote substantive, balanced, and civil discussion. "Substantive" means that it focuses on the options and the reasons for preferring or dispreferring them (this may include narratives and the sharing of experiences); "balanced" means that it involves different perspectives, arguments, and views; and "civil" means that it is respectful [...].
> (List, 2018, p. 468)

Deliberation, thus understood, bears promise to enhance collective decision-making along several routes beyond the obvious fact that the participants will probably become better informed of each other's views in its course. Notably, deliberation represents a significantly more information-intensive procedure than voting: as we have already considered in the case of QV, voting that only records a person's ordinal preference is informationally impoverished. Relative to any aggregation method, deliberation allows for much richer information intake. Benson (2019) even considers it potentially superior to decentralized competitive markets in this regard. Also, it may help to establish a "meta-consensus" on the relevant dimension of the problem at hand and increase the probability that the resultant preferences will be single peaked, thus avoiding cycles in collective choices (Dryzek and Niemeyer, 2006) that represent the most prominent technical setback pertaining to the use of majority rule (see Chapter 2).

Still, from the perspective taken in this book, these are secondary concerns. As we have already discussed, voters' ignorance is less detrimental than meets the eye, as far as it breeds random mistakes. The emergence of cycles is probably also quite rare. Systematic mistakes, that is, political irrationality triggered on grounds of gullibility, naivety, or rational irrationality, appear a much more pressing issue. It is therefore of prime interest if deliberation can also help to limit their frequency. Intriguingly, it has been suggested that "careful institutional design [of deliberation]—involving participant diversity, facilitation, and civility norms—enables well-known problematic psychological biases and dynamics to attenuate or disappear" (Dryzek *et al.*, 2019, p. 1146). It is this claim that I shall focus upon.

To assess deliberative democracy's promise as a cure to political irrationality in a way consistent with our previous discussion, I shall examine it through the lens of the mechanism design problem. Accordingly, I shall treat deliberation as a procedure that changes the incentives for the participating citizens in a way that may limit politically irrational behavior. For the sake of this exercise, two assumptions inherent to the economic approach—which I have utilized throughout the book—need to be reemphasized.

The first assumption is motivational neutrality: to the extent that people are self-interested and sensitive to material or reputational incentives in the regular walks of life, they will remain so in any deliberative setting. This assumption goes against the grain of many a deliberative democrat's disdain for self-interest and their faith that deliberation will transform people into a more altruistic version of themselves (cf. Mansbridge *et al.*, 2010). In my model, any increase in citizens' public-mindedness—relative to the status quo—needs to be explained through a change in incentives (cf. Landa and Pevnick, 2021, p. 51).

The second assumption is that the deliberative reform must be workable from the viewpoint of cost-benefit analysis: namely, it cannot be prohibitively costly to implement on a meaningful scale. This precludes any schemes that would call for avoiding post-deliberative preference aggregation on the grounds that reaching consensus is necessary, for instance. Not only because consensus may be infeasible in principle given irreconcilable competing interests, but also because it tends to generate exorbitant decision-making costs: the negotiations can be protracted, plagued by opportunistic preference misrepresentations, and fortify the status quo. Additionally, the citizens' opportunity costs of participation need to be considered, as these restrict the projects of mass deliberation. In short, any proposal that would expect the democratic citizens to expend unrealistic amounts of effort and time is impractical. What works experimentally may not be scalable to proportions necessary to bring about meaningful change in a mass democratic system. For instance, while "deliberative polls" with dozens or even hundreds of participants may perform amazingly, a scheme where all citizens would be invited to participate in deliberation—a Deliberation Day (Ackerman and Fishkin, 2004)—would represent an immensely complicated and costly solution to the problem of deliberation.

Even with these assumptions at hand, the field of reforms to promote democracy's deliberative aspect remains broad. To enable a sufficiently detailed examination, I shall limit the scope of my attention to Hélène Landemore's project of *open democracy* (Landemore, 2020). There are several reasons for this: she puts the scalability problem at the center stage (Landemore, 2020, pp. 64, 206), appreciates the issue of incentives (Landemore, 2020, pp. 45–46, 204), and is technologically informed (Landemore, 2021). All these features align her proposal well with the intent of this book. A note of caution: my approach will be significantly more "economistic" than Landemore's own and thus perhaps somewhat normatively impoverished relative to her original analysis.

Instead of trying to manage the next to impossible task to get a meaningful part of the whole mass of democratic citizens to deliberate while otherwise keeping in the confines of the liberal democratic system, Landemore suggests a radical change in the way political representation is conceived. Elections are to be replaced with a lottery that produces a random sample representative of the populace at large. The citizens chosen via this lottery would become lottocratic representatives tasked to deliberate and ultimately produce binding political decisions via a majority vote. For the sake of preserving representativity, participation of the lottocratically selected citizens may be mandatory similar to jury duty (cf. Landemore, 2020, pp. 90, 97). In short, Landemore envisions an "open mini-public" as the central body of collective choice. It represents

> a large, all-purpose, randomly selected assembly of between 150 and a thousand people or so, gathered for an extended period of time (from at least a few days to a few years) for the purpose of agenda-setting and law-making of some kind, and connected via crowdsourcing platforms and deliberative forums (including other mini-publics) to the larger population.
>
> (Landemore, 2020, p. 13)

From my economistic viewpoint, there are several noteworthy features of the proposal. First, both lottocratic representation and employment of the majority rule—whatever their other virtues—serve as cost-saving measures. Instead of bearing the costs of scaling deliberation to the citizenry at large, it is only the selected sample that engages in it while being adequately compensated for their efforts. Consensus during deliberation is not required; deliberation is followed by an aggregative phase when decisions are made via majority rule, eliminating the threat that a decision will be blocked by an intransigent minority.

How about the incentives, though? Intriguingly, Landemore appears committed to the view that incentives may represent a key to eliminating political irrationality: in her view, the empirically recorded inconsistencies between democratic ideals and citizens' actual behavior can be attributed to the current institutional setup of liberal democracy: "[… It] is not that we have the wrong ideal of democracy. Instead, it is that we have the wrong institutional translation of it" (Landemore, 2020, p. 45). If so, what incentives do democratic citizens have not to misbehave in their role of lottocratic representatives?

There are two distinct categories of incentives to consider: material incentives and social incentives. The former has to do with a greatly increased probability of casting a pivotal vote that the lottocratic representatives—and representatives in general—enjoy compared to regular citizens. Being more decisive concentrates one on the substantive trade-offs involved in the issue at hand. One's own well-being is at stake since one creates the rules that will bind one as well, and one's influence upon their shape is far from negligible. The latter arises from the fact that representatives find themselves in the spotlight, being observed and judged by their peers, but also by the public at large. Here, one's reputation is at stake, often with tangible long-term consequences. While the two kinds of incentives are not necessarily at odds, the likelihood of their conflict is significant. Where social incentives push one via the reputation-management channels toward displaying public-mindedness, material incentives stimulate narrow self-interest. And not always can self-interest be defended by demonstrating its social desirability.

Both the increased pivotality probability and the increased social pressure distinguish a lottocratic representative from a regular citizen. But their position is distinctive compared to an elected representative too. While the size of both the elected and the lottocratic chamber of representatives may be similar or identical, what differs is the number of the terms in office one may reasonably expect. In a liberal democracy, incumbents are famously difficult to defeat, often leading to life-long political careers. In a lottocracy, the political professionalization would be minimized. Given that the probability to be randomly selected to a high-level decision-making body is minuscule, lottocratic representatives need to count only with a single term in the office. Moreover, their tenure may be relatively brief: Landemore (2020, p. 142) emphasizes the need for periodic rotation as a corrective to the threat of misuse of power. This alters the incentive calculus, of course.

Let me concentrate on the material incentives first. From their perspective, the one-off nature of the lottocratic representation may diminish the pressure to please the crowds. It is a generally accepted claim in behavioral political economy, that politicians interested in reelection face strong pressure to pander to political irrationality if it is sufficiently widespread (Lucas and Tasić, 2015). The breathing space provided by lottocracy may therefore be welcome—at least if deliberation works the promised way and leads to collective choices less plagued by systematic biases that so often characterize the intuitive understanding of political issues (Boyer and Petersen, 2018).

However, the absence of prospects for a long-term political career also has some rather worrisome ramifications, recently highlighted by Landa and Pevnick (2021). Since the one-off nature of the lottocratic tenure is given by the basic features of the system, perhaps the most important choice variable in designing its implementation is the tenure's length. Unfortunately, there exists a particularly disconcerting trade-off that needs to be considered. Longer tenures create more powerful lottocrats and increase the probability of the misuse of power. In particular, longer tenures provide better opportunities for the interest groups that hope to sway their decision-making in their preferred direction. The more decisions that a given lottocrat has a chance to influence, the more attractive a partner for a mutually beneficial relationship with special interests they become. While outright corruption can perhaps be precluded, the problem of revolving doors looms particularly large in a lottocracy since a sustained political career is not an option (Landa and Pevnick, 2021, pp. 54–55). Support for the interest groups' agenda can be rewarded with a promise—perhaps an implicit one—of a lucrative job after one is released from their service as a representative.

Brief tenure diminishes the opportunities for the outsized influence of interest groups, but at a significant cost. It may encourage short-term, predatory thinking and certainly does not do away with the incentives that lottocratic representatives have to follow their own narrowly self-interested goals. Moreover, it exacerbates the risk of bureaucratic capture (Landa and Pevnick, 2021, p. 64). Short-term representatives have a lesser incentive—and a much-diminished opportunity—to achieve the political expertise necessary for an autonomous orientation in procedural matters and the capability to hold one's ground vis-à-vis a professional public servant. This is a task challenging for a career politician, let alone a lottocratic representatives torn out of their regular life for a brief moment.

Moreover, in deliberative settings, the threat of third-party meddling is more pronounced than elsewhere, given the need for "curating" the discussion. Apparently, proper facilitation and moderation are key for the benefits of deliberation to emerge: their role is to keep the discussion within the confines of its proper theme and encourage participants to consider the arguments of either side, while giving no hint regarding their own opinion (Fishkin *et al.*, 2021, pp. 1468–1469). In experimental settings, where no political decisions are made by the deliberative assembly, it is perhaps easy to presume that only moderators with a genuine interest regarding the quality of deliberation will be interested in participating. However, if the same procedure would be used "for real," that is, with binding political choices as an outcome, there would arise mighty incentives for the moderators to nudge the deliberative process toward a specific outcome. Arguably, this issue of third-party interventions into the democratic process requires more sustained attention in democratic theory than it has received so far (Smith, 2009, p. 169).

Still, while the risks of bureaucratic capture and revolving doors are significant, perhaps they can be attenuated by the social incentives that eclipse the material ones in Landemore's (2020) proposal. It must first be noted that, given the assumption of motivational neutrality, I do not consider social preferences to be of a different nature than material incentives in any ultimate sense. It is just that the pressure they exercise derives from the influence of one's choices as a lottocratic representative on one's personal reputation and social status. For an overwhelming majority of people, becoming a pariah is neither pleasant nor lucrative. Also, lottocratic representatives would be less thick-skinned than today's career politicians who are both self-selected and professionalized to withstand a significant amount of scorn.

The lottocratic representatives are regular people called upon to proclaim and defend their position in front of the other representatives and in the view of the general public. Given human evolved sensitivity to the others' opinion of themselves and obsession with social status discussed in Chapter 3, the hope is that the social incentives will press them to become "their own best self" and take their task with great seriousness not just because of the immediate material stakes but also for the sake of their public standing. As Landemore (2020, p. 203) paints the picture of a lottocratic assembly, the need for deliberation creates "discursive accountability" because credible and publicly acceptable reasons must be given to justify a position one defends. If need be, reputational concerns can be further stimulated by a reputation-tracking mechanism familiar from today's digital sphere: peer evaluations of the lottocratic representatives would be accessible together with a record—probably permanent and searchable—of their activities (Landemore, 2020, p. 204). Simply put, it is the transparency of the lottocratic assembly's dealings—and the social incentives it creates—that should secure the representatives' accountability where the prospect of a second term is missing.

However, social incentives should not be treated as a single homogeneous category. Deliberation is expected to transform its participants' preferences. If it is only the lottocratic representatives who deliberate, their preferences will thus diverge from the preferences of the public at large. Suppose the regular democratic citizens are prone to "emporiophobia," that is, an intuitive distaste toward the markets (Rubin, 2014), but deliberation tends to attenuate this bias. Since we cannot presume that the mass of democratic citizens will have the resources (or the propensity) to follow the assembly's debates in any detail, the median views of the representatives and the people will grow apart. Therefore, we need to distinguish two kinds of social incentives: internal ones where the representative's deliberative peers are concerned, and external ones, which pertain to the public at large.

Internal social incentives come from within the lottocratic assembly. They depend on how much a representative values their reputation in the eyes of the other representatives. However, such reputation tracking can only be achieved when the size of the lottocratic representative body is limited enough for its members to know each other personally (cf. Fishkin *et al.*, 2021). The more anonymous the deliberative assembly, the lesser is the power of the internal social incentives. When considering an upper limit for a size of a group strongly bound together on reputational grounds, the famous Dunbar's number—that is, 150—comes to mind, which corresponds with the lower bound of Landemore's proposal on the size of deliberative assembly in an open democracy. However, the more limited the size of the assembly, the less likely it is that it will be representative of the population at large, as random sampling can deliver representativeness only with large numbers.

External social incentives are provided by the general public. Unfortunately, their alignment with the internal ones cannot be expected. On average, regular citizens will be much less sophisticated than the representatives themselves simply because they lack the privilege of having deliberation as their full-time job. The public at large will not undergo any debiasing process. On the contrary, they will possess very limited information about the particulars of the ongoing deliberative process, and this information will be skewed. Selective media coverage will emphasize the "infotaining," spectacular moments of the deliberative process rather than the substantive ones. In particular, imagine the digital Synopticon of social media presenting the ongoing deliberative process as a variation on the Big Brother reality show.

After their, quite possibly brief, tenure is over, it is the lottocratic representative's reputation with the mass public rather than a reputation with their peers that will determine their fate. External social incentives can thus derail the deliberative process making the representatives pander to the crowds, tempting them to build up a public reputation via rationally irrational partisanship, intransigence, or just mirroring the popular biases. In this vein, Chambers (2004) warns from the detrimental influence of "plebiscitory reason" which provides arguments that—instead of aiming to persuade the fellow deliberators—are fitted to manipulate the public, pander to its worst instincts, and build a flattering image of the speaker in its eyes.

Consequently, the relative strength of the internal versus external social incentives may be decisive for open democracy's success. Much depends on finding the proper balance between internal and external social pressures. Too much shielding from the exterior and open democracy will lack legitimacy among the masses; too little shielding and it will not deliver the promised epistemic and political goods. Thus, the greatest challenge for open democracy seems to lie in finding the optimal degree of transparency and optimal balance between the social and material incentives. One key issue is the publicity of the ballot. Given increased pivotality, a secret ballot would eliminate the influence of social incentives, probably leading to selfish voting and loss of legitimacy. On the other hand, a public ballot may lead to the external social incentives dominating the internal ones. Does a semi-public ballot, where only other representatives can access the information regarding one's vote, represent a workable solution?

To appreciate the complexities that open democracy faces, consider the Icelandic experiment which Landemore (2020, chap. 7) uses as her paradigmatic case study. The constitutional proposal created in the experiment has been criticized by international observers for offering an overly extensive list of vaguely phrased rights that would create "a strong risk that the public takes them as promises to ensure high living conditions" (Venice Commission 2013, p. 7). Did the criticized formulation arise on account of the unforced force of a better argument? Or does it reflect material self-interest of the majority of lottocratic representatives—that is, nothing else than tyranny of the majority—who took the opportunity to redistribute from the haves to the have-nots? Or should we seek the "plebiscitory reason" behind it? The answer is, of course, elusive, but it nevertheless appears crucial for the evaluation of open democracy's potential.

All things considered, can open democracy provide a better bulwark against political irrationality than liberal democracy? From the proposals covered so far, it is the most forceful in its work with incentives. It fully appreciates the problematic incentives of citizens in liberal democracy and strives to change their predicament. One important step in the right direction—judging from the perspective of the Sovereignty Principle—is to endow the lottocratic representatives with agenda-setting power. These features make open democracy less reliant on third-party benevolence unless bureaucratic capture succeeds. Given that lottocratic representatives have their necks on the line—both materially and socially—their motivation to jealously guard their normative authority against third party incursions is considerable.

At the same time, the proposal lags behind the marginal reforms such as boosts and budges in the degree to which it is behaviorally informed. There is just too little explicit concern for the findings of behavioral science. True, the mechanism of deliberation bears significant promise to attenuate some of the most dangerous pathologies of contemporary politics, such as group polarization (Fishkin *et al.*, 2021). However, it is also possibly quite fragile in the face of quirks and imperfections of human reason (Smith, 2014). While it is perhaps difficult to do anything about gullibility in a non-paternalist setting, a detailed analysis of how specifically naivety and rational irrationality are to be disincentivized in open democracy is still necessary. The heretofore apathetic regular citizens would be suddenly torn out of their regular walks of life and put into a situation that includes great stakes to "get their political preferences straight" before a binding vote. But will the setup facilitate a swift overcoming of their initial naivety? Will the preparatory phase and length of their tenure be sufficient for that? With rational irrationality, the case is yet more complex due to the unresolved issue of the proper balance between internal and external social incentives. In short, there is still a long way to go for open democracy to become truly behaviorally informed.

An Anti-Psychological State

Where does the above overview of the landscape of democratic reform leave us when trying to fortify democracy for the digital age? While there is no paucity of proposals, even the most sweeping ones promise only a limited solution to the problem of political irrationality in the current technological ecosystem. In "The Landscape of Democratic Reform" section, I have put forward several questions to guide an assessment of the available reform proposals:

1 Is the reform behaviorally informed?
2 What is its predicted efficacy vis-à-vis the various forms of political irrationality?

3   What mechanism does it suggest for recovering people's preferences that will be treated as normatively binding?
4   Does it presume third-party benevolence?

While the preceding discussion has been structured to propose a tentative answer to each of them, a concise overview is necessary. Table 5.1 provides a back-to-back comparison of the reform proposals encountered so far. Nudges and shoves represent behaviorally informed paternalism, boosts and budges are marginal reforms, and, finally, QV and open democracy stand for the radical reform.

What is the normative key to interpreting the table? In the light of the preceding considerations, I suggest the following reading.

Since the perspective of this volume is instrumental, it implies the need for democratic institutions that are functional with people as they are, not as they should be. With behavioral sciences steadily increasing the available stock of knowledge pertinent to this issue, I take it as a distinct advantage if a reform proposal takes this knowledge explicitly into account, even if critically so. The *Behaviorally informed* box in the table should therefore read "yes."

When it comes to political irrationality, we can be fairly confident in its growing prevalence and its threat to the quality of the outcomes of the democratic social choice (see Chapter 3). But its specific functioning is much more controversial. Politically irrational outcomes could be triggered by gullibility, that is, "hardwired" biases of the human mind that are impossible to eliminate; naivety, that is, adaptable but not yet optimally adapted heuristics that can be improved via learning; or rational irrationality where politically irrational behavior is a side effect of rationally pursuing nonpolitical goals, reputation management in particular. The latter two causes of irrationality are sensitive to incentives that influence the speed of learning and the motivation to treat the task at hand with due diligence. In contrast, gullibility can only be reduced via an environmental design—choice architecture, broadly understood—to dispose of irrationality's triggers. Since there is no conclusive evidence regarding the relative prevalence of each of the three causes, I consider broad-spectrum remedies ceteris paribus preferable. The *Effective against gullibility/naivety/rational irrationality* line should therefore contain a "yes."

For those committed to the Sovereignty Principle, the *prima facie* attractive attitude toward a possible occurrence of irrationality—that is, toward the threat of systematic mistakes—is to uncover what an individual really wants and help them to choose the proper actions to achieve their goals. However, this implies a need for the identification of "true" preferences, a task that generates more problems for democracy than it solves (see Chapter 4). Thus, interventions that are not built around the notion of behavioral micromanagement appear more attractive and the *Requires identification of "true" preferences* should include a "no."

A concern closely related to this is the point at which individuals' choices count as a normatively binding revelation of preference. At this point, I take the preference purely pragmatically, not to imply any particular assumptions

Table 5.1 The landscape of reform

	Nudges	Shoves	Boosts	Budges	Quadratic voting	Open democracy
Behaviorally informed	Yes	Yes	Yes	Yes	No	Minimally
Effective against Gullibility	Yes	Yes	No	Yes	No	No
Naivety	Yes-ish	Yes	Yes	Yes	No	Yes
RI	No	Yes	No	Yes?	No	Potentially
Requires identification of "true" preferences	Yes	Yes	No	No?	No	No!
Revealed preference normatively binding	Conditionally (environmental, micro)	Conditionally (environmental, micro/macro)	Unconditionally	Conditionally (environmental, macro?)	Unconditionally	Conditionally (processual, macro)
Presumption of third-party benevolence	Strong	Strong	Weak	Depends on transparency (possibly strong)	Depends on the agenda-setting mechanism (probably strong)	Not necessarily strong
Information input	Restricted	Restricted	Unrestricted	Restricted	Unrestricted	Unrestricted

Note: RI: rational irrationality.

about the consistency or stability of the ranking: I just mean that with democracy, one must eventually take what the people choose as imperative. There is a spectrum of ways how to approach this issue. On the one extreme, preferences are admitted only if revealed in a well-designed (i.e., supportive of "true preference" revelation) choice environment. Accordingly, behaviorally informed paternalists micromanage one environment and one bias at a time, inevitably leading to complex, technocratic solutions. On the other extreme, revealed preferences are unconditionally accepted as bearing a normative authority. This is the case with reforms that only offer people tools (such as boosts or voice credits) and then let them decide any way they see fit, no further questions asked. Finally, in the middle of the spectrum, we can find proposals that put specific requirements on the process preceding the choice or the environment in which it takes place while keeping the requirements relatively general in nature. So, open democracy only lets the lottocratic representatives vote after proper deliberation, and budges aim to preclude manipulative kinds of communication. Any preference revealed after the proper process has taken place is then accepted as normatively binding. Due to these complexities, it is more difficult to proclaim what the row *Revealed preference normatively binding* should optimally contain. My tentative answer, given in the light of the concerns about both political irrationality and third-party violations of the Sovereignty Principle, is that unconditional deference and deference conditional on environmental micromanagement are both dominated by the option to condition the binding choice by macro-level criteria.

Another criterion closely related to the issue of true preferences is the *Presumption of benevolence.* The proposed reforms differ in their vulnerability to third-party violations of the Sovereignty Principle. Broadly speaking, the less transparent the intervention, and the more indirect people's consent to it, the more one needs to rely on the various choice architects, agenda setters, or mediators to pass on an opportunity to commit value imposition. Here, I recommend a cautious stance. Although many liberal democratic governments have lately been showing their citizens a benign face, history teaches caution. The adage "trust, but verify" comes to mind. The less reliant does the reform leave democratic citizens on third-party benevolence that cannot be properly verified (and enforced, if need be), the more should it count to its benefit.

Finally, the *Information input.* This criterion targets the ability of the resultant setup to process information regarding preferences (i.e., the "normative information") scattered among the society's members. However well they may be grounded in science, strict technocratic requirements on when and how the preferences need to be revealed to be recognized as normatively binding impoverish the informational base of collective choice since they restrict the information input. At the same time, mechanisms that allow for recording preferences' intensity enhance the input. Overall, the system of collective choice able to process more normative information will also be more capable in democracy's promise of responsivity to people's preferences. The last line in the table should therefore read "unrestricted."

From this evaluative perspective, each of the examined reforms has serious setbacks as already discussed. Let me summarize the most pressing issues.

- Nudges and shoves are most dependent on true preference identification and rely extensively on third-party benevolence. Their propensity toward technocratic micromanagement also throttles the information input since people's valuations are only admitted through a narrow pathway. In relative terms, these restrictions elevate the importance of the political channel of preference revelation: hardly an unadulterated blessing in times of a democratic crisis. In terms of effectivity against the various triggers of political irrationality, shoves show general promise, but nudges cannot defuse rational irrationality since they eschew altering the incentives.
- Boosts can only help where people face incentives to apply their enhanced competencies when making their choices. This is rarely the case in the political context. Boosts' built-in unconditional deference to revealed preference is thus worrisome because no mechanism to bolster the signal of the normative information from the noise of the systematic mistakes is offered.
- Budges suffer, above all, from an unclear delimitation of what counts as a manipulative method of communication. If the delimitation remains as arbitrary as it currently stands, it results in an overreliance on third-party benevolence and the threat of value imposition looms large. The informational input concerning people's valuations of alternatives may also be overly restrained, especially where limitations to freedom of speech are to be introduced.
- QV's expected performance is most threatened by the weak incentives toward political rationality. The existing proposals are technically sophisticated, but they have not yet come to terms with the findings of behavioral science. With a low probability of pivotality, QV does not discourage political irrationality, and its potential to enhance the inflow of normative information in collective decisions thus cannot come to fruition. Agenda-setting is another pressing issue with agenda uncertainty looming particularly large. The threats of collusion and organized interest groups' outsized influence have also not been dispelled so far. These concerns raise the specter of third-party value imposition.
- Open democracy offers an audacious vision of restructuring democratic citizens' political incentives. However, the vision is currently only tangentially informed by the findings of behavioral science. In their light, it appears of essence to find the proper balance between the material incentives and the social incentives of both the internal and the external kind. Open democracy is at risk of putting too much weight on external social incentives, especially if the more radical calls for transparency—including open ballot or digital reputation tracking—were heeded. Another worrisome aspect is the dependence of deliberation's success on third-party management of the due process. If deliberative assemblies are employed to make binding

political choices, the various facilitators and mediators will be well-positioned to skew the outcomes in their favored direction.

What is the route forward then? As we have seen, the discussion about the implementation of the findings of behavioral science in the public sphere has been dominated by paternalism. Paternalists pursue a dream of a government empowered by the most up-to-date techniques of behavioral manipulation to minimize people's self-defeating behavior. So arises a Psychological State as a behaviorally informed Leviathan. For the reasons already stated, I consider this vision a treacherous will-o'-the-wisp against the background of the democratic crisis and digital revolution. Anyone committed to the democratic values incorporated in the Sovereignty Principle I urge to caution.

Still, the threat of political irrationality appears real enough with the democratic equilibrium of liberal democracy not necessarily able to maintain it within manageable proportions indefinitely. Complacency thus hardly represents a dominant alternative to paternalist efforts. Fortunately, a third road could be passable. It lies in designing an antipode to the Psychological State: an *Anti-Psychological State*.

Despite its name, the Anti-Psychological State does not turn its back to the findings of behavioral sciences, which may indeed provide a key to saving democracy from the technologically catalyzed onslaughts of political irrationality. However, its design employs these findings in ways that minimize the threat of third-party value imposition smothering people's voices. Many tools requisite for such a task are already available. Indeed, they have been covered on the previous pages. While each of the non-paternalist proposals I have examined has its fair share of drawbacks vis-à-vis political irrationality, I am going to demonstrate that they compensate for each other's weaknesses while their strengths work in synergy. I suggest they represent complementary building blocks of the Anti-Psychological State.

No doubt, an Anti-Psychological State can take many distinct forms and not all promising building blocks have been considered in this volume. Nonetheless, one needs to start from somewhere. Therefore, let me sketch one specific way the marginal and radical reforms could be combined in a mechanism of collective choice designed to minimize political irrationality without violating the Sovereignty Principle.

The foundational principle of the Anti-Psychological State I am about to outline can perhaps best be summarized as "boost—deliberate—vote quadratically." Open democracy serves as its basic template because it is the only one of the proposals discussed that goes far enough in reshaping the incentives of regular democratic citizens. Or at least those selected for service as lottocratic representatives. Thus, a random sample of the adult populace would be drawn for mandatory participation in a deliberative body tasked with making binding political choices. As we have seen, open democracy's main vulnerabilities are the susceptibility of the deliberation process to third-party manipulation and the possible overweighting of external social incentives which may sway the representatives from substantive considerations within the deliberative assembly toward posturing directed at the non-deliberative public at large. Could we use boosts, budges, and QV to alleviate these shortcomings?

Currently, the common practice at deliberative assemblies is to present the participants with "balanced and authoritative information" (Fishkin *et al.*, 2021, p. 1466) pertinent to the issue(s) at hand. Since any delimitation of "balanced and authoritative information" will remain forever vague, its selection represents remarkably delicate moment vulnerable to an unwelcome third-party scheme. Certainly, this problem may not be manifest during experimental deliberation where the participants possess no decision-making power. But consider how different the situation would be if the deliberative assembly were called upon to deliver a binding decision concerning an important political issue. Little wonder Landemore (2020) conceives a more dynamic information environment where the representatives would maintain an active connection with the public at large via crowdsourcing platforms, while also engaging their own capacities to look up information and call upon experts for consultation. However, this is not a cure-all setup: neither the possibly outsized external social incentives nor the facilitators' sway over the process of deliberation have been addressed. Crowdsourcing could easily become dominated by lynching mobs or interest groups' shills trying to impress their opinion on the deliberators. Expert testimonies are difficult to interpret, let alone assess with respect to their epistemic merit (Goldman, 2001).

Boosts and budges bear a promise that open democracy's problems could be much diminished. Boosts build competencies. These competencies are often useful in a broad range of contexts and cheap to acquire. Think of a crash course in elementary statistical reasoning and information literacy (Hertwig and Grüne-Yanoff, 2017) or a training session in mediation not very different from the one currently given to third-party facilitators. Where the baseline knowledge of regular citizens is low, the most important lessons can often be boiled down to a simple checklist (McIntyre, 2018) or a few intuitive principles (Gigerenzer, 2014). Open democracy already provides strong incentives to overcome one's naivety. But a suitably constructed educative session preceding the deliberation period could much expedite the process and save the representatives from a costly trial-and-error adaptation. Even better, boosts would promote lottocratic representatives' epistemic independence and diminish their reliance on third-party facilitation or information selection making bureaucratic capture less of a concern.

How about budges? Note that they represent the only potentially non-paternalist bulwark against gullibility. If irrationality is deterministically triggered in some circumstances, the only solution is to remove the trigger or at least diminish the frequency of encountering it. Budges could thus prove useful in designing the communication channels for the lottocratic representative in such a way that the substantive information gets through but efforts to exploit rationality's bounds are blocked. For instance, rules may specify the admissible format of expert testimonies. It could be mandated to present information in its most intuitive form, such as natural frequencies, or in ways that optimally resonate with the competencies built during the representatives' training session. Even the expert selection process could be rule-based so that the assembly identifies the experts to summon only through the specification of general qualification criteria—for example, requisite education, experience, publication record, public service—to avoid bias. Other budges could then regulate the crowdsourcing process and the process of deliberation itself.

A vital question is whether these boosts and budges can be constructed in a transparent enough fashion so they can be guarded against third-party manipulation. For example, crowdsourcing certainly cannot be moderated in the haphazard and arbitrary way in which digital platforms currently regulate their content (see Chapter 3). Thus, boosting and budging must be rule-based to the maximum possible extent and eliminate the use of third-party discretionary judgment wherever practicable. This seems quite possible in many instances. In case of boosting, the training sessions could be standardized, prerecorded, and accessible online to the general public in the form of massive online open courses free for anyone to attend at will. Similarly, all the standards pertaining to the form in which outside information is delivered or accessible to the assembly would need to be publicly available online. The key principles of openness and peer review that have been perfected within the scientific discourse (cf. Kitcher, 2011) could find their use in the public debate regarding the structure of these interventions.

The complementarity between boosts and open democracy is bilateral. Open democracy provides incentives for the lottocratic representatives not only to take the training sessions seriously but also to use their newly acquired or upgraded competencies during the deliberation and choice process. It is unlikely that an individual could improve their decision-making but was lax about doing so: open democracy greatly increases the stakes in the realm of both social and economic incentives. Simultaneously, open democracy does away with the unconditional deference to revealed preference: the "boost them and let them choose" chain gets interrupted by the deliberative session in between. Of course, the lottocratic representatives are not forced to change their initial stance on issues, but they certainly have every opportunity to learn other people's viewpoints, acquire new information, and consider the relative strength of their position before they finally get to make a binding choice.

Where boosts and budges fortify open democracy against third-party manipulation, QV could help it find balance among the various incentives, material, and social. While the original version with vote-buying appears even more impractical with open democracy than with general suffrage, the opposite is the case for QV with voice credits. Consider the following scenario: after the deliberative session establishes the agenda, walks over the pros and cons of each proposal, and generally "does its thing," the aggregative phase of the collective decision-making uses QV instead of a simple majority rule. Each representative receives an equal amount of voice credits to be allocated among the various issues on the agenda based on the relative intensity of their preference. This preserves equality among the representatives but enhances the amount of normative information solicited: we learn not only which proposals the representatives support and oppose, but also much about these issues' relative weight. Where simple "yes" or "no" comes in an infinite stock, spending credits on the individual items of the agenda brings the opportunity cost of any additional vote lively to mind.

Even better, a constrained voice credit budget combined with the growing price of an additional vote may help restrain the outsized influence of external social incentives. Suppose Roger, a lottocratic representative, decides to dedicate his efforts to pandering to the public at large instead of a substantive deliberation with his peers. He expends all his energies on raising issues of symbolic importance and feeding the flames of "culture wars" to create an opportunity to grandstand, impress the crowds, and flatter their prejudice. In such a rationally irrational strategy, Roger sees the promise of advancing his career after his tenure as a representative concludes: having numerous followers always comes in handy, especially in the digital age.

QV makes Roger's strategy more costly in relative terms. With a simple majority vote, one can monomaniacally promote a single issue but still gets to vote on all of them with equal force. With QV, Roger will be expected to "put his money where his mouth is" and spend his voice credits in ways consistent with his rhetoric. Otherwise, the success of his strategy will be threatened since people are generally sensitive to marks of insincerity (Mercier, 2020). Do note that on the margin, Roger's extremism will be quite ineffective due to the quadratic pricing scheme employed: he must sacrifice 25 potential votes on 25 other issues to gain 5 actual votes on his signature issue. Given Roger also faces material incentives to vote on issues that concern his well-being, the price of grandstanding may prove too steep. Also, his peers in the assembly are well-positioned to countermand his extremism with a modest outlay of voice credits if they cooperate.

Moreover, QV could diminish the threat of interest group capture. The constrained voice credit budget and the growing marginal cost of a vote make it harder for the interest groups to exercise strong influence over the assembly's choices. Each credit spent for the sake of one group means one credit less to support another, exacerbating their competitive struggle. Also, persuading a few representatives via, say, an implicit promise of the revolving door, will mean a lesser advantage since large unidirectional spending does not provide all that much extra influence on the margin, becomes easily noticeable, and simpler to counter by a coordinated action of the remaining representatives.

Where QV helps open democracy, open democracy returns the favor. Although QV optimally requires substantial numbers of voters, experimental evidence suggests it works reasonably well with a relatively low number of participants (Goeree and Zhang, 2017; Quarfoot *et al.*, 2017). The limited numbers of lottocratic representatives then represent a clear benefit. With a compulsory participation, the endogenous turnout problem (Kaplow and

Kominers, 2017) disappears. And small electorate means high stakes, that is, provides the incentives so sorely missing from the original QV proposals. Lottocratic representatives will be motivated to carefully plan how to spend their credits. Moreover, since agenda-setting is broadly in the hands of the assembly itself, the problems of agenda manipulation and agenda uncertainty all but disappear. One only gets to vote once it has been already established what the items on the agenda are going to be.

How about collusion? With open democracy, voting blocs certainly remain a possibility. But the threat they represent is much diminished. Since the lottocratic representatives will be well-informed due to the preparation process, the resources at their disposal, and their deliberative sessions, their voice credit spending cannot be easily shifted merely by providing some additional bits of information. The concerns by Goodman and Porter (2021) can thus be laid to rest. Weyl's (2017, pp. 81–87) attempts to dispel the concern regarding collusion also hold much more sway under open democracy than otherwise: incentives to defect are indeed substantive and those opposing the bloc's agenda are in well-positioned to thwart its efforts once they became apparent.

All in all, the marginal and radical reforms discussed in this chapter show considerable mutual compatibility. Certainly, the existing sketch of the Anti-Psychological State remains rough and preliminary. But it points toward a road out of the democratic crisis that may be passable. While much theoretical and empirical work remains to be done, it appears that findings of behavioral science that inform boosts and budges can be frugally combined with the mechanism design insight and audacity of vision that characterize QV and open democracy. Through their synergy, political irrationality may yet be contained within a democratic institutional framework, even if currently inflamed by the digital revolution.

Conclusion

The landscape of democratic reform is richly populated. But four recent proposals stand out in their promise to address the problem of political irrationality via non-paternalist means. Some of them are "marginal," that is, target the problem against the static background of the liberal democratic institutions. Others envision a radical refashioning of the basic rules of the political game. Can they give a credible of fortifying democracy for the digital age?

As a solution to political irrationality, each of the proposals shows important weaknesses under a closer scrutiny. The marginal reforms—*boosts* and *budges*—are well-informed behaviorally but do not reshape the incentives democratic citizens face in their political choices. The radical reforms—*QV* and *open democracy*—strive to redesign the incentives but do little to come to terms with the findings of behavioral science. In addition, case-specific problems tend to plague each individual proposal.

But hope is certainly not all lost. It appears that the marginal and radical reforms I have considered can be woven together to work in synergy. I suggest they mutually compensate for each other's weaknesses and compile their strengths. As a result, we may yet construct an Anti-Psychological State, that is, a political order optimized to counter political irrationality relying on the findings of behavioral science but also retaining a commitment to the Sovereignty Principles threatened by paternalism. Open democracy, reinforced with boosts, budges, and QV appears one of the alternatives to liberal democracy. Its virtues are preserved but the resilience toward the onslaughts of political irrationality in the digital age is enhanced.

Notes

1 Still, consider the upswing of dictatorships corresponding with the introduction of the first truly mass medium, that is, the radio. The demise of Weimar Republic in the early 1930s and the ascent of the Third Reich represents a particularly salient example (Adena *et al.*, 2015). Democracy's triumph over totalitarianism in the 20th century was not predetermined.
2 The short-term boosts show greater resemblance to nudges and require greater caution. When Sims and Müller (2019) argue that there is no normative difference between boosts and nudges, it appears we should be especially careful when boosts come to be conceived overly broadly to resemble interventions into choice architecture.
3 Arguably, this is why the boosters include nudge-adjacent changes to choice architecture: fallible heuristics that cannot be updated or overwritten can still be directed.
4 Post-election, all the money spent on buying votes is distributed equally among all the citizens which makes the system budget neutral and partially compensates the losers. However, this feature of the proposal is perhaps not essential and creates its own problems: see Patty and Penn (2017).
5 If the price of additional votes grows too slowly, the most intense special interests capture the election; if it rises too steeply, the outcome will converge to what the 1p1v rule would deliver (Lalley and Weyl, 2018, pp. 34–35).

Bibliography

Ackerman, B.A. and Fishkin, J.S. (2004) *Deliberation Day*. New Haven: Yale University Press.

Adena, M. *et al.* (2015) 'Radio and the Rise of The Nazis in Prewar Germany', *The Quarterly Journal of Economics*, 130(4), pp. 1885–1939. doi:10.1093/qje/qjv030.

Akerlof, G.A. and Shiller, R.J. (2015) *Phishing for Phools: The Economics of Manipulation and Deception*. Princeton: Princeton University Press.

Alemanno, A. and Spina, A. (2014) 'Nudging Legally: On the Checks and Balances of Behavioral Regulation', *International Journal of Constitutional Law*, 12(2), pp. 429–456. doi:10.1093/icon/mou033.

Archer, A., Engelen, B. and Ivanković, V. (2019) 'Effective Vote Markets and the Tyranny of Wealth', *Res Publica*, 25(1), pp. 39–54. doi:10.1007/s11158-017-9371-4.

Arrow, K.J. (1963) *Social Choice and Individual Values, Second edition*. New Haven: Yale University Press.

Bächtiger, A. *et al.* (2018) 'Deliberative Democracy: An Introduction', in Bächtiger, A. et al. (eds) *The Oxford Handbook of Deliberative Democracy*. Oxford, UK: Oxford University Press, pp. 1–32. doi:10.1093/oxfordhb/9780198747369.013.50.

Benson, J. (2019) 'Deliberative Democracy and the Problem of Tacit Knowledge', *Politics, Philosophy & Economics*, 18(1), pp. 76–97. doi:10.1177/1470594X18782086.

Boyer, P. and Petersen, M.B. (2018) 'Folk-Economic Beliefs: An Evolutionary Cognitive Model', *Behavioral and Brain Sciences*, 41, pp. 1–65. doi:10.1017/S0140525X17001960.

Chambers, S. (2004) 'Behind Closed Doors: Publicity, Secrecy, and the Quality of Deliberation', *Journal of Political Philosophy*, 12(4), pp. 389–410. doi:10.1111/j.1467-9760.2004.00206.x.

Dryzek, J.S. *et al.* (2019) 'The Crisis of Democracy and the Science of Deliberation', *Science*, 363(6432), pp. 1144–1146. doi:10.1126/science.aaw2694.

Dryzek, J.S. and Niemeyer, S. (2006) 'Reconciling Pluralism and Consensus as Political Ideals', *American Journal of Political Science*, 50(3), pp. 634–649. doi:10.1111/j.1540-5907.2006.00206.x.

Fishkin, J. *et al.* (2021) 'Is Deliberation an Antidote to Extreme Partisan Polarization? Reflections on "America in One Room"', *American Political Science Review*, 115(4), pp. 1464–1481. doi:10.1017/S0003055421000642.

Gigerenzer, G. (2010) *Rationality for Mortals: How People Cope with Uncertainty*. New York; Oxford: Oxford University Press.

Gigerenzer, G. (2014) *Risk Savvy: How to Make Good Decisions*. New York: Viking.

Goeree, J.K. and Zhang, J. (2017) 'One Man, One Bid', *Games and Economic Behavior*, 101, pp. 151–171. doi:10.1016/j.geb.2016.10.003.

Goldman, A.I. (2001) 'Experts: Which Ones Should You Trust?', *Philosophy and Phenomenological Research*, 63(1), pp. 85–110. doi:10.2307/3071090.

Goodman, J.C. and Porter, P.K. (2021) 'Will Quadratic Voting Produce Optimal Public Policy?', *Public Choice*, 186(1–2), pp. 141–148. doi:10.1007/s11127-019-00767-4.

Grüne-Yanoff, T. (2018) 'Boosts vs. Nudges from a Welfarist Perspective', *Revue d'economie politique*, 128(2), pp. 209–224.

Grüne-Yanoff, T. and Hertwig, R. (2016) 'Nudge Versus Boost: How Coherent Are Policy and Theory?', *Minds and Machines*, 26(1–2), pp. 149–183. doi:10.1007/s11023-015-9367-9.

Hertwig, R. (2017) 'When to Consider Boosting: Some Rules for Policy-makers', *Behavioural Public Policy*, 1(2), pp. 143–161. doi:10.1017/bpp.2016.14.

Hertwig, R. and Grüne-Yanoff, T. (2017) 'Nudging and Boosting: Steering or Empowering Good Decisions', *Perspectives on Psychological Science*, 12(6), pp. 973–986. doi:10.1177/1745691617702496.

Kaplow, L. and Kominers, S.D. (2017) 'Who Will Vote Quadratically? Voter Turnout and Votes Cast Under Quadratic Voting', *Public Choice*, 172(1–2), pp. 125–149. doi:10.1007/s11127-017-0412-5.

Kelly, J.T. (2012) *Framing Democracy: A Behavioral Approach to Democratic Theory*. Princeton: Princeton University Press.

Kitcher, P. (2011) *Science in a Democratic Society*. Amherst: Prometheus Books.

Lalley, S.P. and Weyl, E.G. (2018) 'Quadratic Voting: How Mechanism Design Can Radicalize Democracy', *AEA Papers and Proceedings*, 108, pp. 33–37. doi:10.1257/pandp.20181002.

Landa, D. and Pevnick, R. (2021) 'Is Random Selection a Cure for the Ills of Electoral Representation?', *Journal of Political Philosophy*, 29(1), pp. 46–72. doi:10.1111/jopp.12219.

Landemore, H. (2020) *Open Democracy: Reinventing Popular Rule for the Twenty-First Century*. Princeton: Princeton University Press.

Landemore, H. (2021) 'Open Democracy and Digital Technologies', in Bernholz, L., Landemore, H., and Reich, R. (eds) *Digital Technology and Democratic Theory*. Chicago, IL: University of Chicago Press, pp. 62–89. doi:10.7208/9780226748603-003.

Levine, D.K. (2020) 'Radical Markets by Eric Posner and E. Glen Weyl: A Review Essay', *Journal of Economic Literature*, 58(2), pp. 471–487. doi:10.1257/jel.20191533.

List, C. (2018) 'Democratic Deliberation and Social Choice: A Review', in Bächtiger, A. et al. (eds) *The Oxford Handbook of Deliberative Democracy*. Oxford, UK: Oxford University Press, pp. 462–489. doi:10.1093/oxfordhb/9780198747369.013.14.

López-Guerra, C. (2011) 'The Enfranchisement Lottery', *Politics, Philosophy & Economics*, 10(2), pp. 211–233. doi:10.1177/1470594X09372206.

Lucas, G. and Tasić, S. (2015) 'Behavioral Public Choice and the Law', *West Virginia Law Review*, 118, pp. 199–266.

Mansbridge, J. et al. (2010) 'The Place of Self-Interest and the Role of Power in Deliberative Democracy', *Journal of Political Philosophy*, 18(1), pp. 64–100. doi:10.1111/j.1467-9760.2009.00344.x.

McIntyre, L.C. (2018) *Post-truth*. Cambridge, MA: MIT Press.

Mercier, H. (2020) *Not Born Yesterday: The Science of Who We Trust and What We Believe*. Princeton: Princeton University Press.

Ober, J. (2017) 'Equality, Legitimacy, Interests, and Preferences: Historical Notes on Quadratic Voting in a Political Context', *Public Choice*, 172(1–2), pp. 223–232. doi:10.1007/s11127-017-0409-0.

Oliver, A. (2013) 'From Nudging to Budging: Using Behavioural Economics to Inform Public Sector Policy', *Journal of Social Policy*, 42(4), pp. 685–700. doi:10.1017/S0047279413000299.

Oliver, A. (2015) 'Nudging, Shoving, and Budging: Behavioural Economic-Informed Policy', *Public Administration*, 93(3), pp. 700–714. doi:10.1111/padm.12165.

Oliver, A. (2018a) 'Nudges, Shoves and Budges: Behavioural Economic Policy Frameworks', *The International Journal of Health Planning and Management*, 33(1), pp. 272–275. doi:10.1002/hpm.2419.

Oliver, A. (2018b) *Reciprocity and the Art of Behavioural Public Policy*. Cambridge; New York: Cambridge University Press.

Patty, J.W. and Penn, E.M. (2017) 'Uncertainty, Polarization, and Proposal Incentives Under Quadratic Voting', *Public Choice*, 172(1–2), pp. 109–124. doi:10.1007/s11127-017-0406-3.

Posner, E.A. and Stephanopoulos, N.O. (2017) 'Quadratic Election Law', *Public Choice*, 172(1–2), pp. 265–282. doi:10.1007/s11127-017-0415-2.

Posner, E.A. and Weyl, E.G. (2015) 'Voting Squared: Quadratic Voting in Democratic Politics', *Vanderbilt Law Review*, 68(2), pp. 441–500.

Posner, E.A. and Weyl, E.G. (2017) 'Quadratic Voting and the Public Good: Introduction', *Public Choice*, 172(1–2), pp. 1–22. doi:10.1007/s11127-017-0404-5.

Posner, E.A. and Weyl, E.G. (2018) *Radical Markets: Uprooting Capitalism and Democracy for a just Society*. Princeton: Princeton University Press.

Quarfoot, D. et al. (2017) 'Quadratic Voting in the Wild: Real People, Real Votes', *Public Choice*, 172(1–2), pp. 283–303. doi:10.1007/s11127-017-0416-1.

Rizzo, M.J. and Whitman, G. (2019) *Escaping Paternalism: Rationality, Behavioral Economics, and Public Policy*. Cambridge; New York: Cambridge University Press.

Rubin, P.H. (2014) 'Emporiophobia (Fear of Markets): Cooperation or Competition?', *Southern Economic Journal*, 80(4), pp. 875–889. doi:10.4284/0038-4038-2013.287.

Sims, A. and Müller, T.M. (2019) 'Nudge Versus Boost: A Distinction without a Normative Difference', *Economics and Philosophy*, 35(2), pp. 195–222. doi:10.1017/S0266267118000196.

Smith, A.F. (2014) 'Political Deliberation and the Challenge of Bounded Rationality', *Politics, Philosophy & Economics*, 13(3), pp. 269–291. doi:10.1177/1470594X13488355.

Smith, G. (2009) *Democratic Innovations: Designing Institutions for Citizen Participation*. Cambridge; New York: Cambridge University Press.

Véliz, C. (2021) *Privacy Is Power: Why and How You Should Take back Control of Your Data*. Brooklyn: Melville House.

Venice Commission (2013) 'Opinion on the Draft New Constitution of Iceland'. Available at: www.venice.coe.int/webforms/documents/?pdf=CDL-AD(2013)010-e (Accessed 10 July 2021).

Weyl, E.G. (2013) 'Quadratic Vote Buying', *SSRN Electronic Journal*. doi:10.2139/ssrn.2003531.

Weyl, E.G. (2017) 'The Robustness of Quadratic Voting', *Public Choice*, 172(1–2), pp. 75–107. doi:10.1007/s11127-017-0405-4.

Yeung, K. (2017) '"Hypernudge": Big Data as a Mode of Regulation by Design', *Information, Communication & Society*, 20(1), pp. 118–136. doi:10.1080/1369118X.2016.1186713.

Conclusion
The Road Ahead

Writing in the late 2021, the news from democracy's frontline is not exceedingly cheerful. The malaise of 2016 is still with us. While fears of an imminent collapse of the liberal democratic order would be certainly premature, so would be the hopes that it has finally caught a fresh breath. Joe Biden's ascendance into the White House to replace Donald Trump has been marked by the infamous Capitol Riot and the subsequent unwillingness of more than a few US representatives to disavow its legacy. Some of Europe's populists are in retreat, but it may be temporary. The tension between the "old" EU countries and Poland or Hungary is more pronounced than ever. Regime change movement in Belarus has been brutally suppressed. Concurrently, the COVID-19 pandemic has exposed in a broad daylight the catastrophic ineptitude of bureaucratic infrastructure and political leadership in many advanced liberal democracies and unleashed a wave of misinformation perhaps yet unseen. What is to be done?

Democratic skeptics may be enjoying their "we told you so" moment: in their view, democracy is inevitably inept, and the recent events are just making it obvious, once again. Democratic optimists, caught on their back foot, struggle to explain how the current problems do not stem from democracy but from the lack of it: since *proper* democracy is resistant to failure—let alone repeated and stubborn one—trouble must be caused by the obstacles put into the way of people's will by the liberal democratic institutions.

My book attempts to navigate the territory between the two camps. It approaches democratic theory from a methodological standpoint guided by the economic approach. In the honorable tradition of the "imperialist" rational choice, it puts preferences, incentives, and equilibria at the center stage. Like the skeptics, it refuses to endow the democratic citizens with angelic motivations and takes very seriously the worrying empirical findings regarding their blunders. However, like the optimists, it retains faith in the capability of the regular citizens to make sound political decisions.

It is true that the manifestations of citizens' capability often fall short of its potential. But a lack of democratic responsivity is not the sole culprit, probably not even the most vexing one. A specter of political irrationality should haunt each democratic idealist: what if the government "of the people, by the people,

DOI: 10.4324/9781003274988-7

for the people" is hamstrung by the prevalence of systematic mistakes in the people's judgment and choice? Accordingly, this book takes political irrationality as the most severe threat to democratic order which needs to be accounted for. It views democratic political order as a—potentially fragile—equilibrium to be maintained between staying responsive to people's preferences and not giving in to the centrifugal forces of political irrationality.

As I show throughout the book, it is most notable that political irrationality is not of a single origin. Sometimes, it is triggered by the use of heuristics that have arisen as adaptations to our ancestral environment of small-scale groups lacking sophisticated division of labor. Such heuristics can be considered "hardwired," as far as they are triggered outside of our voluntary control and cannot be updated: no amount of training or reflection makes one perceive the lines in the Müller-Lyer illusion as of equal length. As a result, there is some amount of gullibility in each of us. Applied to current political issues, heuristics adapted to an ancestral environment often misfire. However, political irrationality is also malleable, likely to a considerable extent. Many heuristics and mental models can be learned (or unlearned) to improve performance in a specific choice environment, like the one of social media and modern politics. If past mistakes entail sufficiently salient feedback, we can improve our understanding of the world, overcome our naivety, and do better in the future. Political irrationality also results—as an externality—from our rational pursuit of goals merely tangential to the political issue at hand. Humans are social animals rightly obsessed with their reputation and status. If we need to signal loyalty to our allies and friends, epistemic irrationality is a small price to pay, especially if it is as inconsequential as single citizen's political beliefs (and actions) in mass democratic politics. Thus, rational irrationality also needs to be accounted for.

It may well be that gullibility represents a hard constraint on democracy's potential. But so it does for oligarchy, autocracy, or any other regime where humans are in charge. It would be foolish to repudiate democracy on gullibility's account. For there can be little doubt that liberal democracy has served us remarkably well. It has achieved an immense, unprecedented success, in fact. But its institutional blueprint may be growing obsolete as its underlying equilibrium is threatened by the digital revolution and epistemic democratization it brings. The concern that drives this book's interest in reform is that liberal democracy's bulwarks against political irrationality may be too weak to withstand the barrage of technologically catalyzed misinformation cascades.

Perhaps the most popular existing cure for irrationality is the one offered by the behaviorally informed paternalists. There can be little doubt that their remedies—be they of a coercive or "libertarian" kind—are effective to change human behavior in directions desired by the policymakers. However, my account is cautious regarding the prospects of paternalism to save democracy from political irrationality. Although their commitment to the Sovereignty Principle of value non-imposition via subscription to the "as judged by themselves" (AJBT) standard of welfare improvement is laudable, its implementation leaves much to wish for. Paternalists' efforts to address irrationality in consumption—which is

174 Conclusion: The Road Ahead

generally less controversial than political irrationality—end up overloading the political channel through which people's preferences are transmitted. With no transparent way of how the AJBT standard could be withheld and people's true preferences identified behind the mess of their actual choices, paternalists end up relying on discretion, not rules. Therefore, implementation of paternalist policies—which tend to take a shape of precisely targeted micro-interventions and meticulously crafted choice architectures—means either that democratic citizens must be extremely watchful to detect potential misuse, or that policymakers' benevolence must be strongly presumed. Given what we know about democratic citizens' habitual behavior, the former road does not appear passable and the latter one is overly risky, especially in the stormy waters that democracy currently navigates. The paternalist way of weeding out irrationality on an *ad hoc* basis may all too easily undermine the responsivity of liberal democracy to the citizens' value judgments. Paternalism protects the political system from the threat of political irrationality, but it also makes it increasingly inert vis-à-vis regular people's preferences (albeit not to the preferences that the rulers and their choice architects posit people have or should have). The resulting fortress may be quite impenetrable—if inelegant—but in place of its original garrison, it can end up hosting a predatory soft-authoritarian regime or a technocracy that serves a well-sanitized fetish of an idealized human but not the actual people.

How about a non-paternalist way to battle irrationality? I examine both the marginal improvements that could bolster democracy's defenses and the radical proposals to restructure its fundamental rules. All these solutions, as far as they may provide a workable defense against political irrationality, represent a bet on the efficacy of incentives and learning. Thus, except for budges (behavioral regulations), they cannot reduce gullibility since the only protection against it is trigger-avoidance. Nonetheless, they promise an effective treatment of both naivety and rational irrationality. Given how badly incentives are currently set up for a regular citizen in mass democratic choice, the weight of such promise should not be discounted as the room for improvement appears large. After all, a complete elimination of irrationality—even if desirable—remains a pipedream. What democracy needs to accomplish is to keep political irrationality within manageable proportions. *Liberal* democracy's ability to achieve this goal may be faltering. If so, democracy may need to be reformed. In that case, I suggest we follow the line of what I call an *Anti-Psychological State*.

An Anti-Psychological State is a general label for the institutional design crafted with a specific intent to discourage political irrationality while not sacrificing democratic responsivity. For that purpose, it must draw on several sources of inspiration. The first is mechanism design: proper incentives must be put in place to motivate the democratic citizens to make use of their best abilities in service of democratic collective choice and feed the aggregation mechanism as much relevant information—inevitably scattered across many minds—as possible. The second is behavioral science: it is crucial that an assumption of a perfectly rational, even hyperrational, agent does not sneak in as it is prone to do in the technical mechanism design treatises. The exercise of institutional design must be undertaken in acute awareness of the current state of knowledge regarding the quirks and limitations of human rationality. From behavioral science, it should also draw methodological inspiration: namely that theoretical speculation can only carry us so far before the need for systematic experimental testing sets in. The third source of inspiration is democratic theory that delivers original and ambitious visions of possible reform.

Accordingly, my example of how an Anti-Psychological State could look like combines "open democracy's" radical rethinking of political representation, mechanism design insights of quadratic voting, and behaviorally informed boosts and budges to further decision-makers' competences and shield them from attempts to exploit the bounds of their rationality. I demonstrate a remarkable complementarity of these proposals: the shortcomings of each of the building blocks are neatly compensated by the strengths of another. Boosts and budges can empower the lottocratic representatives to become less susceptible to bureaucratic capture and third-party manipulation in general. Quadratic voting hinders interest group capture and penalizes excessive pandering to the public at large. In turn, open democracy provides the incentives necessary for each of the other measures to work their intended way.

There remain two final questions to address: "Is this really the time for those who believe in democracy to embrace a vision of radical reform?" and "Is there any way how such a reform would be practically feasible?"

As far as the first question is concerned, I have only a cautious answer to offer. Certainly, any radical reform is risky compared to gradually patching up an established system. No matter how much experimentation precedes the reform, it would be naïve to deny that it would be a step into a largely uncharted territory. Only after the reform is implemented, we can gradually discover all the unintended consequences and the unknown unknowns that come in its path. Experimentation is vital, but it cannot dispel uncertainty. Therefore, my answer is conditional on three "big ifs." Namely:

1   If the current democratic crisis is likely enough to set liberal democracy on a path of a terminal decline;
2   if the degrading ability of liberal democracy to contain political irrationality is a major trigger of this crisis;
3   and if it is not already too late for an ambitious project of an institutional overhaul;

then embracing radical reformism along the lines suggested in this book—especially in its own vision of an Anti-Psychological State—appears prudent, despite the inherent risks. Otherwise, I consider marginal fixes a preferable option, albeit a caution with respect to paternalism remains advisable since disavowing radical reform does not subtract anything from the arguments presented against it.

This brings me to the "how" of the reform. Suppose one commits herself to the quest of a radical reform of democratic institutions. Is it in any way realistic that such a quest could succeed? Certainly, the current political establishment has little incentive to seek reform altering the rules of the game that brought them to power. At the same time, gaining mass support among the public requisite for any such reform's success would require means a long uphill battle. Where to start?

I do not purport to have a particularly good advice as to the specifics of a viable transition strategy. My excuse is that, apparently, neither does anybody else. On the bright side, much work has already been done to raise awareness of the alternatives to the current system and their potential, especially by the deliberative democrats (Bächtiger *et al.*, 2018). Some radical reform ideas have become influential enough to stimulate substantial innovation, often with a non-negligible impact on the practical politics (Sintomer, 2018). However, elected officials are understandably reluctant to cede too much real power—as opposed to, say, merely coopting of the citizens in an advisory role—to deliberative or lottocratic bodies of questionable legitimacy among the broad public. The speed of tangible change in the ways of democratic decision-making remains glacially slow. The odds are that most democratic citizens are still completely unaware of any viable alternatives to the habitual institutional setup. Much less have they become fervent supporters of its reform.

Nonetheless, there are also reasons for hope. As Landemore (2020, p. 207) points out, governance in online communities perhaps more easily allows for experimentation than the traditional political settings. Similarly, relatively small-scale decision-making on issues of local interest could present a welcome first step toward more ambitious reforms. Variations on open democracy could be tried locally, perhaps instead of direct democracy which has been gaining some popularity without offering any remedies to political irrationality (likely a recipe for a disaster). Also, the mandate of the alternative bodies of representation could be limited to specific questions—perhaps those where purely allocative problems concerning public goods are concerned and any distributive issues excluded, if we are to take inspiration from the discussions surrounding quadratic voting.

Private philanthropy could also be included. Effective systems of governance are at least as important for human flourishing as clean energy and access to freshwater. After all, social technologies have long been recognized as key to development along with physical technologies, if not prior to them (Beinhocker, 2006). So, perhaps the philanthropists will find interest in designing new systems of governance and negotiating its employment in meaningful political decisions. Similarly, private business could be interested in experimenting with different setups to engage consumers in substantive decisions. If nothing else, their public image could benefit from such manifestation of a democratic sentiment in organizations otherwise quite hierarchical.

I am well-aware these last remarks are exceedingly speculative and vague. At the same time, academics are hardly best positioned to notice all the existing opportunities to introduce a democratic reform. Therefore, I want to conclude with a plea to benevolent politicians, public servants, philanthropes, and entrepreneurs, that is, the practically minded people among us who have the insight and resources necessary. This book is down-to-earth in its concentration on incentives: maybe too crass for many a democratic theorist. But perhaps this makes it better positioned to speak to the practical people around.

The acceptance of an economic approach to the analysis of social phenomena does not equal cynicism about the role idealism may play. While I assert that a viable democratic system cannot be based on a blind faith in third-party benevolence—be it composed of experts on politics, administration, behavioral science, or anything else—this is not the same as claiming that no idealistic, genuinely benevolent people in the positions of power exist. It is them who can most easily make a difference to see opportunities for democratic reform where no one else would notice them.

Any social change starts with persuasion. If this book persuades some of its readers to ponder how the often-speculative ideas of democratic theory viewed through the lens of behavioral political economy could be used in service of human flourishing, it has not been a waste of ink and paper.

Bibliography

Bächtiger, A. *et al.* (eds) (2018) *The Oxford Handbook of Deliberative Democracy*. Oxford; New York: Oxford University Press.

Beinhocker, E.D. (2006) *Origin of Wealth: Evolution, Complexity, and the Radical Remaking of Economics*. Boston: Harvard Business Review Press.

Landemore, H. (2020) *Open Democracy: Reinventing Popular Rule for the Twenty-First Century*. Princeton: Princeton University Press.

Sintomer, Y. (2018) 'From Deliberative to Radical Democracy? Sortition and Politics in the Twenty-First Century', *Politics & Society*, 46(3), pp. 337–357. doi:10.1177/0032329218789888.

Index

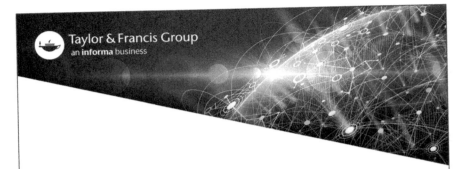

Printed in the United States
by Baker & Taylor Publisher Services